the food of france

the food
of france

a regional celebration by **sarah woodward**

with a foreword by **raymond blanc**

food photography by **richard jung**

kyle books

In memory of Oscar

This edition published in 2006 by Kyle Books
An imprint of Kyle Cathie Limited
general.enquiries@kyle-cathie.com
www.kylecathie.com

Distributed by National Book Network
4501 Forbes Blvd., Suite 200
Lanham, MD 20706
Phone: (301) 459 3366 Fax: (301) 429 5746

ISBN (10-digit) 1-904920-43-8
ISBN (13-digit) 978-1-904920-43-4

Project editor Caroline Taggart
Design Geoff Hayes
Maps Tyrel Broadbent
Copy editor Morag Lyall
Editorial assistant and picture research Vicki Murrell
Index Sarah Ereira
Home economy Linda Tubby
Styling Penny Markham
Production Sha Huxtable and Alice Holloway

The Library of Congress Cataloguing-in-Publication Data
is available on file.

Printed in Singapore by Kyodo Printing Co Pte Ltd

contents

Foreword by Raymond Blanc   7

Introduction   8

Paris and the Ile-de-France   10

Alsace-Lorraine   20

The North and Champagne   36

Normandy   48

Brittany   62

The Loire   74

Le Centre   88

Burgundy and the Rhône valley   100

The Alps   114

Aquitaine and Poitou-Charentes   124

The Basque country   138

Languedoc-Roussillon   150

Provence   166

Corsica   182

The French West Indies & the Ile de la Réunion   192

Index   204

Acknowledgements 208

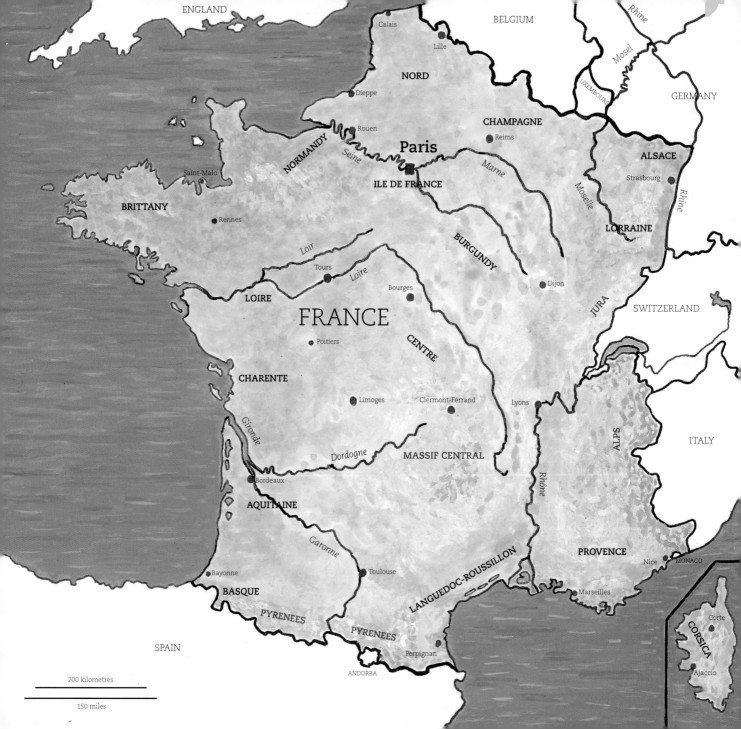

foreword by raymond blanc

Sarah Woodward kick-started her career in 1990 by winning the *Independent* newspaper's Cook of the Year Competitionwhich involved cooking lunch for me in my own kitchen at Le Manoir aux Quat'Saisons. I take real pleasure in the fact that she has worked in Paris and gone on to live half the year in France. We often hear people say that France is losing its food culture, and succumbing, like the rest of the developed world, to convenience food and fast food. But because of the time she has spent in France, Sarah knows better than this.

Yes, our culinary patrimony is in some danger. But it is by no means lost. I know from my own experience that, behind every Michelin-starred chef, there is a mother or grandmother whose cooking still had some connection to the soil of a particular region of France. We chefs may not even have learned the recipes of these women who have always nourished us, but the taste of the dishes they prepared for us is almost in our bloodat the very least it's something we'll never forget. Our mother's specialities may not have been the canonical version of these dishes, but they all have that special authenticity that comes from being prepared in the proper way, using the correct ingredients and, above all, in the right place, reflecting the *terroir* of their origin.

So even when a French cook is transplanted (as I myself have been) to a different country, we carry with us some essential baggage, those memories of taste, smell and texture that allow us to recreateas well as anyone is able to do this at allour own corner of France. Sarah's book celebrates this, and long may it continue.

introduction

The supposed demise of French food has been much written about in recent years. According to the various doom-mongers among the media and politicians alike, many French schoolchildren do not know that milk comes from cows, the French housewife has forgotten how to cook, you cannot get a decent affordable meal in a local restaurant and most Michelin-starred chefs have become more interested in the decor and crystal ware of their restaurants than the food.

There is of course a degree of truth in all these exaggerated statements, but in my experience food, and the passion for it, is very much alive and well in France today. Above all, the French like to talk about their food: what they ate yesterday, what they will eat today, what they have bought for tomorrow's meal, how such and such a dish should be prepared. And children are taught (or expected) to eat much the same as the adults.

French food is deeply rooted in its ingredients and seasons. Above all, though, it is regional. Certain dishes may be eaten across the country at certain festive timesoysters on Christmas Eve, kid or baby lamb at Easter, for exampleand around the country the first cherries and *pêches de vigne* (literally, peaches from the vine) of summer and the truffles and wild mushrooms of autumn are cause for celebration. The party, however, takes place in the region where the fruits are grown or the mushrooms and truffles are found in the woods.

Suggest to a Marseillais that a cook from Alsace can prepare a decent bouillabaisse and you will be greeted with pure scorn; a scorn similar to that heaped on a Marseillais who offers a choucroute. The Alsatian would be accused of not having the right rock fish and the Marseillais would indubitably fail on both the sausages and the pickled cabbage. Or so I have been told. There are, too, many topics for debate. Does the best foie gras come from

Alsace or Périgord, for example, and are the chickens of Bresse better than those from the Gers? Impartial observers who might answer such questions are hard to find.

France remains a country you can travel across and sense a difference in ingredients and methods as you move from region to region or season to season. There will always be someone to tell you about the best local market, restaurant or dish, usually at some length. And they tell you with pleasurethey want you to get it right.

Much of the secret lies in the shopping. There are plenty of splendid markets and suppliersand affordable ones at that, frequented by the local inhabitants. Naturally, the supermarkets have made their mark, but provided you do not rely upon them entirely that is all to the good for those with busy lives. In the Mediterranean south a supermarket will have a vast array of fresh shellfish on ice; in the north and east you will find local sausage and freshly cooked choucroute; towards the mountains cheese is cut from huge wheels. Even in the grandes surfaces there is a feel for the regionality and seasonality of food. And where else do you find service stations on the motorway that sell local products as well as petrol and hamburgers?

But if the regionality of French food is entrenched, one of my biggest challenges in writing this book was how to define the regions. France has after all 95 départements, excluding those of the Domaines d'Outre Mer (of which Guadeloupe, Martinique, French Guiana and Ile de la Réunion are the principal ones). I felt it important to include a section on the French cooking of overseas. *Cuisine antillaise* in particular has in recent years had plenty of influence on restaurant cooking on the mainland, with an increasing and sometimes even wilful use of spices (I am reminded of an especially misguided dish of duck with vanilla sauce served to me in Provence). Another regional French cuisine that is often ignored by books on French cooking, of whatever language, is that of Corsica. The cooking of the islands is easily circumscribed (with the possible exception of that of Saint-Martin, which is half French and half Dutch and, yes, the culinary division does show). The borders are not so easily drawn on mainland France, where inevitably gastronomic influences bleed into each other across the country.

In broad terms I have tried to follow the over-arching political definitions of the regions of France. Sometimes this has been easier to do than at other times: few would dispute that either Normandy or Brittany stand alone, both historically and gastro-nomically (and even, with their coastlines, to a certain extent geographically). Some regions also fall together naturally, such as Alsace and Lorraine, and Burgundy down into the valley of the Rhône. Champagne may not be too delighted at being linked to Picardy and the north but the cooking, largely as result of the ingredients, has much in common (though I can sense a shudder in Reims as I write those words).

There are anomalies in the cartographers' politically dictated view of France, however, which a cook cannot agree with. Technically the center is linked as a region with the Val de Loir, with the Vallée de la Loire being a distinct entity to the west. For me, though, the valleys of the Loir and the Loire have a very similar and rather delicate approach to food, reflecting the fact that they were once the game larders and orchards for the Kings of France, while the center is the hilly region of Auvergne and the Massif Central, bordering onto Limousin, where the dishes are altogether more robust, reflecting the harsher climate.

Similarly, Provence is linked technically to the southern Alps, but its cooking is so distinct as to deserve a separate chapter. The very southern part of Aquitaine bordering Spain bears no relation gastronomically to the region around Bordeaux and so I have included a section cheekily entitled the Basque Country (no political overtones intended). In short, the regions in this book are defined by what goes on in the fields, the markets and the kitchens rather than government offices.

All of which is possible because one of the pleasures of shopping and eating out in France is that you can still expect regional specialties to be located in their specific areas. Of course you will find rillettes de Tours in your traiteur in Paris but everyone knows where they come from, just as Camembert comes from Normandy, choucroute from Alsace, tomates farcies from Provence. One of the factors that protects this rooting of food is the system of awarding certificates of Label Rouge and Appellation d'Origine Contrôlée to particular produce, which, if undoubtedly bureaucratic, also shows a dogged determination to hold on to local agricultural and gastronomic tradition. But just as important is the insistence that a certain dish can only be prepared using local ingredients in the regional way.

As a result I have not, for example, included a recipe for bouilla-baisse because the rock fish necessary to prepare it are simply not available away from the Mediterranean coast (and a defined area of it at that; try buying rascasse, or scorpion fish, in Perpignan and you will have trouble, whereas a few hundred kilometres up the coast in the market in Marseille every fish stall has a pile of fish especially destined for bouillabaisse, or soupe de poissons). Of course, one can be too purist: the inhabitants of Castelnaudary will have you believe that a correct cassoulet can only be prepared with the local variety of white bean, but white haricot beans do perfectly well (though I must admit I usually buy mine ready prepared in a jar). But on the whole, in these days of global supply, an insistence on local ingredients is to be celebrated.

There is a word in French that is widely used about food and that is 'correct'. It is meant as a compliment but it also underlines an innate understanding. A butcher, a fishmonger, a restaurant, a market stall, a baker can all be 'correct' but above all a meal is 'correct' and dishes are prepared 'correctement'. Which means not just that they are well cooked, but that local standards and traditions have been followed.

In reality, every cook has their own version of even the most classic of dishes. And thank goodness for thatthe slavish following of recipes has no place here. In France recipes are still passed down from mother to daughter (and father to son come to that, thinking of the dynasties of French chefs), each of whom add their own twist and techniques. French cooking is classic but also evolving, especially right now. French food, with its emphasis on good seasonal ingredients and regional variations, is right back in fashion. If, indeed, it ever went out of it.

The island of France, Paris and its environs. From a gastronomic point of view, all the food of France in the end gravitates to the capital. Do you want to eat choucroute, often of a better quality than you will find in Alsace itself? Then head to any number of brasseries, the vast restaurants named breweries due to their popularity with the beer-drinking refugees from Alsace-Lorraine who fled to the capital after the Franco-Prussian War of 1870.

Looking for a plateau de fruits de mer? The very best of the seafood from the Norman and Breton coasts comes to Paris, to be cleaned, shucked and arranged on ice by the écailleurs on the street outside the many seafood restaurants. Fancy some classics from the Loire Valley, perhaps a fillet of the river fish sandre, cooked in cream, and a tarte aux mirabelles? There is a small restaurant up a back alley in the 10th arrondissement, which offers just such specialties. Provided you know where to look.

A Bar at the Folies-Bergère, 1881–2, by Edouard Manet

For Paris is a city of secrets, jealously guarded by its inhabitants. The big, famous brasseries are easy to find and you will rarely eat badly at them, assuming you order with a due degree of caution (that is, keep it simple). But what is more elusive is that café du coin where each day's plat du jour is carefully cooked rather than just reheated in the microwave. They do still exist. It's just that no one, especially the Parisians, wants to tell you about them.

One good way of finding them, though, is to go to one of the many local markets of Paris. In 1136 Louis VI (nicknamed, appropriately enough, Louis the Fat) chose an area in the center of Paris known as Les Champeaux to open a new food market. Over the centuries this grew in importance, soon becoming known as Les Halles. Les Halles had a chequered history, almost closing down during the Hundred Years War, though by the sixteenth century it was back in thriving business. It was soon joined by numerous street markets, insalubrious affairs according to Voltaire, who wrote: 'we blush to see public markets set up in narrow streets, spreading their dirtiness, scattering infection and causing regular disorder.' But street markets were in Paris to stay, unlike Les Halles, which in 1973, after a long battle, was finally moved a few kilometres south of the city, to Rungis.

Voltaire might have been disappointed to know that Parisians remai very fond of their food markets, which these days are positively chic Of course, there are the daily market streets where the shops spill out onto the sidewalk, as in the Rue Mouffetard in the 5th arrondissement, down from the Place de Contrescarpe, the Rue de Montorgueil in the 2nd, just off Les Halles, and the Rue de Buci in th

Traffic Island on Boulevard Haussmann, 1880, by Gustave Caillebotte

hazelnuts is especially good). There is an organic bread stall, an olive merchant, a couple of butchers offering game in season as well as the more usual meats, a range of vegetable stalls (I have even bought zucchini flowers in early summer), and two wine stalls. In short, everything you need for the weekly shop, except perhaps a porter.

The market closes promptly at 12.30. The traders need to eat before their journey home, and they expect to do so well. I always feel reassured when Madame bustles over, spreads a clean piece of paper on the table, plonks down some water and bread and tells me what is the dish of the day. Hopefully it will be a classic such as *hachis parmentier*, made with the leftovers of the previous day's pot-au-feu, or *petit salé aux lentilles*. Honest food of the sort that you are unlikely to prepare for yourself at homeat least if you are eating for one. The café du coin is made for the solitary diner.

Of course, all the best restaurateurs in France also have to make their mark in the capital, which is excellent news provided you have an expense account. But for me the real pleasure of food in Paris is in the shopping. They may be under threat from property developers, but for the moment each quartier still has its local shops, which stay open at times convenient to workers, so that you can pick up provisions on the way home from the office.

People living in the center of Paris shop every day, even if it is just to pick up their baguette. Paris can be a lonely city, as I found when I first lived there in my early twenties, but the shopkeepers provide a lifeline, to disorientated foreign students and elegant elderly ladies alike. Each purchase is a reason for lengthy and animated conversation before returning to a small and solitary apartment.

There is only one problem: the food is too tempting. The traiteurs of Paris know just how to persuade you to buy too much. This is ready-prepared food of the highest order, displayed with artistry, especially in the shop windows of the smarter districts. No wonder then that the Parisienne, planning a dinner party, will often turn to her traiteur and her pâtissier rather than her own cooker.

smart 6th arrondissement. Or, for a street with a distinctly Middle Eastern flavor, try the rue de la Goutte d'Or in the 18th. But most districts also boast a once or twice weekly open-air food market, which attracts suppliers from often surprisingly long distances around the country. And a lot of these take place on a Sunday.

One of the best Sunday markets to visit is in the Place Monge in the 5th arrondissement. The compact square is packed with enticing stalls, though as elsewhere clothes sellers are slowly creeping in. But there is still the foie gras producer who weekly makes the trip from Gascony to offer his superior (and pricy) product; a fishmonger from the north coast who offers splendid oysters and flat fish; several excellent cheese stalls, including one that specializes in the cheeses of the Alps, with fine aged Comté, rich Beaufort d'été from cows who grazed the summer pastures, and vast slabs of Emmental, as well as a wide choice of saucisson (the one with

The waiter in a Parisian brasserie

There is a unique quality to the experienced waiter in an old-fashioned Parisian brasserie. Treading a fine balance between overt rudeness and extreme efficiency, weaving between the tables head and tray held high, he (it is almost always a he) knows just how to put you in your place should you query a dish or a wine. Yet if you are prepared to consult him in his wisdom, appreciate his consummate professionalism on a very busy evening, and even indulge him in a little repartee, there is in my experience no waiter in the world to beat him.

These days, language doesn't come into it. Try French by all means but unless your accent is perfect you will like as not be answered in English. No, it is simply a question of attitude. You must make it clear from the very beginning that you are not a customer to be trifled with. Your meal must be just solike that of the elegantly coiffed elderly lady sitting opposite, probably with a small dog on her knee. You, like the waiter, have standards.

And when it goes right, it is perfect. Paris is one of the few places in the world where I positively enjoy eating alone. No one blanches if you indulge yourself in half a dozen oysters and a glass of white wineinstead, the shellfish are produced with a flourish, together with the shallot vinegar, the pain de seigle, the mound of butter served in a small white pot. Madame would like to follow with the lamb cutlets? How would she like them cooked? And perhaps a green salad and a glass of a petit Bordeaux to accompany them? Attentive but unobtrusive service, guaranteed to make you feel at ease. Of course, it can also go horribly wrong. In my time I have had some spectacular shouting matches with Parisian waiters, though I like to think I earned some respect for complaining in the first place.

potage crécy
crécy soup

radis au beurre
radishes with butter

Two towns, Crécy en Brie in Picardie and Crécy en Ponthieu in the Ile de France, claim credit for this soup. Both are famous for their carrots (and the former also for the battle fought here during the Hundred Years War) but since it was the Parisian chef Escoffier who produced a refined version I incline towards the latter for the soup. There are three keys to its success. You must use young fresh carrots (though not necessarily small ones), not old cracked ones. You must cook the vegetables slowly at first and simmer them at length once the broth has been added. And the broth must be of excellent quality, deep in flavor. There are times when a bouillon cube will do, but this is not one of them.

Serves 4 to 6

3 pounds carrots, peeled and chopped into fine rings
white of 1 small leek, chopped
2 shallots, preferably the long, thin variety,
   peeled and finely chopped
1 pound red potatoes, peeled and diced
2 teaspoons brown sugar
sea salt
3 tablespoons unsalted butter
6 cups concentrated chicken or vegetable stock
1 tablespoon finely chopped parsley

Place all the vegetables in a large pan, together with the sugar, a generous sprinkling of salt (be careful if your stock is at all salty) and the butter. Stew gently, stirring from time to time, about 30 minutes. The vegetables should soften, not brown. Add the stock, bring to a gentle simmer, cover and leave barely to bubble, about 1 hour. Remove from the heat and as soon as it is cool enough liquidize in several batches, though not too smooth—the soup should have some texture. Check seasoning, sprinkle with parsley (some cooks also add a little knob of butter) and serve.

This makes for a simple but stylish hors d'oeuvre or a nibble with aperitifs. It is important that you get the longer, milder radishes rather than the rounder, hotter variety. Restaurants tend to serve the butter in little white pots but a slab on the side of the plate is fine by me. What is important, as with any deceptively simple dish, is that all the ingredients must be top quality.

Serves 4

20 long radishes
a good hunk of butter, preferably beurre demi-sel
   de Bretagne
salt, preferably fleur de sel

Wash the radishes well and trim, leaving a little of the green stalk attached to each. Chill for an hour or so and serve with the butter, salt and some good bread (pain de Poilâne is ideal, but any good French country bread will do). The idea is to spread a little butter on the end of each radish, dip in the salt, and crunch.

crudités

carottes rapées
shredded carrots

The lucky French cook can pop into their traiteur of an evening and pick up a range of sliced and dressed vegetables—*carottes rapées*, shredded carrots, *céleri rémoulade*, celeriac in a mustardy mayonnaise, and *betteraves*, beets in a parsley vinaigrette, are my three favorites. These days, you can also buy them in the supermarkets, but for my money they are best freshly prepared. And if you don't have a traiteur on your doorstep, provided you have an effective food-processor, they are easy to make at home. A careful dressing, a hot and crusty baguette and possibly a slice or two of pâté and you have supper.

A portion of each of these three crudités serves 4 as a light supper or 6 as a first course

1 pound carrots, peeled and shredded
2 shallots, peeled and finely chopped
1 tablespoon white wine vinegar
a pinch each of sea salt and white sugar
4 tablespoons extra virgin olive oil
1 tablespoon sunflower oil

Mix together the carrots and shallots. Whisk together the vinegar, salt and sugar, then slowly whisk in the oils and stir well. Leave to stand before eating, about 30 minutes.

céleri rémoulade
celeriac salad

juice of ½ lemon
1 celeriac, around 1 pound in weight
sea salt and freshly ground black pepper
1¼ tablespoons Dijon mustard
4 tablespoons mayonnaise

Bring a large pan of water with the lemon juice to the boil. Peel the celeriac and grate coarsely. Blanch, 30 seconds, then drain well. As soon as it is cool enough to handle, squeeze out any remaining liquid. Season. Stir the mustard into the mayonnaise and mix into the celeriac.

salade de betteraves
beetroot salad

1 pound small beets, in their skins
sea salt and freshly ground black pepper
1 teaspoon Dijon mustard
juice of ½ lemon
2 tablespoons extra virgin olive oil
2 tablespoons sunflower oil
1 tablespoon finely chopped flat-leaved parsley

Scrub the beets well and boil in salted water, 40 minutes. Drain and as soon as they are cool enough to handle, top and tail and peel off the skins. Chop the flesh into small chunks and season well. Whisk together the mustard and lemon juice then slowly add the oils until you have an emulsion. Dress the beets while still warm. Sprinkle with the parsley just before serving.

View of the Marché des Innocents, c. 1840, by Philippe Benoist

poireaux vinaigrette
leeks vinaigrette

Another simple, old-fashioned dish which turns the leek into a splendid starter. It has the added advantage of tasting better if it is prepared in advance. It is sometimes served with chopped hard-cooked egg scattered over the top, or with sauce gribiche (see next recipe).

Serves 4 as a first course

8 medium-sized leeks
1 wine glass each of olive oil and white wine
8 peppercorns
8 cilantro seeds
4 bay leaves
sea salt

Trim the green part of the leeks and set aside (they are useful in making stock). Cut the leeks in half across and make a cross-shaped incision at each end. Wash well.

Put the leeks in a heavy pan in which they will all lie flat and add the oil and wine, together with the spices, bay leaves and a generous sprinkling of salt. Bring to the boil, turn down to a simmer, cover and leave to cook, 15 minutes. Allow to cool in the liquid and serve with bread, spooning the liquor over the leeks.

sauce gribiche

France has always been proud of its sauces; the nineteenth-century statesman Talleyrand's most damning comment upon his return from the United States was that he had 'found a country of 32 religions but only one sauce', the implication being that such paucity of culinary if not religious thought could never happen in France. I am not personally much of a one for sauces but I do think that sauce gribiche, which some claim is named after a general in Napoleon's army, is worth the small effort. Another explanation for the name is that it comes from the old Norman word, derived from the Dutch *kribbich*, for 'grumpy old woman', because it is a *sauce relevée*, in which the eggs must bind. It is a piquant, bright green sauce, traditionally served with poached tongue or calf's head (*tête de veau*), but it goes just as well with leeks vinaigrette.

Serves 4

3 eggs
8 small dill pickles, finely chopped
2 shallots, peeled and finely chopped
zest and juice of $1/2$ unwaxed lemon
a good handful of flat-leaved parsley, stalks removed
a few leaves of tarragon
sea salt and freshly ground black pepper
2 teaspoons Dijon mustard
generous ½ cup extra virgin olive oil

Hard-cook the eggs, 10 minutes, and peel as soon as they are cool enough to handle. Chop finely and mix with the pickles and shallots. Chop the herbs finely. Mix some seasoning and the lemon juice into the mustard and slowly beat in the olive oil, so that you have a thick emulsion. Add the egg, pickle and shallot mixture, the lemon zest and the herbs.

rognons de veau à la moutarde
veal kidneys with mustard

Veal kidneys are worth seeking out for this bistro favorite. Traditionally they were roasted whole in their robe of suet, but I find that makes them too greasy. Provided they are roasted quickly in a very hot oven and you are prepared to eat them rosy pink, they have enough fat to keep them moist. But they do need a good old-fashioned sauce, and the kick of good mustard.

Serves 4

2 whole veal kidneys, fat removed
2 tablespoons Dijon mustard
sea salt and freshly ground black pepper
about 1 teaspoon all-purpose flour
1 small glass of Madeira
a bunch of watercress

Preheat the oven to maximum (normally 475°F). Smear half the mustard over the kidneys and season well. Put them in a roasting pan into which they fit snugly and roast in the oven, turning them once halfway through cooking, 20 minutes.

Drain any excess fat from the kidneys, reserving a tablespoonful, and cut them in half lengthways, discarding any gristle. They should be rosy pink in the middle. Wrap them in foil and set aside, 5 minutes.

In a separate pan, mix the flour with the reserved fat from the kidneys. Add the remaining mustard and the Madeira. Allow to bubble, stirring all the time.

Remove the kidneys from their foil and slice across. Add to the sauce and turn a few times. Serve straight away, with watercress on the side.

salade tiède aux oeufs et lardons
warm salad with eggs and bacon

Basically eggs and bacon on lettuce, but careful preparation is needed: the lettuce leaves should be crisp and bitter, the bacon of good quality, the eggs very fresh, the dressing suitably mustardy and nicely emulsified. In fact, the kind of dish that reflects a good French cook's attention to detail, even when using the simplest of ingredients.

Serves 4 as a first course or 2 for lunch

1 large frisée lettuce, well washed
4 tablespoons olive oil
¼ pound smoked bacon, preferably cut into lardons or cubes
4 shallots, peeled and chopped
1 tablespoon shallot or red wine vinegar
4 large fresh eggs
1 garlic clove, peeled and cut in half
4 slices of French bread, chopped into croûtons
1 tablespoon finely chopped tarragon

For the dressing
2 teaspoons Dijon mustard, tarragon-flavored for preference
sea salt
1 tablespoon shallot or red wine vinegar
2 tablespoons extra virgin olive oil
2 tablespoons sunflower oil

Drain the lettuce leaves well and arrange in a large serving dish. Heat 1 tablespoon olive oil over a medium heat and add the bacon and shallots. Fry, stirring occasionally, 10 minutes, and then deglaze (which means nothing more than stirring around to remove any residues from the pan) with the vinegar.

Meanwhile, bring a pan of water to the boil and add the eggs. Boil for 5 minutes, remove from the heat, and leave to cool in the water another 5 minutes before rinsing well in cold water.

Make the dressing by beating together the mustard, a generous pinch of salt and the vinegar, then adding the two oils (you can beat them in but the easiest and quickest way is to use a sealed jam jar and shake).

As soon as the eggs are cool enough to handle, peel them and cut in half. Arrange over the lettuce. Heat the remaining oil with the halved clove of garlic, and as soon as it is hot add the croûtons of bread. Fry, turning all the time, until nicely browned, 2 minutes. Remove with a slotted spoon and drain on paper towels, discarding the garlic.

Add the bacon and shallots, together with any pan juices, to the salad, followed by the croûtons. Sprinkle over the tarragon, pour over the dressing, and serve.

blanquette de veau
white veal stew

Often described as cooked *à l'ancienne*, this is a soothing, old-fashioned dish, of the sort that you hope to find as the plat du jour in your local café. It get its name from the white-coloured sauce, though I always use non-crated veal, which can be detected by its rosier hue and is now widely available.

Serves 6

4½ pounds shoulder of veal, cut into large chunks and trimmed of fat
1 large carrot, peeled and chopped into chunks
1 large white onion, peeled
2 cloves
2 fresh bay leaves
some sprigs of parsley, preferably flat-leaved
a few leaves of celery, if available
6 or 8 whole peppercorns
$1/2$ teaspoon sea salt
½ pound button mushrooms, washed and sliced
6 tablespoons unsalted butter
1 tablespoon olive oil
½ pound shallots, peeled
1 tablespoon all-purpose flour
1 teaspoon Dijon mustard
2 egg yolks

steak tartare

Place the veal in a heavy pan with the chopped carrot, the onion studded with the cloves, the herbs, peppercorns, salt and just enough water to cover. Bring to the boil, skim off any froth and discard, then turn down to a slow simmer. Cover and cook until the meat is very tender, 2 hours.

Meanwhile, gently cook the mushrooms in a quarter of the butter and the olive oil until tender, then reserve, discarding the juice (this seems a shame, but if you add it to the sauce your blanquette will not have its eponymous whiteness). Do the same for the shallots, taking care that they do not brown. Each will take around 20 minutes, and are best cooked in separate pans. Preheat the oven to 300°F.

When the veal is cooked, drain away the stock, which you should reserve (though you can discard the vegetables and herbs), and put the meat, together with the mushrooms and shallots, in an earthenware serving dish in the preheated oven to keep warm. Melt the remaining butter in a heavy pan and stir in the flour to make a roux (not a brown one, naturally) and then the mustard. Slowly stir in enough stock to make a thick sauce and allow to bubble for several minutes. Remove from the heat, leave to cool for a few minutes, then whisk in the egg yolks. Check the seasoning, pour over the meat and serve, preferably with boiled white rice.

A sunny autumn Sunday morning in Paris. A cup of coffee, a croissant and a visit to a flea market, or *marché aux puces*, in the south of the city. By midday, thoughts turn to lunch. And there is a café du coin, where steak tartare is on offer, with frites on the side. Do we want to season it ourselves? Yes, we do; after all, we like to concoct our own Bloody Marys. Each plate of finely ground beef comes with half an eggshell poised in its center, the yolk of the raw egg brilliantly yellow. Arranged around the beef are little piles of chopped cornichons, or small dill pickles, pink shallots, capers, parsley. A cruet set of Worcestershire sauce, Tabasco, Dijon mustard, sel de Guérande and coarse black pepper is set before us. The very thin, salty frites arrive crisp and piping hot. There is a carafe of chilled Brouilly sitting on the white paper tablecloth, brought automatically. Bliss.

Serves 2

1 pound best quality ground steak
sea salt and freshly ground black pepper
2 fresh free-range eggs
some small dill pickles
some capers, well rinsed
some chopped red onion or shallot
Dijon mustard, Worcestershire sauce and Tabasco

Season the meat well and pound to a paste by wrapping it in clingfilm and bashing it with a rolling pin. Break the eggs carefully, so that you have two intact half-shells. Return the yolks to the half-shells, and use the whites for another purpose. Divide the meat into two, spread onto two plates, make a well in the center of each and put a half eggshell, egg yolk within, into each well. Serve with the various condiments so you can season it to your taste.

tarte au citron
lemon tart

There is almost always a lemon tart on offer on the brasserie menu, but too often the pie crust is leaden, the filling too sweet. I like mine sharp and light.

Serves 6 to 8

For the pie crust
generous 2 cups all-purpose flour
a pinch of salt
generous ¼ cup sugar
 ¼ sticks unsalted butter, chilled
yolk of 1 large egg
iced water

For the filling
5 eggs, separated
scant ½ cup sugar
juice and zest of 3 large unwaxed lemons
1 level teaspoon cornstarch
a pinch of salt
unsalted butter, for greasing tin
confectioners' sugar

îles flottantes
floating islands

First make the pie crust by sifting the flour, salt and sugar together. Chop the butter into small cubes and then, either in the food-processor or working quickly with fingers you have first dipped into iced water, crumble the butter and flour mixture together. Now add the egg yolk and just enough iced water to make the pie crust bind together—between 2 and 4 tablespoons. Work as little as possible, wrap in plastic wrap and chill.

For the filling, beat the egg yolks with two thirds of the sugar until light and creamy. Stir the lemon juice and zest into the egg mixture. Carefully sift in the cornstarch, making sure there are no lumps. Pour the mixture into a heavy-based pan, set over a gentle heat and cook, stirring continually, until thickened, about 5 minutes. Do not allow to boil or the mixture will curdle. Leave to cool, stirring from time to time with a wooden spoon to prevent a skin from forming.

Preheat the oven to 350°F. Roll out the pie crust thinly and line a 8–10 inch tart pan, which you have liberally buttered (it's better not to use a loose-bottomed tin or the mixture may seep out). Prick several times with a fork and place the tart pan in the fridge, 10–15 minutes. Bake blind in the oven, 10 minutes.

Beat the egg whites with the remaining sugar and the pinch of salt until very stiff. With a wooden spoon gently fold into the lemon cream then pour this mixture into the pie crust. Return to the oven and cook until the surface is very lightly browned and the filling risen up, 20–25 minutes. Serve just warm, sprinkled with a little confectioners' sugar and with crème fraîche or sour cream if you like. The tart is also good cold.

Crème anglaise: literally, English cream, but named for a properly made English custard, that is, one based on vanilla-scented milk, sweetened with caster sugar and thickened with egg yolks. But what to do with the leftover egg whites? The French solution was to turn them into part of the pudding itself, puffy little white islands floating in a sea of yellow sauce. This is another bistro classic, which is fiddly to make but at least can be prepared in advance.

Serves 4

2 cups whole milk
½ vanilla bean
4 large fresh eggs
a pinch of salt
½ cup superfine sugar
5 cubes of brown sugar

Scald the milk by just bringing to the boil with the vanilla bean and leave to cool. Remove any skin. Carefully separate the eggs (it is important that no yolk is left with the white). Whisk the egg whites with the salt until firm, adding a quarter of the sugar halfway through the process. The egg whites should stand in firm peaks.

Bring the milk back to just below a simmer—it should not boil. Drop a few tablespoons of the sweetened egg white into the milk at a time: your aim is to have either eight or twelve *oeufs à la neige*, as they are called. As soon as they are set, lift them out with a slotted spoon, set aside and repeat the process.

Beat the egg yolks with the rest of the sugar until the mixture is a deep yellow in color and of a thick consistency. Strain the milk in which you have just cooked the egg whites and over a gentle heat add slowly to the egg yolk mixture, whisking all the time. Do not under any circumstances allow to boil or the mixture will separate. The 'custard' is ready when it is just thick enough to coat the back of a wooden spoon and no more.

Finally, prepare the caramel by simply melting the brown sugar cubes with a little water; it is ready when you have a brown liquid, well before it starts to set. Leave to cool, at least 10 minutes. Place the egg whites in the custard, pour over the caramel, and chill well before serving.

alsace-lorraine

Whenever I think of Alsace-Lorraine, the autumn months come to mind, when this north-easterly region of France comes into its own. The fruit trees are laden with quetsch, a local variety of small dark plum, mirabelles, a yellow plum, and reine-claudes, or greengages, just waiting to fill the open tarts for which the area is famous. Morning mists hang over the vineyards, ideal conditions for the grapes that will go to make the vendange tardive, or late harvest wines. A vast array of pumpkins and gourds are displayed outside farmhouses in wooden wheelbarrows. Meanwhile in the weinstübe of Strasbourg the new season's cloudy wine is served from jugs, accompanied by bowls of freshly picked walnuts.

Pumpkins and gourds in an Alsace market

This is not a region to comply with classic picture-postcard views of France. The wine villages of Alsace may be impossibly pretty, but with their timbered frames and geranium-filled hanging baskets, they vie in appearance towards the architectural style and decoration

of their German neighbours, who were often in sway over the region. Alsatian is a guttural language and the fact that local dishes have names such as baeckhöfe and flammekuche rather gives the game away.

The plateau of Lorraine, meanwhile, lying before the swell of the hills of the Vosges, is rarely perceived as a gastronomic haven. Yet, as an important area of pig breeding, Lorraine provides the raw materials for many of the dishes of the more famous Alsatian cooking. The French influence has subtly refined traditional dishes over the decades. The local choucroute, as served in Metz, is a world away from the German sauerkraut.

The Alsatians have developed their own more extravagant versions of the dish, sometimes served with river fish rather than sausages and cuts of pork. In smarter Strasbourg restaurants the choucroute royale involves pouring a half bottle of champagne over the steaming pile of cabbage (rather a waste, in my view). A properly made quiche lorraine, a light pastry case filled with just good smoked bacon, thick cream and fresh eggs, is a sheer delight, a revelation after so many offerings that traduce the name.

Niedermorschwihr village, Haut Rhin, Alsace

My brother and his family have lived in Alsace for nearly two decades and my favorite local meals have been taken with them at the *fermes auberges* in the wine villages of Alsace or the pine-clad hills of the Vosges. There is rarely much choice, and sometimes none at all. Seating is often at shared tables, and the waiting is generally by the cook of the house. The food is unlikely to be light, but the meal will be based on local ingredients – game in season, or river fish such as pike and eel, or rabbits, kid or chickens bred on the farm. Sometimes the meal will be as simple as *bibelkas*, fresh cheese mixed with herbs and served with bacon and potatoes, with a slice of fruit tart to finish, possibly with a chilled glass of the eau de vie into which so much of the fruit of the orchards is distilled.

The region is nonetheless rich in Michelin-starred restaurants, encouraged by the presence of the European parliamentarians, plus the fact that this is a wealthy part of France. The burghers of Strasbourg will defend the quality of their foie gras, served with a glass of Gewürztraminer, over that of the Gascon variety any day. At the famed Auberge de l'Ill, on the banks of the river of that name in the isolated village of Illhausern, the house specialty (apart from a whole black truffle cooked in ash) is the truffled foie gras terrine. But even in this temple to gastronomy the fillet of venison is served with *kneppfla*, a form of dumpling, with fromage blanc.

It was in the woods of the Vosges that I picked my first ever wild mushroom, a cep, known in America as king boletus. These are still the only mushrooms I dare to pick in the forest, as they are virtually impossible to confuse with any poisonous variety. The sun was slanting through the trees, my then tiny nephew was running on ahead (he is now a strapping rugby player), and there was a sunlit glade full of mushrooms. We filled our basket and after a long journey home behind tractors groaning with just-picked grapes we cooked the ceps straight away. Perhaps that is why I believe that the best things in Alsace-Lorraine happen in autumn.

asperges blanches au jambon et trois sauces
white asparagus with smoked ham and three sauces

Alsace is famous for its thick white asparagus, which were first cultivated in 1873 in Hoerdt, at the behest of one Pasteur Heyer. The raised asparagus beds are now a familiar sight as you travel around the region, as are the delicately tied bunches of asparagus in the June markets. Never ones to do things by halves, Alsatians traditionally serve their asparagus with not one but three different sauces: a vinaigrette, a hollandaise and a sauce mousseline, which is essentially hollandaise 'let down' with cream. They also like to serve three different kinds of ham, the so-called jambon de Paris (cooked white ham), some smoked ham and some paysan, or country, ham. I stick to the smoked only.

It is vital when cooking asparagus to keep their tips out of the boiling water (they should cook in the steam). There are special asparagus pots designed for this purpose, but tying the asparagus together in a bundle with string and standing them upright in a pan works perfectly well.

Serves 4

12 fat white asparagus stalks
4 slices of smoked ham

For the three sauces
Vinaigrette: 1 tablespoon white wine vinegar, 1 teaspoon tarragon mustard, sea salt, 2 tablespoons sunflower oil, 2 tablespoons extra virgin olive oil, freshly ground black pepper (optional)

Hollandaise: 3 tablespoons white wine, water, 3 yolks from large free-range eggs, 1 stick best quality unsalted butter, chilled, sea salt, ½ lemon

Sauce mousseline: half of the hollandaise and 2 tablespoons full-fat crème fraîche or sour cream.

Carefully wash any dirt from the asparagus and with a potato peeler gently peel the tough outer layer from the stalks. Bring a pan of salted water to the boil. Cook the stalks according to size (prick with a fork to check), between 10 and 15 minutes, and drain.

To make the vinaigrette
Mix together the vinegar, mustard and a good pinch of salt. Slowly beat in the two oils until you have a thick emulsion. Add a few grinds of pepper if you wish, though it does rather spoil the appearance of the vinaigrette.

To make the hollandaise
For years I have used a slightly altered version of Elizabeth David's recipe for sauce hollandaise, although as she correctly points out it is not one to please the purists, who would argue for nothing but eggs and butter. I like the touch of flavor given from the white wine, though you can also use white wine vinegar for a more pronounced taste.

It is really very easy to make and I always do it the old-fashioned way in a glass bowl set over simmering water (it is important that the base of the glass bowl should not be in contact with the water or the eggs will scramble). Others swear by the food-processor and melted butter but I don't think this gives the same consistency to the sauce.

So – briefly boil down the wine with 1 tablespoon water until you have less than 1 tablespoon liquid left. Let it cool. Beat the egg yolks well in a glass

bowl and add in the reduced liquid. Cut the butter, which should still be chilled, into small pieces.

Put the egg mixture over the pan of just simmering water and start whisking. Add the butter a piece at a time and don't add any more until the previous piece has melted. Keep going until either you have used up all the butter or the sauce has reached the consistency you like (personally, I prefer it not too thick). If at any time it gets too hot, either add a few drops of cold water or lift the bowl briefly away from the pan of water. When the sauce is finished remove from the heat, add a little salt and a squeeze of lemon juice. Hollandaise is served tepid.

This is a quicker process than it sounds but if the sauce does separate, then you can usually retrieve it by whisking an egg yolk in another bowl and slowly beating in the separated sauce. But as long as you are reasonably patient, you shouldn't have to do so.

To make the sauce mousseline
Whisk the crème fraîche until stiff and carefully fold it into the tepid sauce hollandaise.

Have the three sauces ready and serve the asparagus hot, with the ham on the side.

soupe aux choux avec foie gras
cabbage soup with foie gras

The key to this soup is leftovers. It was devised by a French housewife who found herself with some cabbage that had already been cooked with a chicken or guinea fowl, and some stock from the same bird. A few potatoes to thicken the mixture and possibly a splash of beer to enliven it and lunch was on the table. The addition of toast spread with foie gras is of course something else altogether – but then in a French farmer's household foie gras is not the luxury item it is perceived to be elsewhere.

Serves 4 to 6

1½ pounds precooked Savoy or other green cabbage – if you don't have any leftovers, then braise it briefly with a little smoked bacon, a scrap of onion, a knob of butter and some salt and pepper
1 pound red potatoes – Desirée, Red Bliss or Cal Red—peeled and roughly chopped
6 cups mild chicken stock
generous ½ cup (a small bottle) French lager (optional)
4 slices of French bread, toasted at the last minute
4 thin slices of preserved foie gras (optional)

Mix together the cooked cabbage, potatoes, stock and lager, if using, in a deep, heavy pan. Bring to the boil, turn down to a simmer and cook uncovered until the potatoes are tender, 45 minutes. Liquidize and season to taste. If you want to reduce it further, return to the heat until the desired consistency is reached. Before serving, spread the hot toast with the cold foie gras if you are using it and float a slice in each bowl.

tarte à l'oignon
onion tart

Quiche lorraine may be more famous but Alsatians prefer their tart thinner, crisper, filled with nothing but onions, cream and eggs. Perish the thought of cheese. It is usually served as a first course (no-one ever said Alsatian cuisine was light) but dished up with a green salad it makes a splendid supper. Traditionally it is served with a salad of dandelion leaves, or *pissenlits* (see page 32), but corn salad also works well. I like to scatter warm lardons of smoked bacon over the salad, together with a splash of white wine vinegar.

Serves 6 to 8 as a first course or 4 as a main course

for the pie crust
2 cups all-purpose flour
a good pinch of salt
1 stick unsalted butter, chilled and chopped into pieces
1 whole egg, beaten
iced water

for the filling
5 tablespoons butter
6 large Bermuda onions, peeled and sliced into fine half moons
a pinch each of salt and sugar
3 eggs, beaten
¾ cup crème fraîche or sour cream
a good pinch of nutmeg
sea salt and freshly ground black pepper

To make the pie crust, sift the flour with the salt and sugar and then, either in the food processor or with your fingers (which you have first dipped in a bowl of iced water), crumble in the butter. Add the beaten egg and just enough water to form a dough—a few tablespoons at most. Work the dough as little as possible, wrap in parchment paper and chill in the fridge for 45 minutes.

For the filling, melt two thirds of the butter in a heavy-based pan, then add the sliced onions, salt and sugar. Cook the onions as slowly as possible—they should lightly caramelize but turn no more than golden, about 30 minutes. Leave to cool.

Preheat the oven to 400°F. Choose a large shallow tart pan, ideally rectangular in shape, and grease it liberally with the remaining butter. Put in the refrigerator for 5 minutes while, on a floured surface, you roll out the dough as thinly as possible. With your fingers, spread the dough over the pan, making sure it comes well up the sides. Pop it back in the refrigerator, another 10 minutes.

Whisk together the eggs and crème fraîche with the nutmeg and seasoning, taking a light hand with the salt but adding plenty of pepper. Add the cooled onions and then pour the lot into the chilled pie crust. Transfer immediately to the oven. It is a good idea to place some foil on a baking sheet below the tart in case the filling spills over as it puffs up.

Bake until lightly browned on top, 25–30 minutes. Cool for 10 minutes, then serve warm.

le foie gras frais avec son pain d'épices
fresh foie gras with spiced bread

I include this dish in Alsace-Lorraine because I especially like the combination of fresh foie gras with pain d'épices, which the region is famous for. Cooking lobes of foie gras is a slightly fraught business as if you leave them in the pan too long they will literally melt—so get everything ready before you start. The onion compote can be prepared well in advance.

Serves 4

3 red onions, peeled and sliced into fine half moons
1 dessertspoon goose or duck fat
1 tablespoon brown sugar
1 tablespoon red wine vinegar
4 slices of fresh foie gras
sea salt and freshly ground black pepper
4 slices of pain d'épices

Put the onions, fat, sugar and vinegar in a heavy pan and sweat slowly over a gentle heat, stirring regularly, until the onions are soft and caramelized. This will take around 40 minutes.

Heat another heavy pan over a high heat. Season the foie gras and fry briefly for 2 minutes on either side. Place a piece of foie gras on top of each slice of pain d'épices, add a small pile of the caramelized onions on the side, and serve straight away.

parfait de foies de volaille
chicken liver parfait

Often described as fake foie gras, this is a rich and unctuous mixture which I used to make as a student. Serve it with nothing but toast.

Serves 4 to 6, depending on the size of your pots

½ pound chicken livers
¾ cup dry white wine (Riesling is ideal)
6 tablespoons unsalted butter, softened
salt and freshly ground black pepper
a pinch each of ground allspice and mace
⅓ cup full-fat crème fraîche or sour cream

Wash the livers well and cut away any fat or greenish-tinged pieces. Bring the wine to the boil in a small pan and add the livers. Bring back to the boil and cook for precisely 3 minutes. Drain and leave to cool, discarding the wine (or keep it for stock or soup).

When the livers are thoroughly cooled, purée them in the food-processor with the butter, generous seasoning and the spices. Whisk the crème fraîche until stiff and fold it into the chicken livers. Pack into small pots; if you are going to keep the parfait for a day or two before serving, you may like to cover it with a layer of clarified butter.

a choucroute festival

The little town of Riedwihr, in the countryside between Strasbourg and Colmar, is a quiet place most of the time, but, for the last thirty-five years, on one weekend at the end of September it comes to life. For this is the time of the choucroute festival and Riedwihr is the self-styled Alsatian capital of choucroute, owing to its particular soil which is ideal for growing cabbages. Over the two days over 2,000 pounds of pickled cabbage will be consumed, along with countless sausage, cuts of smoked pork and bottles of Riesling.

As we approached, we thought we might be in the wrong place, such was the silence—though the fields of cabbages did provide a clue. But as we neared town we were reassured by a steady stream of solid burghers in their Sunday best, marching purposefully forward. Their destination, and ours, was a vast marquee, where huge cabbages were suspended from the ceiling and hundreds of tressle tables set out. Later there would be dancing, with elderly matrons preferring to waltz with each other rather than their husbands. But first came the serious business.

I have eaten choucroute for decades in the brasseries of Paris but this was some of the most delicious I have ever tasted, a delicate yellow in color, full of flavor and in no way sour, despite the German name of sauerkraut. This, it was explained to me, was because it was the new season's crop. The enormous cabbages, some up to 20 pounds in weight, are harvested in August. Is it a particular kind of cabbage? I asked Frieh Lucien, member of the *sapeurs et pompiers*, or firemen, who are always in charge of these kinds of events in France. White cabbage, he replied (in fact traditionally choucroute is made with a variety of cabbage known as Quintal d'Alsace).

The outer leaves and core are removed using a specially designed machine and the inner leaves finely shredded. Nothing more than salt is added—the dish makes its own brine. Traditionally the brining took place in wooden barrels, and some locals still produce it this way, but on a large scale steel vats are used. By the last weekend in September the choucroute has reached perfection.

But first it must be cooked. The pickled cabbage is rinsed and then heated in goose fat. Spices including cumin and cilantro seeds, juniper berries, peppercorns and cloves are added, together with a sprinkling of thyme and a secret ingredient, whose identity—of course—couldn't be divulged. Copious quantities of Riesling are poured into the cauldrons and the choucroute cooked gently, giving off a delicious aroma.

Traditionally a choucroute garnie is served with the local sausage known as *knack*, two types of bacon, smoked and salted, and a piece of palette de porc fumé. Plain boiled potatoes and some mustard are the only other accompaniments. And then, as the people of Riedwihr and their visitors demonstrated with gusto, elbows out and heads down. My nephews and niece, two out of the three born and bred in Alsace, showed me the way with enthusiasm.

poule au riesling
chicken cooked in riesling

Alsace's answer to the Burgundian coq au vin, this is a soothing dish which requires a tender boiling fowl rather than the tougher cockerel. Without wishing to sound too precious, it really should be made with Riesling rather than another grape varietal, although you could use a Riesling from the New World just as easily as one from Alsace. It is at its best served with buttered fresh egg noodles.

Serves 4

1 plump boiling fowl
2 large carrots, peeled
2 shallots, peeled
1 bottle of Riesling
½ pound button or other white mushrooms
2 tablespoons unsalted butter
sea salt and freshly ground black pepper
juice of ½ lemon
scant ½ cup heavy cream
yolk of 1 large fresh egg

Wash the chicken inside and out and pat dry. Cut the carrots across at fine intervals into rounds; dice the shallots. Choose a heavy-lidded Dutch oven into which the chicken will just fit and place the bird in it breast side down. Add the carrots and shallots together with the wine. Bring to the boil as slowly as possible. Remove any scum, cover and leave to cook very slowly, 2 hours (you can transfer to a slow oven at this stage, if you prefer).

Wipe the mushrooms with a damp cloth (or wash them) and slice them if they are larger than button. Put in a separate pan with the butter, some seasoning and the lemon juice. Cook gently until the juices run, 10 minutes or so.

Turn the chicken breast side up and add the mushrooms together with any juices. Cook covered, or back in the oven, another 15 minutes. Meanwhile, heat a serving dish. At this point you might also want to make sure the water is boiling for the noodles.

Joint the chicken into 4 pieces and put them in the warmed serving dish. Whisk the cream with the egg yolk. Remove the vegetable and wine mixture from the heat and whisk in the cream and egg. Return it briefly to the heat but do not allow to boil. Check the seasoning, pour the sauce and vegetables over the chicken and serve.

jarret de porc au raifort
pork hock with horseradish

The preferred cut for this dish is a smoked hock of pork, but this can be difficult to find outside France and Germany due to different butchering traditions, so you can also use a shoulder of pork on the bone. The gammon should first be soaked in several changes of water, then slowly simmered with a whole onion studded with cloves until tender.

The sliced pork should be served hot, but the important point here is the sauce, made with fresh or preserved grated horseradish—categorically not horseradish from a jar, which is mixed with vinegar. The resulting sauce is creamy and mild and should also be served hot.

Serves 4

your chosen cut of pork (see above)

For the sauce
2 teaspoons freshly grated horseradish
scant ½ cup heavy cream
1 teaspoon Dijon mustard
juice of ½ lemon
freshly ground black pepper

Mix everything together and heat gently, stirring all the time. Do not allow to boil. Serve hot, poured over the sliced meat.

médaillons de biche à la crème
medallions of venison with cream sauce

Biche is a female roe deer, and the farmed variety is excellent for this dish as the meat tends to be more tender. Rather Germanic in style, this is often served in Alsace with *spätzle*, little flour and water dumplings not unlike the Italian gnocchi.

Serves 4

4 venison steaks, about ½ pound each
salt and freshly ground black pepper
3 tablespoons butter
1 cup heavy double cream
1 tablespoon redcurrant jelly

Cut the venison steaks into medallions about 1 inch thick across. Season the meat well. Heat the butter in a heavy pan and when it is bubbling add the venison. Cook 3–4 minutes either side, then transfer to a warmed serving dish. Add the cream and redcurrant jelly to the pan, stir well, bring to a bubble and cook for a minute or two. Return the venison to the pan, turn once or twice in the sauce, and serve.

chou rouge aux marrons et pommes
red cabbage with chestnuts and apples

The white cabbage used for choucroute is not the only form of cabbage grown and consumed in the north-eastern regions of France: red cabbage is also very popular in the cold months, especially to accompany roast goose at Christmas.

Serves 6 to 8 as a side dish

1 large red cabbage, around 5 pounds
2 tablespoons goose or duck fat
1 large white onion, halved, peeled and sliced
    into thin half moons
2 fat garlic cloves, peeled and finely chopped
sea salt and freshly ground black pepper
3 cloves
1 stick of cinnamon
a pinch of mace or nutmeg
1 tablespoon brown sugar
1 tablespoon white wine vinegar
¼ pound peeled and cooked chestnuts
2 eating apples, peeled and chopped
1 glass of white wine

Cut the cabbage into quarters and remove the core. Slice the cabbage into thin half moons. Choose a heavy, oven-proof pan large enough to take all the cabbage, and for which you have a lid. Melt the goose or duck fat over a moderate heat then add the onion and garlic. Sweat gently, stirring regularly, until softened but not browned, 15 minutes. Now add the sliced cabbage and stir well to coat in the fat. Season and add the spices, sugar and vinegar. Cover and leave to cook, stirring from time to time so that it does not stick, 30 minutes.

Preheat the oven to 300°F. Add the chestnuts and apples, transfer to the oven and cook, covered, for about 1 hour. The cabbage always tastes better when reheated.

baeckeoffe
stew of pork, lamb and beef

Literally meaning the baker's oven, this slow-cooked dish of mixed meats and potatoes was traditionally served on Monday, having been baked overnight in the oven that had been used for the Sunday roast. Highly decorated earthenware dishes can still be found on sale in Alsace for this family classic, but whatever you cook it in the important detail is to have a tight fitting lid and to seal it with an old-fashioned flour and water paste to prevent steam from escaping.

Serves 6 to 8

1 pound shoulder of lamb, off the bone
1 pound chuck steak
1 pound sparerib of pork, off the bone
2 large white onions, peeled and sliced into fine
    half moons
2 leeks, trimmed of the green, white part
    finely sliced
bouquet garni composed of a few sprigs of fresh
    parsley, a couple of bay leaves and a sprig of
    thyme
2 cups Alsatian Riesling or Pinot Blanc wine
freshly ground black pepper
2 pounds red-skinned potatoes
sea salt
2 tablespoons goose fat or butter

The night before you intend to serve the baeckeoffe, cut all the meat, trimmed of its fat, into bite-sized pieces and place in an earthenware dish together with the onions, leeks, bouquet garni, wine and a generous seasoning of pepper. Leave to marinate overnight, at room temperature covered with a clean cloth if the weather is cool; otherwise in the refrigerator.

The next day, preheat the oven to 300°F. Peel the potatoes and slice finely (this is easiest in a food-processor but you could also use a mandolin slicer). Arrange a layer of the potatoes over the base of an earthenware or other heavy pot with a lid, season with salt, then add the beef. Follow with another layer of potato slices, season with salt again, then add the pork. Repeat the process with the lamb. Pour in the wine from the marinade, having removed the bouquet garni, and mix the onions and leeks with the remaining potatoes. Arrange this mixture over the meat.

Cover the pot and seal the edges with a flour and water paste, made by mixing some all-purpose flour with just enough water to make a thick paste, rolling it out and placing over to cover the surface of the pot. Crimp down with your fingers all around the edges. Bake 3–3½ hours. To serve, first break open the flour and water paste with a sharp knife. A sharply dressed green salad and some strong mustard are all that is needed as an accompaniment.

salade de pissenlits
dandelion salad

In the Lorraine in spring they take their dandelions so seriously that the leaves are grown under pots, so that they do not turn a deep dark green and become too bitter for this warm salad, known locally as *chaude meurotte*.

If you can't find dandelion leaves (and you must look for ones that have not been sprayed with chemicals), then the frisée lettuce is a good substitute. The important point is the deglazing of the pan in which the bacon has cooked with vinegar. The salad must be served absolutely straight away, before the leaves wilt under the heat of the bacon and vinegar. Further to the east, in the Vosges, slices of hard-cooked egg or cooked potato and sliced shallot are often added.

Serves 4 as a first course

1 pound dandelion or other bitter salad leaves
½ pound lardons fumés or cubes of smoked bacon
2 tablespoons sunflower or ground nut oil
2 tablespoons red wine vinegar
sea salt and freshly ground black pepper

Wash the dandelion leaves very well to remove any grit and dry carefully in a clean dish-towel. Put the lardons and oil in a heavy pan and fry over a medium heat until crisp, stirring regularly, 4–5 minutes. Add the vinegar, allow to bubble for a minute, then tip the entire contents of the pan over the salad leaves. Add a little salt and plenty of pepper, toss well and serve absolutely straight away, before the leaves wilt under the heat of the bacon and vinegar.

tarte aux quetsches
plum tart

The small oval-shaped black plums known as quetsches are a speciality of the region, where they are made into eau de vie, jellies and conserves as well as used in open tarts.

Serves 6 to 8

For the pie crust
2 cups all-purpose flour
a pinch of salt
¼ cup white sugar
1 stick unsalted butter, chilled and chopped into pieces (reserve 2 teaspoons for buttering the tart pan)
1 egg, separated
iced water

For the filling
2 pounds small purple plums (damsons are an excellent substitute for quetsches)
¼ pound ladyfingers
1 egg white, saved from the pie crust
a little superfine sugar for sprinkling

Sift the flour with the salt and sugar and then, either in the food-processor or with your fingers (which you have first dipped in a bowl of iced water), crumble in the butter. Add the egg yolk and just enough water to form a dough—1 tablespoon or at most 2. Work the dough as little as possible, wrap in parchment paper and chill, 45 minutes.

Meanwhile wash the plums, halve vertically and remove the pits. Either crumble the ladyfingers in the processor or smash in a pestle and mortar, to produce fine crumbs.

Preheat the oven to 350°F. Grease a large tart pan, preferably one with a removable base, with the remaining butter. Roll the dough out as thinly as you can, taking care as it is very crumbly—if in doubt, you will do best to spread it across the pan with your fingers. Put the pan in the refrigerator, 40 minutes.

Brush the pastry base with the egg white and then sprinkle over the biscuit crumbs. Lay the plums cut side up on top, in concentric circles. Bake in the oven for 40 minutes.

Leave to cool and serve just warm, scattered with a little superfine sugar (though the leftovers, in the unlikely event that there should be any, are also good cold).

eaux de vie

When my brother first moved to Alsace, he lived on the edge of the Vosges to the north of Strasbourg and he had a favourite, if illicit, Saturday morning outing which I occasionally joined him on. This was to visit the famous house of Bertrand, one of the many distillers of eaux de vie in Alsace, in the pretty neighbouring village of Uberach. Monsieur Bertrand himself (the house was founded in 1874 by his ancestor Joseph) would greet us and propose a *petite dégustation*. Perfectly suitable, he felt, at eleven in the morning.

The problem was what to choose. The classic local eaux de vie are made from the variety of pear known as Williams, the golden mirabelle plums and the small dark quetsch, raspberries, both cultivated and wild, and of course the sour cherries for kirsch. But chez Bertrand the selection was as vast as the rows of bottles. There was spirit made from beer hops or holly berries, sloes or rowan, quinces or elderflower.

On my first visit I resolved one conundrum. One spring I had wondered why some trees in the orchards had bottles suspended from their branches. That was until I saw the bottles of Poire Williams, each with a whole pear inside. The pear grows inside the bottle, which is then topped up with eau de vie.

But good distillers like Bertrand have no need of such tricks to capture the essence of the fruit. The extraordinarily pronounced and clean fragrances that arose from the clear white spirit result from the use of prime fruit picked at its peak of ripeness, and distillation of the fermented fruit by the Holstein method in which the liquid is heated indirectly. Monsieur Bertrand was always proud to show off the family's venerable copper stills, though of course more modern ones were in use, and to explain that his aim was 'to preserve as much fruit as possible, on the nose and in the mouth'.

Eaux de vie or *acqua vitae*, literally waters of life, have a long history and are made the world over and all across France. Correctly served slightly chilled, they are a classic digéstif, and in fancier restaurants the sommelier will often place the balloon-shaped glass on its side at the lip of the table in order to pour the right measure, which should come just to the edge. Some of the very best come from Alsace—and that is directly linked to the abundance from the orchards.

Mirabelle plums

gâteau de nancy
nancy chocolate cake

Nancy and Metz, both of which towns have a reputation for their desserts, cakes and cookies, dispute ownership of this fondant chocolate cake, which is at its best served warm with a dollop of crème fraîche or sour cream.

Serves 6

2 sticks unsalted butter, softened
½ pound best quality bitter chocolate, at least 70% cocoa solids, broken into pieces
4 whole large eggs, separated
scant ¾ cup superfine sugar
a pinch of salt
1 tablespoon all-purpose flour
1 heaped tablespoon ground almonds

Preheat the oven to 375°F and grease an 8-inch deep, round cake pan with butter. Melt the butter with the chocolate over a very gentle heat or, if you are nervous, in a glass bowl over gently simmering water. In either case keep stirring with a wooden spoon and under no circumstances allow the mixture to boil or it will split. As soon as the mixture is incorporated, take off the heat and plunge the base of the bowl or pan into iced water.

Beat the egg yolks with the sugar until they turn creamy yellow. When the chocolate and butter mixture has cooled stir in the yolks and sugar. Whisk the egg whites with the salt until stiff enough to stand in peaks. Carefully stir first the flour and then the ground almonds into the chocolate, butter and egg mixture, making sure there are no lumps. Finally, using a wooden spoon, fold in the stiffened egg white. Spoon the lot into the buttered cake pan and bake 25 to 30 minutes. The gâteau is cooked when a skewer poked into the center comes out clean. Carefully remove from the pan and leave to cool on a metal tray before serving.

gratin de framboises
raspberry gratin

tarte à la rhubarbe
rhubarb tart

The first season's raspberries are so good in the Lorraine that they are served with nothing but a sprinkling of sugar and maybe a splash of the excellent eau de vie de framboise. But later on in their season raspberries are also briefly baked in a gratin, coated with a vanilla-flavoured custard.

Serves 4

generous ½ cup good quality heavy cream
½ vanilla bean
yolks of 4 medium-sized eggs
scant ¼ cup superfine sugar
½ pound fresh raspberries

Bring the cream to the boil with the vanilla bean, remove from the heat and leave to stand, 30 minutes or so. Meanwhile, whisk the egg yolks with the sugar in a pan until smooth enough to leave trails on the back of a wooden spoon. Extract the vanilla bean from the cooled cream and slowly whip into the egg and sugar mix. Heat very gently, stirring all the time, until you have a thick custard. Under no circumstances allow to boil.

Preheat the broiler to maximum and arrange the raspberries in a heatproof gratin dish. Pour over the custard and put under the broiler until the surface is lightly browned—4–5 minutes, provided the broiler is hot enough. Serve straight away.

Looking towards the Vosges Hills, Alsace

The pale pink stalks of forced rhubarb, often known as champagne rhubarb, are a regular feature in the early months of the year in the markets of north-east France and make a splendid filling for an open tart.

Serves 6 to 8

1 quantity of sweet pie crust (see page 32)
2 pounds rhubarb
unsalted butter
1 egg, separated
scant ¾ cup white sugar

Make the pie crust as in the recipe for tarte aux quetsches on page 32. Chill well.

Using a potato peeler, remove the stringy pink outer skin from the stems of rhubarb. Trim the ends. Chop the flesh across into 1-inch segments, chopping any especially large stalks in half vertically as well.

Preheat the oven to 350°F. Butter an 8-inch tart pan well and with your fingers spread out the dough to fill it. Prick all over with a fork. Return to the refrigerator for 10 minutes. Brush the egg white over the base of the tart and the egg yolk around the sides. Sprinkle half the sugar over the pie crust and arrange the pieces of rhubarb in concentric circles over the surface. Sprinkle with the remaining sugar. Bake in the oven until the rhubarb is lightly browned on the surface, about 40 to 45 minutes. Serve the tart warm.

The flatlands of northern France were battlegrounds and it is difficult to drive through them without thinking of the millions who died in the mud and horror here. Border country, this region was fought over long before the two World Wars and frequently changed hands between different powers. A fact, of course, that is reflected in the local cooking.

The wetlands of the Somme yield plentiful fish from the drainage ditches and canals that criss-cross the fields. Some find their way into *waterzooi*, a fish stew, which is strictly speaking a Flemish dish from Belgium over the now French border. For centuries, however, some of this part of France was known as Flanders and much of the local food is interchangeable.

Maisons-Alfort, 1898, by Jean Baptiste Armand Guillaumin

The dish of moules marinières, for instance, is just as popular in Boulogne, Calais, Dunkirk and Lille as it is in Belgium. Eels are still caught, smoked and exported to the Netherlands as well as eaten locally. Herrings are cured on the northern coasts in vinegar with onion, juniper berries and genever or the local version of gin.

The north is beer rather than wine country, and the strong ales traditionally brewed by monks often find their way into the cooking. Beer soup, which was once served heavily sweetened with prized sugar and flavored with expensive spices, is still popular, thickened with bread crumbs rather than flour. Beer flavors rabbit stews, coq à la bière as opposed to au vin, and carbonnade de boeuf. It also finds its way into some of the local range of puddings, cakes, pastries and fritters, which is vast, perhaps reflecting the long and often gloomy winters.

Cheeses are few and far between as this is not cow country, but the ones they do have are strong in flavor, the most popular being Maroilles, which is used in sweet as well as savory tarts. The bright orange briq from the Calais region bears a strong resemblance to aged Gouda. Despite the lack of local variety, one of the most famous fromagers in France comes from Boulogne. Philippe Olivier is one of the best *affineurs* or maturers of cheese in the business and it is a credit to France that such a profession is still a recognized one.

Move across Picardy towards Champagne on the Autoroute des Anglais, so-called because so many English use it to head south, and the land remains resolutely flat until the steep hillock on which sits the medieval town of Laon appears on the horizon. One sunny evening I sat outside a café in front of the twelfth-century Gothic cathedral, admiring the ornate carving around the portal (look out also for the oxen on the twin towers) while I tucked into a tarte (or flamiche as they are known locally) aux Maroilles, accompanied by a little salad of bitter leaves. The square was deserted, even though it was the height of summer. There are many reasons not to push on south too fast.

Shortly after Laon, the magnificent thirteenth-century cathedral of Reims hoves into view, albeit against a background of poor industrial planning. Behind looms the Montagne de Reims, site of some of the most expensive vineyards in the world. It is worth persevering through the suburbs into the city itself, as the cathedral – and especially its façade and rose windows – is stunning. This is a city of exquisite food shops, the famous biscuits *roses de Reims*, or little pink boudoir biscuits, seemingly gracing every other shop window alongside the inevitable foie gras and bottles of champagne.

As regards food, though, you are better off heading into the countryside, unless you are after Michelin-starred restaurants. Vineyards need workers and workers need lunch. One hot August day we drove out of Épernay, home to Bollinger and other famous names, into a neighbouring village in search of a meal. We found ourselves in a little café, oddly decorated with stuffed birds and old posters, where after some discussion as to whether it was too late (it was one o'clock; the French still stick religiously to midi) it was decided we could eat.

There was no menu. A vast pâté was plonked on the table, together with a pot of cornichons and a carafe of red wine. Then, despite the heat, came a very good if difficult to place soup (described, of course, as soupe de légumes), followed by côtes de porc. There was cheese, and a home-made crème caramel. On the dot of two everyone got up to leave. I had the pleasurable impression that

The Maison Krug, Champagne

lunch was taken just as seriously each and every day. This was just a few years ago; who says the French déjeuner is dead?

Further south of Reims lies the half-timbered medieval town of Troyes, once home to the merchants' fairs of Champagne. This is the home of the andouillette, to which the description of tripe sausage does not do justice. I am not a great lover of tripe when stewed or boiled in the style of, say, Caen in Normandy, but an andouillette à la ficelle, carefully broiled so that the skin does not burst, served with crisp, thin, salty frites and strong mustard, is a treat. My friends Marie-Pierre and Gary, who for a long time lived outside Troyes, used to cook it over their wood fire with as much care and attention as some would lavish on fillet steak.

From the fishing ports of Boulogne and Dunkirk to the wealthy burghers' town of Troyes is a long way in food terms as well as historical influences, if not especially in distance, but throughout these regions there is a constancy: food is, and always has been, taken very seriously indeed.

salade de harengs marinés au vin blanc avec pommes de terre à l'huile
salad of wine-marinated herrings with potatoes in oil

Herrings were once big business in the ports of the Pas-de-Calais, and in the fishing towns of Étaples and Boulogne in particular. Nowadays dwindling fish stocks and the sheer economics of the fishing industry mean that the catches are much lower, but you will still find the brasserie classic of marinated herring, served with sliced onions and boiled potatoes, on the menu. In the best of brasseries the dish is served from a central bowl as an hors-d'oeuvre to which you help yourself at will. Each November Boulogne holds a festival of the herring, when you can taste it in its many forms, cured, smoked, marinated in wine or served à la Calaisienne, stuffed with its roe.

For a different and simpler version you could mix ready prepared sweet-cured herrings cooked with onions with boiled potatoes, again cooked in their skins and dressed with a vinaigrette made with a little of the potato cooking liquor, a touch of white wine vinegar, mustard, crème fraîche or sour cream and some fresh chives. This dish is typical of the regions bordering Belgium.

Serves 4 as a light main course

4 small herrings, filleted
2 cups white wine
2 carrots, peeled and sliced
2 white onions, peeled and sliced into fine half moons
a sprig of fresh thyme
2 fresh bay leaves
2 cloves
8 juniper berries
8 black peppercorns
scant ½ cup wine vinegar
½ teaspoon salt
1 pound small waxy potatoes, roughly equal in size

extra virgin olive oil
1 teaspoon Dijon mustard
freshly ground black pepper
1 tablespoon finely chopped leaves of parsley, preferably flat-leaved

Place the herring fillets skin side up in an earthenware bowl, having picked out any stray bones. Put the white wine, carrots, onions, herbs and spices together in a Dutch oven, bring to the boil, turn down to a simmer, cover and leave to cook until the vegetables are just soft, around 20 minutes. Add the vinegar and salt, bring back to the boil and pour immediately over the herring fillets. The fish will 'cook' in the hot marinade. Leave to stand before serving, at least 24 hours (it will keep for several days, even improving in flavor).

To serve, boil the potatoes in their skins, just covered in salted water to which you have added 2 tablespoons olive oil. When almost all the water has been absorbed, check a potato—it should still be firm. Drain and, as soon as the potatoes are cool enough to handle, peel them and dress with a vinaigrette made from 1 tablespoon herring liquor, the mustard, plenty of pepper and 4 tablespoons oil. Don't drain the herrings; eat them with the vegetables from the marinade and the still warm potatoes, sprinkled with parsley.

tourte au potiron
pumpkin pie

In autumn throughout northern France cartloads of gaily colored pumpkins, squashes and gourds are on display. Some are designed to be dried as decoration; others are of the edible variety. A particular favorite is this pumpkin tourte, differentiated from the more familiar tartes by the fact that it has a pie crust top as well as bottom. It can stand alone for supper with a green salad.

Serves 4–6

1¾ pounds pumpkin
1 large shallot, peeled and finely sliced
generous ½ cup whole milk
sea salt and freshly ground black pepper
a good pinch nutmeg or mace
1 pound frozen puff paste
a generous knob of butter
the yolk of an egg, beaten

Preheat the oven to 325°F. Peel the pumpkin, discarding any seeds and strands from the hollow, and roughly chop the flesh. Put in a heavy lidded pan with the chopped shallot, the milk, generous seasoning and the nutmeg or mace. Bring almost to the boil (though be careful that the milk does not boil over), turn down to a simmer, cover and cook until the pumpkin flesh is very soft, about 20 minutes. Take off the lid and boil off any excess liquid, until the pumpkin flesh is almost dry. Mash and leave to cool.

Roll out two-thirds of the paste, line a buttered pie pan with it and spoon the cooled pumpkin mixture into the tin. Roll out the remaining paste and cover the surface, crimping the edges well together. Brush the surface with the beaten egg and bake until the pastry is nicely browned and puffed up, 30–40 minutes. Leave to cool before serving.

velouté de chou-fleur
cauliflower cream soup

soupe à la bière
beer soup

I do not, on the whole, like cauliflower, especially when boiled. I was introduced to this recipe, however, by a menu supplied by Bouchard Père et Fils, who had invited a chef from Reims to cook for one of their regular food and wine matching dinners. He had the temerity to serve cauliflower soup with one of their finer old white Burgundies and I was so intrigued that I felt I must try it (sadly without the old Burgundy). The soup is surprisingly delicate, with none of that whiff reminiscent of school canteens. The key lies in the initial boiling of the cauliflower before combining it with the other ingredients.

Serves 4 to 6

1 nice head of cauliflower, around 1¾ pounds
salt
4 cups chicken broth
1 tablespoon crème fraîche or sour cream
2 egg yolks, beaten

Remove any green outer leaves from the cauliflower and break the head into florets, discarding any stalk. Bring a large pan of salted water to the boil and cook the cauliflower, 20 minutes. Drain well.

Add the drained cauliflower to the broth and whizz in a food-processor until very smooth. Transfer to a saucepan, bring gently to the boil and simmer, 15 minutes. Check for salt but do not add pepper, which would alter the subtle flavors.

Remove from the heat and stir in the crème fraîche and the egg yolks. Beat in well and serve. If you are preparing this in advance, do not bring back to the boil or the soup will curdle.

A simple and very northern soup which, provided you use good-quality home-made broth, makes a splendid winter warmer. Thickening with bread crumbs rather than flour gives an unusual but pleasing texture.

Serves 4 to 6

1 large white onion, peeled and finely chopped
2 tablespoons unsalted butter
1 heaped teaspoon brown sugar
a good pinch of sea salt
1 teaspoon strong French mustard
scant 1½ cups strong French lager
6 cups strong chicken broth
2 cups dry brown bread crumbs
freshly ground black pepper
a good pinch each of nutmeg and cinnamon
2 tablespoons finely chopped parsley
scant ½ cup full-fat crème fraîche or sour cream

Put the chopped onion in a heavy stock pan with the butter, sugar and salt. Cook over a medium heat, stirring regularly, until the onion is nicely browned, about 20 minutes. Stir in the mustard, lager and broth and bring to the boil. Add the bread crumbs, stir well, and simmer, 30 minutes. Leave to cool a little then liquidize and add plenty of pepper and the nutmeg and cinnamon. Stir in the parsley and crème fraîche and serve.

gratin d'endives
endive gratin

The north of France and its neighbour Belgium are famous for their blanched white endive, known locally as witloof, and this is one of my favorite dishes from my childhood—and still one of my preferred winter supper dishes. Ham is often wrapped around the heads of endive, although I like to serve this gratin with cold meats such as ham or pork on the side, as well as some dill pickles and small pickled white onions. These days I also add flavor to the white sauce with beer and mustard. But the sauce is essentially a béchamel, which is attributed to one Louis de Béchamel, Marquess in the court of Louis XIV.

Serves 2

salt
2 large white heads of endive
4 tablespoons unsalted butter
¾ cup all-purpose flour
1 heaped teaspoon Dijon mustard
1 cup strong lager
1 cup whole milk
pinch of nutmeg
freshly ground black pepper
4 slices of jambon de Paris (cooked ham)
  (optional)

Bring a large pan of salted water to the boil and cook the whole endive, 5 minutes. Drain and leave until cool enough to handle. Preheat the oven to 220°C/425°F/gas mark 7.

Melt the butter in a saucepan and stir in the flour. Cook the roux over a gentle heat, stirring all the time until it becomes a delicate caramel color, 5 minutes. Stir in the mustard then slowly add the lager, still stirring all the time. Do the same with the milk, until you have a smooth mixture. Add the nutmeg, a pinch of salt and a generous few grinds of pepper. Leave to cook, stirring occasionally, 5 minutes. The béchamel should be thick.

Meanwhile, cut each endive in half lengthwise and squeeze out any excess water. Wrap each piece with ham, if you are using it, and arrange cut side up in an earthenware dish. Spoon over the béchamel sauce. Bake until the surface is lightly browned and bubbling, 20 minutes. Serve very hot with crusty bread.

arras marketplace

There are few finer market squares in the whole of France than that in Arras, known simply as the Grand'Place—appropriately, as it is truly huge. With its gabled houses in the Flemish style, dating back to the seventeenth and eighteenth centuries, and its arcades beneath, this is a square of elegance and with a sense of history. It is easy to conjure up the cloth fairs and witch trials that have taken place here over the centuries. But above all there is a reek of money.

Arras may have had a troubled history but it has always been wealthy. Regional capital of first the Gauls and then the Romans, under the reign of the Dukes of Burgundy in the fourteenth and fifteenth centuries it became famous for its cloth merchants. In Hamlet Shakespeare refers several times to his characters 'hiding behind the arras', as the rich wall hangings were then known.

The cloth trade moved to Flanders but, under Spanish rule in the sixteenth century, Arras became the centre of the trade in Artois grain, a cereal grown on the rolling hills around the city. Wealth accumulated under the Spanish, so much so that when Louis XIV of France besieged the city in the mid seventeenth century the burghers were reluctant to give way to French rule. The network of tunnels known as *boves* dug into the limestone, which criss-cross underneath the market square, date from this time, and until relatively recently were still used to store food and wine as well as hide in during times of trouble.

Arras may have been just over the border from Flanders, but even today it has a Flemish feel to it, one that is reflected in the foodstuffs on offer in the open-air market in the Grand'Place and the adjoining Place des Héros. Here you will find freshly churned butter, river fish for *waterzooi*, mussels and pickled herrings, piles of bacon and other pork products, potatoes and cabbage. The breads are dark and solid, made from rye and wholewheat. Most characteristic of all, though, are the features of the stallholders and many of their customers. They look, to my eyes at least, as if they have just stepped out of a Brueghel painting.

The Hôtel de Ville [in the Place des Héros], Arras, 1856, by Lewis John Wood

flamiche au maroilles
maroilles cheese tart

A famous patissier in the region in the early sixteenth century, Gohier, was known for his cheese tarts, flavored with the expensive medieval treats of orange-flower water and sugar. From there, so the story goes, came the local tradition of cheese tarts, which soon became savory as well as sweet. In this version the Maroilles, known as the king of cheeses of the north, is baked in a tart. If you cannot find Maroilles, you could use the even more pungent Munster from Alsace.

Serves 4 to 6

1 quantity of pie crust (see page 25)
unsalted butter, for greasing the tin
1 ripe whole Maroilles cheese, around 1 pound, rind removed, the cheese cut into bite-sized pieces
2 tablespoons all-purpose flour
3 large eggs, beaten, plus 1 egg yolk
1 cup 40% fat fromage blanc
a pinch of nutmeg
a pinch of cinnamon
sea salt and white pepper

Make the pie crust as described on page 25 and chill. Preheat the oven to 400°F. Line a buttered tart pan with the pie crust, making sure that the edges are high up the sides of the pan. Prick the pie crust with a fork and chill, 20 minutes. Mix together the cheese, flour, eggs (excluding the extra egg yolk), fromage blanc, nutmeg, cinnamon and seasoning. This can be done most easily in a food-processor but you can also use the back of a fork.

Take the pie crust from the fridge and brush the edges with the egg yolk. Fill with the cheese mixture and bake until the filling is nicely puffed up, 25–30 minutes. Serve hot, with a salad of bitter green leaves such as frisée on the side.

moules marinières
mussels marinières

Belgium claims this dish as its own (especially when served with frites and mayonnaise, as I enjoyed it as a child), but it is just as popular in northern France. Every cook has their own version, adding the whole of the celery, including the leaves, or none at all, shallots instead of onions, more leeks or none, thyme as well as parsley, a swirl of crème fraîche at the end (which turns it into moules à la crème). This is how I was taught to cook it many years ago.

Serves 4 as a main course

around 9 pounds mussels
1 large white onion, peeled and finely chopped
white part of 1 leek, finely chopped
some celery leaves, chopped
2 tablespoons unsalted butter
¾ cup dry white wine
1 bay leaf
pepper, preferably white
1 tablespoon chopped parsley

Scrub the mussels well under cold running water, discarding any that have a cracked shell or don't close when tapped. Debeard them; that is, pull out the little strands sticking out of one side.

Put the onion, leek and celery leaves together with the butter in a lidded pot large enough to take all the mussels. Stew over a gentle heat, stirring regularly, until the onion and leek are soft but not in any way browned, about 15 minutes. Add the wine and bay leaf, bring to the boil and add the mussels. Cover the pan and cook over a medium heat, giving a vigorous shake occasionally to turn the mussels over, 4–5 minutes.

Take the lid off, give the mussels a good stir and leave to boil for 1 minute. Sprinkle with the pepper and parsley and serve straight away—preferably from the cooking pot, with a ladle and spoons for the diners to sup up the liquor.

turbotin sauce hollandaise
brill with hollandaise sauce

Calais is not my favorite town in France but I do have a favorite habit the minute I set foot on French soil there. Just a few minutes' drive from the ferry terminal, overlooking the water, is a small restaurant much favored by the burghers of Calais. It has the correct white tablecloths, smart wine glasses, a series of affordable set menus (I always start with oysters), excellent service and a splendid cheeseboard. But best of all is the thick slice of pearly white brill which they serve with a jug of thick and buttery hollandaise sauce. A few turned potatoes, a quarter of lemon and that is it. Old-fashioned and very, very good. As an alternative, you could use a slice of turbot rather than its little brother brill.

Serves 2 (you could make it for more, but with fish dishes like this which need last-minute cooking I think two is a good number)

1 glass of white wine
2 tablespoons white wine vinegar
a few black peppercorns
sea salt
a few sprigs of parsley
a sliver of lemon zest, unwaxed if possible
2 thick slices of brill, skinned
a sauce boat of hollandaise sauce (see page 22)

Prepare a court-bouillon with everything but the fish, pouring in just enough water to cover. Bring to the boil and simmer, 20 minutes. Slip in the fish and poach gently—the exact time will depend upon the thickness and freshness of the fillets but around 10 minutes is a good guide. The fish should still be firm and pearly white in color. Have the hollandaise ready, keeping warm over a double boiler; take care it does not boil. Lift out the fish carefully and serve straight away with the warm sauce.

darnes de saumon au champagne
salmon fillets in champagne sauce

Classically this dish was made with the freshwater fish pike which, although bony, has a delicate flavour. Nowadays the more easily available salmon is a popular substitute. This is a restaurant style of dish, lending itself to fast cooking, and of course the key is the rich sauce, which justifies high prices.

Serves 4

4 thin fillets of salmon, skin and pin bones removed
sea salt and white pepper
¼ pound button mushrooms
3 tablespoons butter
generous ½ cup dry champagne
1 heaped tablespoon crème fraîche or sour cream
1 teaspoon finely chopped leaves of fresh tarragon

Preheat the oven to 300°F and put a serving dish in to warm. Season the salmon and leave to stand 15 minutes or so. Meanwhile, cook the mushrooms in half the butter until soft, then transfer to the serving dish in the oven to keep warm.

In the same pan, melt the remaining butter and fry the salmon escalopes 2 minutes on either side. Pour in the champagne and bring to the boil. Cook the salmon a further 2 minutes, then lift out and place on top of the mushrooms. Bring the liquor in the pan to a fast boil and add the crème fraîche and tarragon. Boil until reduced by about a third, 2 minutes, pour over the salmon and serve.

master of champagne

The city of Reims is famous for its champagne houses, of which there are many. But it has been said that 'there is champagne—and then there is Krug'. Master of Wine Jancis Robinson has described Krug as 'one of the most distinctive of champagnes'. One famous couple, who must remain nameless, never travel without a half bottle of it, to drink to celebrate their safe arrival (and send Krug a picture each time to prove the fact). According to Rémi Krug it is also 'the perfect food wine', and he took me on a tour of his home town to prove it.

Krug has been made in Reims since Rémi's German-born great-grandfather Johan-Joseph founded the house in the middle of the nineteenth century, and Rémi still lives next door to the cellars. My first tasting was served not with the traditional sweet *biscuits roses de Reims* but with cheese straws. Next stop was the cheese shop, where we tried the champagne with the local Maroilles cheese, which Rémi insisted should be chalky white in the middle rather than creamy all the way through. Another favored match was with local mirabelles, the tiny yellow plums delicately stewed in sugar syrup.

But that evening Rémi sprang his real surprise. We were eating at the restaurant of a schoolboy friend, who just happens to own and cook at the Michelin starred Boyer les Crayères. I let them choose—and their choice was pig's trotter with lentils. Admittedly it was a boned trotter, stuffed with foie gras, but it wasn't an obvious choice to accompany a fine champagne. However, Rémi had made his point: champagne goes well with all kinds of food. After all, it is only relatively recently that we have started to treat it as an aperitif rather than as a wine to be enjoyed with food.

pintade aux choux
guinea fowl with cabbage

The guinea fowl is a fine bird for eating, appreciated as far back as Roman times, when it was known as the hen of Carthage (the name guinea indicates its African antecedents). In the north of France it is paired with braised cabbage, a one-pot dish that is regularly found on the menus of *restaurants du coin*, or locals, in Paris. The addition of cream cheese is an improvement a neighbor taught me—it keeps the breast of what can be a dry bird moist.

Serves 4

1 plump guinea fowl, around 4 pounds
generous ½ cup cream cheese
a large sprig of tarragon
1 garlic clove, peeled and halved
1¾ tablespoons unsalted butter
1 large cabbage, around 2 pounds
sea salt
½ pound smoked bacon, cut into strips or lardons
freshly ground black pepper
juice of 1 lemon

Preheat the oven to 400°F. Wash the bird and wipe dry, removing any fat from the cavity. Stuff the cavity with the cheese, tarragon and garlic, and smear the butter over the breast. Place the bird upside down in a Dutch oven and roast in the oven, basting with its juices occasionally, 1 hour. Turn the breast side up halfway through cooking.

Meanwhile, remove any tough outer leaves from the cabbage and discard. Cut the cabbage in half, remove the core, then slice the remainder into fine slivers. Bring a large pan of well-salted water to the boil and blanch the cabbage slivers together with the bacon, 3 minutes then drain.

Take the guinea fowl from the oven and remove from the Dutch oven. Add the drained cabbage and bacon, turn in the fat, then add plenty of pepper and the lemon juice, stirring well. Place the guinea fowl on top and cook another 15 minutes. Remove the bird from the oven and leave to rest on a carving board, 5 minutes. Stir the cabbage again and return to the heat.

Carve the bird, arrange the slices on top of the hot cabbage and serve. The only side dish you need is plenty of bread to mop up the juices.

carbonnade de boeuf
beef stewed in beer

Not all French beef casseroles are made with wine; beer (dark rather than lager) is preferred in the north of the country. A Bière de Gard such as Jenlain is ideal, but I have also made this successfully with a good English bitter. The final addition of stale bread to thicken the sauce and mustard to spice it up is classic, though the use of Dijon mustard is not. Locally, a variety of white mustard is normally used but it is both difficult to get hold of out of the region and a touch too hot and sweet for my taste.

Serves 6

6 white onions (the traditional smaller onions rather than the milder variety are best for this recipe)
4 tablespoons lard
1 tablespoon brown sugar
1 tablespoon red wine vinegar
4½ pounds chuck steak, cut into 6 pieces
salt and pepper
bouquet garni made up of a few sprigs of fresh thyme and parsley and a couple of bay leaves, tied together in a bundle
2 cups dark beer
1 tablespoon Dijon mustard
6 slices of slightly stale baguette

Peel and slice the onions into fine half moons. Melt half the lard in a heavy Dutch oven over a gentle heat, add the onion and sweat gently, stirring occasionally, until the onion is softened but not browned, around 20 minutes. Turn up the heat to medium. Add the sugar and vinegar and cook another 2 minutes.

Preheat the oven to 325°F. Scatter the onions over the base of a large dish, preferably one made of earthenware. Heat the remaining lard in the Dutch oven in which you cooked the onions. Season the steak and fry in two batches 2 minutes on either side in order to brown and seal the meat. Place the meat on top of the cooked onions and tuck in the bundle of herbs. Pour in the beer, which should just cover the meat.

Cover the dish with foil and bake 2½ hours, taking it out to stir once or twice, turning the meat and checking there is sufficient liquor (if not, add a little more beer). Ten minutes before serving, remove the bouquet garni, stir in the mustard and push in the slices of baguette. Bake uncovered until the baguette is just browned and has soaked up much of the sauce, about 10 minutes. Check seasoning and serve piping hot.

pain perdu
'lost' bread

There are plenty of puddings across France known as *pain perdu*, all designed to use up stale bread, just as in bread and butter pudding. Brioche is often used but this version is it at its most basic. It is an old-fashioned dish for the selfless mother, who stays at the stove while the youngest and oldest of the family enjoy this simple treat, which must be served really hot.

Serves 4

8 slices of slightly stale white baguette
whole milk
5 tablespoons unsalted butter
2 large eggs, beaten
golden brown sugar
cinnamon

Place the slices of baguette in a dish and pour over just enough milk to moisten but not turn the bread soggy. The exact quantity will depend upon the bread itself.

Heat half the butter in a heavy skillet. Dip each of 4 slices of baguette into the beaten egg mixture and transfer immediately to the sizzling butter. Cook quickly, turning once, until lightly browned, sprinkle with sugar and cinnamon and serve. Discard the first lot of cooking butter and repeat the process for the remaining 4 slices.

salade de fruits au champagne
fruit salad with champagne

There are so many champagne producers that it can be difficult to know where to turn when you want to buy some champagne. The best advice is to try different houses until you find one whose champagne you like and stick to it. Which is why for many years I have been ringing the doorbell of the famille Simonet, in the little village of Villers-Marmery, not far from Ambonnay, who love you to turn up at their house for a dégustation.

Depending on the time of day, *biscuits roses de Reims*, or cheese straws, or little toasts spread with pâté de foie gras might be served with the champagne. But one particularly hot summer's day, when we arrived as usual unannounced, a chilled fruit salad was brought out from the fridge and a generous measure of rosé champagne poured in, which made the fruit bubble in the fizz.

Serves 4

a mixture of summer fruits, all of which should
   be perfectly ripe—white peaches and nectarines,
   American Canteloupe melons, wild strawberries
   or cultivated raspberries would be ideal
white sugar
juice of 1 lemon
rosé champagne

Peel and prepare the fruit: peaches and nectarines should be finely sliced, melons scooped out into balls, strawberries and raspberries washed. Sprinkle generously with sugar and squeeze over the lemon juice. Leave to macerate in the fridge for 30 minutes. Spoon into champagne glasses and top up with the well-chilled rosé champagne.

normandy

Normandy has long stood apart and even now, it doesn't really feel very French. Ceded in AD 911 by Charles III (otherwise, unfortunately, known as Charles the Simple) to the Viking invaders, this blessed part of France gets its name from the *hommes du Nord*—the Norsemen. With its lush pastures, rolling hills, willow-hung streams, tall church towers and half-timbered houses, you could easily imagine yourself over the other side of the Channel in England.

Until, that is, you sit down at the dinner table. Few cooks outside France would serve up the famous local dish of tripes à la mode de Caen. This requires not only every element of the tripe of the ox, including the so-called fourth stomach or maw, but also a whole pre-boiled cow's heel (a calf's foot will not, apparently, do), stewed with carrots and cider. It was traditionally prepared in quantity and cooked in the baker's oven, the baker receiving his own share in return for the favor. No wonder diners needed a *trou normand*, a quick shot of Calvados served between courses, to aid the digestion and create a little more space in the stomach. Nowadays, most people buy their tripe ready cooked from the traiteur—take-away food of a very different nature.

Rouen, the capital of Normandy, is a splendid place to go shopping, with its place du Vieux Marché (where Jeanne d'Arc met her end), surrounded by half-timbered houses and a daily fruit and vegetable market. Serious marketers, however, descend at the weekends upon the marché place Saint-Marc. A trip to the medieval cathedral with which Monet became obsessed or to the high gothic Eglise St-Maclou should precede a splendid lunch, preferably featuring the classic dish of canard rouennais.

Rouen, on the banks of the Seine, was known from medieval times for its merchant population. Wool and hides were brought from

England, and later Scotland, for the tanners and dyers to treat, before they were shipped on to the fairs in the north and Champagne. Sel de Guérande was imported on its way to Paris. Herring fishermen set off from here for the Baltic. Later, with one of the first printing presses in France and boasting its own parliament, Rouen attracted many Spanish and Italian traders. But in their culinary preferences the locals remained most interested in the local produce.

Ask a Norman what the classic cooking of the region involves and the trinity of apples, pork and cream will always get a mention. The ancient apple orchards shape the landscape around these parts and their fruit features in much of the cooking. A Norman apple tart is a thing of beauty, but the use of apples is not restricted to the sweet. Fat pork chops broiled and served with slices of apple cooked in the local butter with lashings of cream and cider are a particular favorite, the lightly smoked black-skinned chitterling sausages, or andouilles, from Vire, accompanied by apples fried in the sausage fat are another.

In between the orchards are the pasturelands where the red and white cows graze, udders full to bursting. Their milk goes to make cheeses famous the world over: Camembert, Pont-l'Evêque, Livarot, Neufchâtel, Brillat-Savarin, all distinguished by their unctuous creaminess. The butter of Isigny tastes like pure cream, while the pots of crème fraîche on sale in every marketplace are so indulgent as to verge upon the wicked. Just as in Ireland, the good green grass also suits horses: most of France's stud farms, or *harras*, including the National Stud, are in this part of the country.

Turn away from the gentle pasturelands towards the sea, however, and a quite different Normandy reveals itself. There are the long sandy beaches which have seen their fair share of death through too many wars, but also plenty of fishing ports, the biggest of which are Le Havre and Dieppe (the pretty port of Honfleur on the other side of the estuary from Le Havre is more favored these days by artists and tourists). The fish landed is generally northern in nature: sole, plaice, skate and brill. Sole à la normande—the fillets of white fish carefully wrapped around a filling of cooked mussels, little brown shrimps and sometimes even oysters and wild mushrooms— was a nineteenth-century Paris restaurant favorite.

The shellfish is exceptional. Look out for the tiny blue-black mussels which are a specialty of the region, cooked with onions, cream and cider. In sight of the cliffs of Etretat, another favorite scene of Monet's, I enjoyed one of my most memorable seafood feasts. The mist was slowly rolling in and we were sitting outside on the increasingly chilly terrace, but we would not be torn away from the tiny freshly boiled crabs, which were produced by the dozen.

I still, though, have the feeling that from a cook's point of view the real Normandy lies inland. My friend Tyrel (a good Norman name) has for some years owned a house near Coutances. He regularly brings me back bottles of Pommeau, the local aperitif made from the must of cider apples and Calvados. It has a flavor very peculiar to Normandy, a mixture of sweetness and spirit and apples. It always reminds me of a lunch I once had in the region known as la petite Suisse, or little Switzerland, for frankly unaccountable reasons—those rolling hills look nothing like the Swiss mountains or even the foothills. It was July but it was pouring with rain and we were cold and wet. Once we reached the restaurant, glasses of Pommeau all round soon restored our spirits.

We sat in front of a roaring log fire and after we had dried off and finished our aperitifs we had the menu du jour: home-made

rillettes de lapin, potted rabbit, served with cornichons, or dill pickles, and small white pickled onions and good bread, followed by noisettes de porc in a cream and apple sauce, some perfect Camembert and a thick slab of pear and almond tart to finish. Simple, and very, very good.

Rouen Cathedral, Effects of Sunlight, Sunset, 1892, by Claude Monet

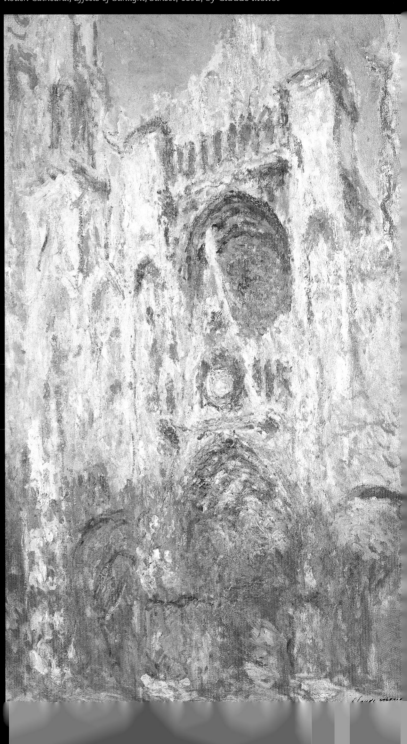

omelette à la mère poulard
mother poulard's omelet

moules à la normande
mussels norman style

La Mère Poulard, who opened her eponymous restaurant on Mont-St-Michel in 1888, was renowned for her omelets. Today many restaurants on the island that has sadly become a tourist trap try (and almost invariably fail) to emulate them. She famously claimed that there was no secret beyond good eggs, fizzing butter and a well-seasoned pan over a hot fire, but then she did make an awful lot of omelets. I would add that my own secret ingredient is really good unsalted butter. There is no shortage of this in Normandy. Also, never try to make an omelet for more than one person at a time, and keep any flavorings, whether they be fines herbes or grated cheese, to a minimum.

Serves 1

2 large, fresh eggs
salt and freshly ground black pepper
a good knob of unsalted butter
a little filling, if you must

Beat the eggs and season. Melt the butter in the pan over a medium heat and when it is fizzing add the eggs. Shake well and add the filling (if you are using it) at this stage. Fold the omelet in half with a wooden spoon, tip out onto a warm plate with the buttery juices and serve straight away with some bread. If you are having salad, eat it afterwards—a vinaigrette with eggs is one of the worst things you can do to your taste buds.

Sitting at a roadside shack staring out across the vast expanses of the Bay of Mont-St-Michel at low tide while our mussels were cooked with cider and cream, I noticed in the distance peculiar-looking vehicles, half boat half tractor, crossing the mudflats, which were studded with poles. Their drivers were busy collecting more of the *moules de bouchot* we were about to eat.

Moules de bouchot are mussels grown in bunches on poles which are exposed at low tide. According to a sixteenth-century manuscript, the tradition goes back to the thirteenth century, when in 1235 a shipwrecked Scot by the name of Patrick Walton found himself in Aiguillon, on the Atlantic coast north of Bordeaux. Looking for food, he put posts into the water, to be exposed at low tide, in order to string his nets to catch seabirds, just as he had back in Scotland. Soon the posts were encrusted with tiny mussels. The first mussel farm was born.

For centuries this method of rearing mussels was restricted to the Atlantic coast, but after the Second World War the method was introduced in the Bay of Mont-St-Michel, where conditions proved to be ideal.

Serves 4 as a first course or 2 as a main dish

6½ pounds mussels
2 shallots, peeled and finely chopped
a handful of flat-leaved parsley, stalks removed, finely chopped
2½ quarts dry cider, preferably Norman
freshly ground black pepper
2 egg yolks
¾ cup crème fraîche or sour cream
2 tablespoons unsalted butter, cut into small pieces

Scrub the mussel shells well under running water and debeard them (that is, pull out the strands that stick out of the side). Discard any that do not close when tapped or that have broken shells.

Preheat the oven to 300°F and put a large serving bowl in to warm. Put the mussels, shallots, parsley and cider in a large pan and add some pepper. Cover and cook over a medium heat, shaking from time to time, until the mussels have opened, 4–5 minutes. Discard any that do not. Strain the liquor from the mussels through a fine sieve into another pan and transfer the opened mussels to the serving dish. Cover with foil and return to the oven.

Working as quickly as possible so that the mussels do not shrivel, whisk the egg yolks into the crème fraîche. Bring the mussel liquor back to the boil, reduce the heat to low, and whisk in the egg mixture. Cook, stirring all the time, for a few minutes, until the mixture thickens sufficiently to coat the back of a wooden spoon (but take care not to boil or it may curdle). Remove from the heat and whisk in the pieces of butter. Check the seasoning, remove the mussels from the oven and pour over the sauce. Stir well and serve straight away with plenty of bread and a spoon for the sauce.

maquereaux dieppoise
mackerel in the style of dieppe

Cooked either in dry cider or white wine (I prefer the latter but it is a matter of personal choice), mackerel are a favorite hors d'oeuvre in both Brittany and Normandy. For best results the fish should be very fresh, sold with gleaming eye and bright skin.

Serves 4 as a first course or light lunch

4 medium-sized mackerel, gutted and heads removed
2 large carrots, peeled
1 large white onion, peeled
6 whole peppercorns
a strip of lemon zest, unwaxed if possible
some stalks of parsley and, if possible, a frond of fennel
2 bay leaves
½ bottle (1½ cups) of dry white wine
1 tablespoon white wine vinegar

Wash the fish well inside and out. Choose a non-reactive pan (this is important unless you want black fish) which has a lid and into which the fish will fit snugly (though don't put them in at this stage). Chop the carrots into fine rounds and slice the onion into fine half moons. Add the peppercorns, lemon zest and herbs, then add the wine, an equal quantity of water, and the vinegar. Bring to the boil quickly then reduce to a slow simmer and cook uncovered, 10 minutes.

Now slip the fish in and cover. The liquid should just simmer over the lowest possible heat, 10 minutes. Remove from the heat and leave to cool in the liquor.

The next stage is up to you. You can, if you have sensitive guests, skin and fillet the fish, in which case you should do so as soon as the fish are cool enough to handle, so that the skin and bones slip off easily. Personally, however, I think the fish taste better if left to cool on the bone—and that's not just for reasons of laziness. In either case, the fish, vegetables and cooking liquor should be transferred to an earthenware bowl and well chilled before serving. The liquor will set to a jelly, which is especially prized. Good bread and unsalted butter are an essential part of the equation.

sole normande
sole norman style

Over the decades this dish has been fancified in many French restaurants, with the fillets of sole wrapped around the filling and cream and cider added to the sauce, but this is the simple housewives' version. You do need fellow diners who are prepared to deal with the rather messy process of eating the cockles and shrimp, but you can always give them a proper finger bowl of warm water complete with a slice of lemon rather than the awful scented wipes which so many restaurants now seem to regard as standard for anyone tucking into their fruits de mer.

Serves 4

4 Dover soles, skinned and filleted (keep the bones and skin for the stock)
½ bottle white wine
several sprigs parsley
salt and freshly ground black pepper
1 onion, quartered with the skin still on
2 carrots, peeled and roughly chopped
½ pound button mushrooms, washed
¾ cup baby shrimp
500g small clams or cockles

Make a stock by adding the fish trimmings, white wine, parsley, seasoning, onion and carrots to 2 cups of water and simmering uncovered, 45 minutes. Leave to cool and then strain.

Preheat the oven to 350°F. Place the sole in a large earthenware dish and scatter over the mushrooms followed by the shrimp and cockles. Pour over just enough stock to cover, cover with parchment paper or foil and bake until the clams have opened, 35–40 minutes. Serve at once with plain boiled white rice.

le caneton aux coings et figues
duck with quince and figs

Just sometimes you strike lucky. We were driving south of Rouen on a miserable rainy evening and had decided to stop for the night rather than continue further south. We found a hotel in the middle of nowhere but it didn't have a restaurant. Madame directed us a few miles down the road. We didn't expect much. We found a feast. The salad of fresh lobster and girolles was exceptional. The home-made foie gras, served with nothing more than coarse salt, was sublime. But the real treat was the roast duck for two, served with quince and fresh figs.

It was only later that I discovered that the area around Rouen has long been famous for its *caneton*, a breed that is half wild and half domesticated duck. These were the ducks used in *la presse*, a contraption popular in Parisian restaurants designed to squeeze the maximum juice from the bones of the roast duck. Though ours was quite moist enough without the need for squeezing.

Serves 2

1 duck, around 3½ pounds
salt
2 large quinces, around 1 pound each
freshly ground black pepper
about 1 cup sweet cider
8 fresh black figs

Preheat the oven to 400°F. Prick the duck all over and salt the skin well. Cut the quinces into quarters (not an easy job—they are very hard) and remove the core. Place the duck in a roasting pan breast side up and surround with the quince. Season the fruit with salt and pepper, then pour in a wine glass of the cider.

Bake the duck 30 minutes, then remove from the oven in order to baste the quince with the juices, and turn the duck so it is breast side down in the roasting pan. Return to the oven and cook a further 20 minutes. Take the bird out again, drain off any excess fat, and add the figs to the roasting pan. Add another good splash of cider. Return to the oven and cook another 20 minutes. Leave to rest 5 minutes before carving and serve with the fruit and the pan juices.

côtes de porc au cidre
pork chops in cider

This makes a simple but delicious supper for two. Sometimes (as so often in Norman cooking) a good dollop of crème fraîche is added to the sauce at the end of cooking but I prefer to leave it out. On the other hand, mashed potato (or a *purée de pommes de terre*, as would be classic in France) and a green salad are essential accompaniments.

Serves 2

2 pork chops on the bone
salt and pepper
2 tablespoons unsalted butter
2 shallots, peeled and finely chopped
2 cups strong dry cider
1 teaspoon Dijon mustard
1 tablespoon chopped flat-leaved parsley

Preheat the oven to 325°F, put a plate in to warm, and heat a ridged grill pan on a medium heat. Season the chops and cook on both sides, turning four times so that you get nice criss-crossed ridge marks. Remove from the pan, put on the plate, cover with foil and keep warm in the oven.

Now you need to work quickly so that the chops don't dry out. Add the butter to the pan in which you have cooked the chops, so that you pick up the meat juices as well, and as soon as it is fizzing add the shallots. Cook, stirring, for a few minutes until softened, then pour in the cider, stir in the mustard and add the parsley. Bring to the boil and bubble 5 minutes. Add the chops to the pan, including any juices that have run, and cook for just 1 minute on either side before serving.

the sheep of mont-st-michel

Early on a hazy morning, the Abbey of Mont-St-Michel appears suspended above the mist, hanging in space like a castle in a Disney film. The thick wall of sea mist dulls all sound. Except, that is, of the ewes, calling their lambs to follow them as they graze their way across the salt marshes. They munch on over sixty different varieties of herbs, a unique mixture which gives the lamb known as *pré-salé* its specific flavor.

Each day farmer Philippe Farcy opens his barn doors directly onto the marsh to allow his sheep out, to mingle with the 4,000 or so belonging to the fourteen other farmers who also have the rights to graze the marshes. The sheep wander many miles over the course of the day but, come nightfall, each returns to its own barn for water and shelter—though Philippe admits that when the new lambs are born, he and his fellow sheep farmers spend a long time each evening on the telephone reuniting each of their flocks.

It is this homing instinct that has done much to preserve the purity of the breed, known as *grévin*, which originates from an English Suffolk cross. It is, Philippe explains, *une race costaude*: hardy, in other words. The flocks go out on the marshes every day, even when the wind and rain are whipping across from the Atlantic. As for attempts to introduce new strains, they have failed because the sheep simply don't know their way home. So each year farmers such as Philippe retain around a quarter of their female lambs to breed from.

There is no problem in selling the rest: restaurants, in Paris in particular, cannot get enough of them. But they face fierce competition from the locals, and in particular Guy Barraux, who uniquely serves only *pré-salé* lamb in his hotel restaurant overlooking the marsh. He buys whole sheep, some four to five a week in the summer season, knowing the *éleveur*, or breeder, each one comes from. The animals are slaughtered and butchered locally and each night Guy broils the meat very simply over a wood fire, as he has for twenty-six years. Every part of the carcass is used. It is no wonder that people come from many miles to eat here. This is food rooted in century-old tradition and I felt privileged to share in it.

faisan à la normande
pheasant norman style

The pheasant is often erroneously thought of as a British bird but with its exotic plumage it is in fact native to Asia. It looks equally at home strutting through the woods and orchards of Normandy—where they cook it better too.

Serves 4

4 breasts of pheasant, skin on
salt and freshly ground black pepper
2 tablespoons unsalted butter
2 shallots or 1 small onion, peeled and finely
  chopped
3 tart eating apples (you want a firm apple with
  a distinctive flavor), peeled, cored, and sliced
2 tablespoons Calvados
scant ½ cup strong dry cider
scant ½ cup full-fat crème fraîche or sour cream

Season the pheasant breasts. Melt the butter in a heavy frying pan and quickly sauté the breasts 2 minutes on each side, until nicely browned. Remove from the pan and set aside for the moment.

Add the chopped shallot or onion to the butter in the pan (if it is looking dry you may need to add another knob) and cook, stirring regularly until soft, 5 minutes. Now add the slices of apple and fry for another few minutes until they are lightly browned.

Return the pheasant breasts to the pan with the apple and onion mixture. Heat the Calvados in a ladle and then set light to it. Pour it flaming into the pan, shaking to distribute the spirit. As soon as the flames die down pour in the cider. Bring back to a bubble and stir in the crème fraîche. Simmer for a few minutes and stir before serving. A celeriac purée goes well with this dish.

boudins noirs
aux pommes
blood sausage
with apples

Blood sausage in France is regarded not as a
breakfast dish but as a starter or a light (well,
this is France) main course. It is generally made in
much smaller sizes than the British black pudding,
and happily dried herbs such as sage are not
allowed anywhere near it.

I especially like it served the Norman way with
fried apples, a cheap and filling brasserie classic.

Serves 4 as a first course or 2 as a main dish

1 pound tart eating apples
juice of 1 lemon
4 small or 2 large blood sausage, around 1 pound
   in total
2 tablespoons unsalted butter
sea salt and freshly ground black pepper
1 teaspoon brown sugar
1 tablespoon red wine vinegar

Peel and core the apples then cut the flesh into
slices about 1-inch thick. Add the lemon juice to
a large bowl of water and soak the slices around
15 minutes.

Slice the sausage across on a diagonal at around
the same thickness as the apples. Melt the butter in
a heavy pan, ideally ridged, over a high heat and
cook the sausage 3–4 minutes on either side, until
browned. Remove with a slotted spoon and set
aside.

Drain the apples well and add to the pan, season,
and fry until nicely browned on each side. Add the
sugar and vinegar and return the sausage to the
pan, turning briefly in the sauce, and cook for
another minute or so before serving.

sorbet au pommes vertes
green apple sorbet

In recent years restaurants, in particular, have developed the traditional *trou normand* (Calvados between courses) into a sorbet, typically made from green apples, over which a little Calvados is poured. In my opinion this is one of the few good uses for a Granny Smith, which is the typical variety of apple grown in the more commercial orchards of the region. The sorbet also goes very well with an apple tart or with *douillons*—fruit turnovers, see page 60.

Serves 6

5 Granny Smith apples
juice of 1 lemon
1½ cups superfine sugar
1¼ cups water
Calvados (optional)

Peel and core the apples and dice the flesh. Place in a bowl of water with the lemon juice and set aside 10 minutes. Meanwhile, mix the sugar into the measured water and bring to the boil. Drain the pieces of apple and add to the now simmering sugar and water mixture. Cook until the apple pieces are just starting to fall apart, 5 minutes.

Leave to cool for about 10 minutes and as soon as cool enough to handle liquidize to a purée. Transfer to a plastic container and place in the freezer. (You can of course use a sorbetière if you are lucky enough to have one.) Stir the sorbet at half-hourly intervals until it is set but slightly slushy, about 4 hours. If you are serving it as a *trou normand*, place round scoops in glasses and top up with a little Calvados.

tarte fine aux pommes
thin apple tart

If you order this in a restaurant, the waiter will generally warn you that you have to wait twenty-five minutes or so, the point being that the tart is best served straight from the oven. Restaurants usually make individual portions in a circular shape; and, just as they do, I feel no shame in using ready-made puff paste. I tend to use a rectangular tart pan, as it is easier to lay the apple slices in rows rather than concentric circles. You can serve the tart just as it is or flambéed with Calvados.

Serves 4 to 6

½ pound packaged frozen puff paste, defrosted
all-purpose flour
5 or 6 tart eating apples, around 1½ pounds
4 teaspoons brown sugar
3 tablespoons unsalted butter
2 tablespoons Calvados (optional)

Have ready a thin rectangular tart tin, which you have buttered lightly and placed in the fridge. Preheat the oven to 200°C/ 400°F/gas mark 6. Roll out the pastry on a floured board and spread in the tart tin, cutting off any overlapping edges. Return the tin to the fridge.

Just before you are ready to cook, peel the apples. Slice the flesh as thinly as possibe into half moons, discarding the core. Take the paste from the refrigerator and, working quickly, layer the apple slices in overlapping lines across. Sprinkle with the brown sugar, dot with the butter and bake until the apple slices are golden and the rim of the tart slightly puffed, about 40–45 minutes.

The tart is delicious eaten warm from the oven but for added drama you can also flambé it. Heat the Calvados in a ladle, set light to it and pour over the tart—standing well back. I have also had this served with a Calvados cream, simply whipped sweetened cream into which a little Calvados has been stirred.

douillons
pear turnovers

tarte aux poires et amandes
pear and almond tart

Normandy has almost as many pear orchards as apple trees, the fruit often being made into perry, just as the apples are used for cider, Pommeau and Calvados. But plenty of fruit remains for dessert and one of the favorites are these douillons.

Serves 6

3 large, round, slightly under-ripe pears (the variety known as Doyennes de Comice, which often have their stalks sealed with a blob of red sealing wax, is ideal)
unsalted butter
1 pound packaged frozen puff pastry
all-purpose flour
6 teaspoons quince or apple jelly
yolk of 1 large egg

Preheat the oven to 325°F. Peel the pears, cut in half and remove the core, stalk and base. Arrange the halved pears on a buttered baking sheet and put a small knob of butter in the cavity of each half. Bake until just tender, about 40 minutes.

Meanwhile, roll out the paste as thinly as possible on a floured board and cut into 6 rectangles. Take the pears out of the oven, turning the heat up to 350°F, and place each pear, halved side up, in the middle of a piece of paste. Drop a teaspoon of the jelly into the cavity of each half. Crimp the paste over the fruit, trimming off any excess, and brush the surface with the egg yolk. Repeat with each pear (traditionally the paste is shaped into a pear shape, but that is going a little far). Bake until the pastry is puffed up and golden, 30 minutes, and serve with crème fraîche or sour cream.

Another pear pudding, this time with halved pears baked in an almond cream spread on a short, buttery base. The dish is also prepared with apples and is a favorite in the local patisseries.

Serves 6

For the pie crust
1 stick unsalted butter
2 cups all-purpose flour
a pinch of salt
¼ cup white sugar
1 egg yolk
iced water

For the almond cream
1 stick unsalted butter
¾ cup superfine caster sugar
⅔ cup ground almonds
1 tablespoon eau de vie de poire (optional)
1 whole egg
1 teaspoon all-purpose flour

For the topping
6 small ripe pears
good quality apricot jam or conserve

First make the pie crust by crumbling the butter into the flour with the salt and sugar (this can be done in the food-processor, though I do it by hand—it is a matter of minutes, and it helps if the butter is first softened and your hands are cold). Beat the egg yolk and add to the mixture, together with just enough iced water for the dough to coagulate. Roll into a ball as quickly as possible (this very short dough needs minimum handling), wrap in plastic wrap and chill 30 minutes.

Meanwhile, make the almond cream by simply whizzing together all the ingredients. (This is definitely a case for the food-processor if at all possible. If you don't have one then first cream together the butter and sugar then add the remaining ingredients.)

Preheat the oven to 400°F. Butter a rectangular or square tart pan liberally (if you use a round one then it will be difficult to fit in the pears). Take the chilled dough from the refrigerator and spread it round the pan with your fingers (it is too short to roll), making sure it comes up the sides. Return to the refrigerator for 10 minutes.

Peel the pears, halve and core them and cut through the rounded side at very fine intervals, leaving the top intact (the idea is that if pressed down on the pear will spread out in a fan shape). If you do this in advance, make sure you put the pears in water to which you have added the juice of a lemon so that they don't turn brown.

Take the chilled dough out and spread the almond cream all over the base. Carefully press the pears into the cream. Bake 30 minutes.

Meanwhile, melt the apricot jam over a gentle heat. Reduce the oven temperature to 350°F and take out the tart. Brush the melted jam over the top of the pears and return the tart to the oven a further 20 minutes. Leave to cool a little before serving. The tart is at its best served warm, accompanied by a little crème fraîche.

Moated manor house at Coupesarte

Say Brittany and most people think of the shore. Its Gaelic name of Armor even means 'country near the sea'. This is a land of rocky coves on a sharply indented coastline, eroded granite and sandstone cliffs tumbling into a rough sea, headlands stretching out into the water and occasional gently curving bays with fine white sand. And for me Brittany is the home of the plateau de fruits de mer.

Pointe du Chateau on the Cotes d'Armor, Brittany

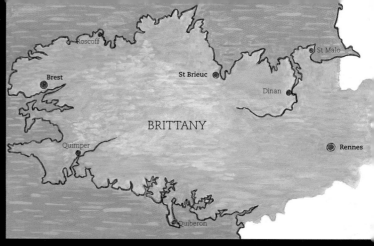

I came to Brittany relatively late in my travels around France. My Italian friend Danny was marrying his French wife Marion (now mother of his four daughters), whose parents' *maison secondaire* is near St Brieuc, and it was here that they chose to hold the wedding. The day before many of us guests went out for a seafood dinner and I have never seen such a spectacular array of shellfish. Seated with a view of rockpools over which the waves crashed, we tucked into spider crab, oysters, both the flat native variety known as *belons* and Pacific, raw clams and mussels, fat boiled whelks dipped in shallot vinegar, juicy prawns with a rich home-made mayonnaise, tiny *crevettes grises*, or brown shrimps, and a lot of lobster, all washed down with plenty of cold white wine, crusty baguette and lashings of the local butter. It is a wonder that we made it to the next day's ceremony at all.

Away from the jagged coastline, Brittany is a harsh place, with its granite-built houses, windswept fields and deep river gorges leading out to estuaries. Known locally as the *argoat*, or wooded country, these days it is largely denuded, as ever since Roman times the ood has been cut for fuel. Nowadays on the flat lands artichokes, onions and potatoes are widely cultivated, finding their way into such classic local dishes as *cotriade*, the fisherman's stew with potatoes, and stewed artichoke hearts. The pink onions, which the so-called Onion Johnnies used to sell from their bicycles in England, are found in most savory dishes.

Brittany always reminds me of Cornwall in England (the south-west is still known as Cornouaille), which is not surprising as it was settled by ancient Britons fleeing from Anglo-Saxon invaders, and just like that other outlying region it remains a place of myth and legend. In particular many of the Arthurian tales are set in central Brittany, around the Fôret de Trécesson, and the two lands are also linked in the tragic story of Tristan and Isolde, on which Wagner based his opera. Independent of France until the fifteenth century and acquired as a result of the marriage (politically motivated, of course) in 1491 of Charles VIII and Anne of Brittany, the area remains in many ways a land apart.

Perhaps in reaction to a perceived degree of paganism, the Breton countryside is full of churches, with no fewer than nine cathedrals, and Brittany is renowned for its pardons, when thousands gather to seek forgiveness for their sins. Pious women certainly dress up for church: Brittany remains famous for its traditional costumes, of which the tall lace headdresses are the best known. These days, pardons apart, you are most likely to see these white lace creations perched upon the hair of galette and pancake makers in the local market square. The Breton galette, made from buckwheat flour and often topped with cheese or ham, is the ultimate fast food, washed down with a glass or two of the local cider rather than wine.

With the exception of the pilchards and mackerel for which Quimper in particular is famous (and which once upon a time, right through until the mid twentieth century, brought much wealth to the region), seafood, and shellfish in particular, is reserved for celebratory meals; the everyday diet of the Breton, especially in the cold months, features plenty of pig (blood sausage, chitterling, smoked sausage and ham), usually served with potatoes. Come early summer both sweet green peas and local strawberries are popular, while the lamb that has fed on the salt marshes is especially prized.

Fishing baskets at Le Conquet, Finistere

And then there is the Breton butter, often flavored with local salt and just made to go on *pain de seigle*, or rye bread, with your Quiberon oysters, and the thick cream used for the rich lobster dish known as *l'armoricaine*, after the original name of the region (owing to a mistake by someone writing the menu in a Parisian restaurant, it is now sometimes also called à l'americaine). Look forward to a glass of chilled Muscadet or the rougher Gros Plant, a view over a rocky coastline from an outside table, a platter of shellfish to be picked over at leisure. Though Brittany has one other feature in common with Cornwall: it rains rather a lot.

fricassée d'artichauts
artichoke stew

Brittany is famous for its artichokes, which grow especially well on the saline land. This is a dish to satisfy a vegetarian, though they are few and far between in France.

Serves 4 as a light supper

4 large globe artichokes or 8 smaller ones
1 lemon, cut in half
2 tablespoons vinegar
3 tablespoons unsalted butter
16 small shallots or small onions, peeled but left whole
sea salt and freshly ground black pepper
1 teaspoon brown sugar
1 teaspoon all-purpose flour
2 cups medium-dry cider
1 bay leaf
2 sage leaves
1 tablespoon chopped flat-leaved parsley

This dish needs fresh artichokes (canned ones, which are already cooked, would disintegrate), but preparing the hearts is less daunting than it might appear. First snap off the outer leaves – they should break at the base. With a sharp knife, cut across the artichoke just above the choke and immediately rub the cut surface with the cut lemon. Cut out any remaining hairy choke and with a peeler scrape off the base of any remaining dark leaves. Immediately place the artichoke hearts in a bowl of water with the vinegar to prevent them discoloring while you are preparing the base of the stew.

Heat the butter in a wide, heavy, large pan and add the shallots or onions. Season and sprinkle with the sugar. Cook carefully, stirring regularly, until lightly browned, 10 minutes. Add the flour and stir well.

Drain the artichoke hearts and add to the pan. Slowly pour in the cider, stirring all the time. Bring to the boil, add the bay leaf and sage, turn down to a simmer, and leave to cook uncovered until the artichoke hearts are tender and the liquid has thickened, 25 minutes. Check seasoning, scatter with parsley and serve.

oeufs en cocotte
baked eggs

The word *cocotte* has two meanings: a kind of pot and (the translation is delicate) a lady of a certain sort – at the kindest a bit of a flirt. I like to think that in the case of the egg, it is covered in cream and cooked in a little china ramekin, concealing its true melting nature. This is certainly a sexy dish, perfect for supper for two.

As is always the case with the simplest of dishes, success depends upon the quality of the ingredients. You need the freshest of eggs and good quality butter and crème fraîche.

Serves 4 as a first course or 2 for supper

butter
4 large, fresh eggs
½ cup finely chopped fresh tarragon
2 tablespoons full-fat crème fraîche or sour cream
salt and freshly ground black pepper

Preheat the oven to 350°F. Butter four ramekins liberally and then carefully break
1 egg into each. Mix together the tarragon and crème fraîche with plenty of seasoning and put a good dollop on top of each egg. Bake until just set, 15 minutes, and serve with a crusty baguette and a green salad if for supper.

crabes bretons
crabs in the breton style

On a hot summer's day the crabs of Brittany are delicious just as they are, served with good bread, butter, lemon and a small pot of mayonnaise, but in the winter months try their flesh baked, mixed with cream and herbs and stuffed back into the shell.

Serves 2 as a main dish or 4 as a first course

2 medium-sized dressed crab, in their shells
2 large shallots, preferably the chicken thigh variety
30g unsalted butter
200ml white wine
2 tablespoons full-fat crème fraîche
1 teaspoon chopped tarragon leaves
1 tablespoon chopped parsley leaves
sea salt and freshly ground black pepper
a pinch of nutmeg

Remove the flesh from the dressed crab and set aside in a cool place. Scrub the shells of the crab well. Preheat the oven to 200°C/400°F/gas mark 6.

Peel the shallots and chop them finely. Melt the butter in a heavy pan over a gentle heat and sweat the shallots for 15 minutes, stirring occasionally, until soft but not browned. Now pour in the wine, turn up the heat and allow to bubble vigorously until the wine is all but evaporated. Reduce the heat to medium, stir in the crème fraîche and chopped herbs and cook for a few minutes, stirring all the time. Add the crabmeat to the pan, together with plenty of seasoning and the nutmeg. Stir a few times to break up the crabmeat and remove from the heat.

As soon as the crab mixture is cool enough to handle, pack into the two crab shells. Bake in the oven for 10 minutes, until the mixture is lightly browned. Serve straight away – in the shells if there are just the two of you, on serving plates if there are four.

huîtres gratinées
oysters in cheese sauce

A dozen oysters, served on a bed of ice, with shallot vinegar, pain de seigle and good butter is my favourite autumn starter, especially if I don't have to open the oysters myself. (A useful tip though: oyster knives are now sold with little oyster-shaped rubber holders, to make sure the oyster doesn't slip as you prise it open.) For those who are a little oyster-shy, however, this rich dish is a good introduction.

Serves 4 as a first course

16 fine oysters
3 tablespoons unsalted butter
2 tablespoons all-purpose flour
1 tablespoon white dry vermouth (Noilly Prat is ideal)
1¼ cups whole milk
2 tablespoons dry breadcrumbs from a baguette
1 tablespoon finely chopped flat-leaved parsley
2 tablespoons finely grated hard cheese, such as Gruyere
freshly ground black pepper

Open the oysters over a pan to catch the juices and then sieve the juice – you should end up with around 1 cup. Scrape out the oysters and keep cool. Place the deeper half of each shell in hot water and scrub well.

Preheat the oven to 425°F. Make a béchamel sauce by first melting the butter over a gentle heat and then stirring in the flour. Cook for 2 minutes, stirring all the time, until lightly caramel-colored. Add the vermouth, cook 1 minute, and then slowly start stirring in the milk. Once all the milk is amalgamated, cook another 5 minutes, still stirring, until you have a thick sauce. Remove from the heat.

In a separate pan, bring the oyster juice to the boil, reduce to a simmer and then slip in the oysters. Simmer the oysters for 1 minute only, then remove them with a slotted spoon. Arrange the scrubbed shells in a gratin dish and divide the oyster flesh equally among them. Add just enough of the oyster liquor to the béchamel sauce to 'relax' it (around half of the liquor) and then spoon the sauce over the oysters.

Mix together the breadcrumbs, parsley and cheese and scatter over the oysters; season with pepper. Cook in the oven until the sauce is bubbling and the topping nicely browned, 12–15 minutes. Serve straight away.

cotriade
breton fisherman's stew

Marseille has its bouillabaisse and Brittany its cotriade. Despite the fact that both are now served in smart restaurants (and at a price), both have their origins as fisherman's stews, made with the less expensive fish that would not reach a good price in the marketplace. While an authentic bouillabaisse is made with the Mediterranean *poissons de roche*, or rock fish, and lashings of olive oil and garlic, the Breton stew relies on white northern fish cooked with potatoes, carrots and onions. It was often cooked up on the quayside when the fishing fleet returned to harbor, after the fishermen had sorted out the more valuable fish for sale.

Serves 6 to 8

2 white onions, peeled and sliced

2 tablespoons butter

1¼ quarts fish stock (ideally) or water

½ bottle of white wine (Muscadet is ideal)

2 pounds red potatoes, skinned and quartered or cut into eighths, depending upon size

3 large carrots, peeled and cut into chunks

2 garlic cloves, peeled and quartered

2 fresh bay leaves

a large sprig of thyme

sea salt

3 pounds skinned and filleted white fish such as cod and haddock

Gently cook the onions in the butter until tender but not browned, about 15 minutes. In a big heavy pan, mix together the stock or water and the wine. Bring to the boil, turn down to a simmer and add the potatoes and carrots, the cooked onions, the garlic and herbs and a generous sprinkling of salt. Cover and leave to cook until the vegetables are tender but not falling apart, around 20 minutes.

Meanwhile cut the fish into bite-sized chunks, removing any stray bones. Add the fish to the cotriade and cook until the fish is cooked through, another 7–8 minutes. Check the seasoning and ladle the mixture into deep bowls to serve.

coquilles st-jacques au muscadet
scallops in muscadet

The classic Breton dish of scallops is cooked with plenty of the famous Roscoff onions but I find the onion overwhelms the natural sweetness and delicacy of the shellfish. I prefer this other traditional version, scallops gently poached in a creamy white wine and mushroom sauce. It also shows just how differently ingredients are treated in various parts of France: compare it to the robust flavors of the scallops provençale on page 178.

Serves 4 as a first course

½ pound button mushrooms

2 tablespoons salted butter

12 scallops

sea salt

freshly ground black pepper

1¾ quarts Muscadet or other dry, sharp white wine

2 tablespoons crème fraîche or sour cream

1 tablespoon heavy cream

Wash the mushrooms and quarter them. Pat dry then heat gently in a deep-sided heavy pan with the butter – the mushrooms should sweat rather than brown. Cook 5 minutes.

While the mushrooms are sweating, wash the scallops well, making sure all the dark thread is removed. If they have corals, cut them off with scissors and keep them for another dish (they are lovely tossed briefly in oil and sprinkled over a crisp salad). Season the scallops well.

Add the wine to the mushrooms, turn up the heat and bubble 1 minute. Mix together the crème fraîche and cream and add to the pan. Bring back to the boil, reduce to a simmer and slip in the scallops. Cook 5 minutes, turning halfway through. Check the seasoning and serve piping hot.

homard à l'estragon
lobster with tarragon

Brittany is famous for its lobsters, a reputation that was established in the eighteenth century, when the lobster became known as the cardinal of the sea thanks to its red color—when cooked. But for this dish you really must deal with the bluey-grey live lobster.

I still remember the first time I bought a live lobster in Chartres market, right behind the cathedral with its glorious blue stained glass. The fishmonger laughed hard when I expressed my trepidation about cooking it. He was joined by the other customers, redoubtable ladies who told me simply to get the water boiling, put the lobster in, jam on the lid and then leave the kitchen. I remain sadly wimpish about killing live shellfish but there is no doubt that the results do taste better, especially for this lobster dish. At least using the knife method means the lobster meets a swift end, though the resulting nerve twitches are disconcerting. Not then a dish for the squeamish, but the result is a treat—for the diner, if not for the lobster.

Serves 2

1 live lobster, about 2 pounds
1 shallot, peeled and finely chopped
4 tablespoons salted butter, preferably Breton
1 tablespoon finely chopped fresh tarragon
freshly ground black pepper
½ cup Breton or other dry cider
2 tablespoons crème fraîche or sour cream

Preheat the broiler to maximum and bring a pan of salted water to the boil. Kill the lobster with a sharp knife inserted behind the head and then chop the body in half lengthways and remove the claws. I am afraid it will twitch for a minute or two. Spoon out any coral and reserve.

Pound together the chopped shallot, butter, coral and tarragon and add a good seasoning of pepper. Smear this mixture over the flesh side of the lobster halves. Place on a deep-sided broiler pan. If you have a separate oven, preheat it to 400°F.

Add the claws to the boiling water and place the halved lobster under the broiler. Cook both for 10 minutes. Meanwhile heat the cider with the crème fraîche until nearly boiling.

Drain the claws and remove the lobster from under the broiler (the butter, shallot, coral and tarragon mixture should be bubbling—if it is not replace for another couple of minutes).

Arrange the lobster in a heatproof serving dish and surround with the cider and crème fraîche mixture. Place in the hot oven until bubbling, 5–7 minutes, and serve with plenty of bread to mop up the delicious juices.

onion johnnies

Britanny has long been famous for its sweet pink onions, grown around the region of Roscoff and sold on plaited strings. As early as the seventeenth century Breton sailors would take the onions, rich in vitamin C, on their long sea voyages as a protection against scurvy. In 1828 the adventurous Henri Olivier decided to introduce them to the United Kingdom. And so was a tradition born.

It is often said that the Englishman's first stereo-typical vision of a Frenchman between the wars was that of a so-called 'Onion Johnnie', dressed in a striped shirt with a beret on his head and a string of onions suspended from his bicycle. And it may not be far from the truth. The golden age of the Onion Johnnie was the 1920s; in 1929, according to public records, some 1,400 Johnnies imported over 9,000 tonnes of onions from Brittany to the UK.

Typically they were farm workers who would arrive by boat with their share of the onion harvest in the month of July, storing the onions in a rented barn. From then until the end of the year they would tour the local markets on foot and later by bicycle, from which were suspended their strings of onions. They bitterly resented the accusation that they wobbled on their bicycles: that, they claimed, was due to the weight of onions, which sometimes could reach well over 200 pounds.

The Depression followed by the Second World War put an end to the golden era of the Onion Johnnies. But onions continue to be an important crop in the region around Roscoff and recently a museum in memory of those brave men on their bicycles was opened in the town. Meanwhile an application has been made to give the Roscoff onion its very own Appellation d'Origine Contrôlée under French law.

raie au beurre noir
ray in black butter

For this dish you do to butter what you normally never should – you burn it slightly. In fact, it should never go black but a deep nutty brown (there is also a slightly less cooked version known as beurre noisette after its hazelnut taste). It is probably derived from an accident in the kitchen, but has certainly been around a long time; Rabelais even mentioned it, according to the Larousse Gastronomique. The Bretons claim it as their own and serve it with ray, whose strong flavor takes the acidulated sauce perfectly.

Serves 4

2 large ray wings, around 1½ pounds each
4 shallots, peeled and finely chopped
4 tablespoons white wine vinegar
sea salt
6 black peppercorns
a slice of lemon zest, unwaxed if possible
2 bay leaves
a sprig of thyme
6 tablespoons unsalted butter
1½ tablespoons capers, well rinsed or soaked for 20 minutes if preserved in salt rather than vinegar
1 tablespoon finely chopped flat-leaved parsley (optional)

sole meunière
fried sole

Preheat the oven to 300°F and put a serving dish in to warm. Sit both wings flat in a large pan (I often use a roasting pan). Sprinkle over the shallots, 3 tablespoons of the vinegar, some salt and the peppercorns, slice of lemon zest and the herbs. Add just sufficient water to cover the fish. Bring very slowly to the boil and barely simmer, around 15 minutes. The fish is done when the flesh lifts easily off the gelatinous central bone—test with a fork. Lift carefully from the poaching liquor and transfer to the serving dish.

Now you need to act swiftly so that the fish doesn't get cold. Put a heavy pan over a high heat and add the butter, cut into several pieces. As soon as it is fizzing, add the capers. Keep shaking the pan until the butter turns just brown, add the remaining vinegar (carefully as it may spit), then pour, still fizzing, over the fish. Sprinkle with the parsley if you are using it and serve at once.

Fried sole may sound the epitome of simplicity but in reality this is not a dish that is easy to prepare and I certainly never make it for more than two people at a time. It cooks quickly, of course, but you need to get your timing right. One of the most famous of French dishes, it has made its way to restaurants all over the world and is a particular favorite of London's gentlemen's clubs. It should be cooked with Dover rather than lemon sole (in the States I once had the unfortunate mistake of being served a version of flounder) and fried on the bone.

As for having it filleted before your eyes, as some misguided restaurants are prone to offer, I cannot see the point: by the time the fish gets to your knife and fork it will have turned limp and the butter will no longer be fizzing hot as it should be.

Serves 2

2 smallish Dover sole, skinned on both sides but left on the bone (you can remove the heads and tails if you like, especially if you don't possess a pan large enough to take both the fish side by side)
sea salt and freshly ground black pepper
all-purpose flour
6 tablespoons unsalted butter
1 tablespoon olive oil
juice of ½ lemon
1 tablespoon very finely chopped flat-leaved parsley, stalks removed

Preheat the oven to 350°F and put two serving plates in to warm. Season the fish well and dust very lightly with flour. Choose a non-stick pan into which both the fish will fit (in French kitchens they have large oval ones especially for the purpose). Put the pan over a medium heat and add half the butter together with the olive oil. This latter addition is not strictly 'correct', but it stops the butter from burning.

When the butter/oil mixture is almost fizzing, add the fish. Fry until nicely browned and the flesh lifts easily off the bone, around 4–5 minutes on either side. The exact time will depend upon the thickness of the fish, but I always prefer to use smaller ones so they cook quickly. Transfer the fish to the plates and keep warm. Discard the oil in which the fish has cooked, making sure you scrape out any leftover bits of skin or bone. Add the rest of the butter to the pan, make it fizz, add the lemon juice and parsley, pour over the fish and serve straight away.

lotte à l'armoricaine
monkfish armoricaine

Under Roman rule the coastal region of the area now known as Brittany was called Armorica. The rocky outcrop off the western coast of France has had many names, including Gaul prior to the Roman conquest and Lesser Britain (hence Breton) when it was returned to Celtic control, but the Latin name has stuck to this classic preparation for the firm flesh of both monkfish and lobster. It is best served with plain boiled white rice.

Serves 4

2 pound monkfish or goosefish tail
sea salt and freshly ground black pepper
all-purpose flour
1 small white onion, peeled and chopped
2 shallots, peeled and chopped
1 garlic clove, peeled and diced
6 tablespoons unsalted butter
1 tablespoon Calvados
¾ cup dry cider
1 cup canned plum tomatoes
2 sweet eating apples, peeled, cored
   and quartered

Skin the fish if it has not already been done and remove the flesh from the central bone so you have two fillets. Cut the fillets across at 1 inch intervals. Season well and dust with flour.

Gently cook the onion, shallot and garlic in half the butter in a heavy pan, stirring occasionally until softened but not browned, 15 minutes. Turn up the heat and sauté the seasoned monkfish for 1 minute on either side. Add the Calvados and set light to it. Shake the pan until the flames die down then pour in the cider and the tomatoes, breaking them down with the back of a wooden spoon. Add the apples, turn down to a simmer, cover and leave to simmer, 15 minutes.

Meanwhile, preheat the oven to 300°F and put a serving dish in to warm. Remove the chunks of fish with a slotted spoon and transfer to the dish. Cover with foil and return to the oven to keep warm.

Bring the cooking liquor to the boil and boil uncovered to reduce, 5 minutes. As soon as it is cool enough, liquidize, then whisk in the rest of the butter, cut into small pieces. Pour over the monkfish, return to the oven for 5 minutes and serve.

Breton Peasants, 1894, by Paul Gauguin

poulet au cidre
chicken cooked in cider

You can also make this dish with a whole chicken roasted in the pot, but to avoid the carving process I prefer to use chicken legs and thighs. It is important, however, to use meat on the bone, in order to get the full flavor. A purée of potatoes is the classic accompaniment, but plain boiled white rice makes for a lighter dish.

Serves 4

4 chicken legs and thighs, preferably from a free-
  range and grain-fed bird
sea salt and freshly ground black pepper
3 tablespoons unsalted butter
6 shallots, peeled and finely chopped
2½ quarts dry cider, preferably Breton
2 eating apples, peeled and diced
2 tablespoons full-fat crème fraîche or sour cream

Wash the chicken legs and thighs well and pat dry with a clean cloth. Choose a heavy pan in which the pieces of chicken fit snugly and melt the butter over a low heat. Add the shallots and sweat gently 10 minutes. Remove the shallots with a slotted spoon and set aside. Now turn up the heat and add the pieces of chicken. Cook for a few minutes on either side, until nicely browned. Return the shallots to the pan and add the cider. Bring to the boil, then reduce the heat so that the liquid is simmering, cover and leave to cook, turning the pieces of chicken halfway through, 20 minutes.

Add the apples to the pan, together with the crème fraîche. Leave to cook uncovered another 15 minutes, check the seasoning, and serve.

rôti de veau aux fonds d'artichauts
roast veal with artichoke hearts

In Brittany the local artichoke hearts are sold ready prepared in the markets, sitting in a bowl of acidulated water to stop them discoloring. They make a splendid accompaniment for a roast of veal.

Serves 4

1 veal rib roast on the bone, around 3½ pounds
salt and freshly ground black pepper
a sprig or two of rosemary
4 garlic cloves, unpeeled
1 large glass of white wine
4 globe artichokes
juice of 1 lemon

Preheat the oven to 400°F. Season the veal well, especially on the fat. Place in a roasting pan into which it will just fit, tuck the rosemary and garlic cloves underneath, pour in the white wine and cover with foil. Roast standing on its base, bones upright, 30 minutes.

Meanwhile, prepare the artichoke hearts as described on page 65. Bring a large pan of salted water to the boil and cook the hearts 5 minutes. Drain.

Take the veal from the oven and push the artichoke hearts underneath the meat, adding a little more wine if needed. Return to the oven for another 30 minutes and rest 10 minutes before serving. The meat should be rosily pink.

galettes

The galette, a flat pancake made from a simple mixture of flour and water, has a long history. All the civilizations of the Old and New Worlds have had their versions, whether made from wheat flour, rice, maize or other cereals. But the Bretons have their own special version, made from the buckwheat that the Crusaders first brought from Asia (hence the French name sarrasin).

Buckwheat is not in fact a cereal, although it has similar nutritional qualities. It is a plant, with heart-shaped leaves and yellowy white flowers and, surprisingly, comes from the same family as sorrel and rhubarb. It has a distinctive nutty taste and is used to make blini in Russia, soba noodles in Japan, pasta in Italy – and of course galettes in Brittany, where it thrives particularly well in the acid soils.

Records show that the first cast-iron galetoires, the flat sheet on which the galette is cooked, appeared in the fifteenth century. Soon no Breton market was complete without a galette or crêpe stand, with their portable ovens. Customers might buy other ingredients in the market, bacon or eggs or sausage, and bring them to the stand to be cooked alongside the galette, which was always eaten standing up.

Nowadays there are restaurants serving galettes, where you can sit down and eat the pancake with a knife and fork, perhaps accompanied by a bottle of cider. But to me this doesn't feel right. I prefer to stand and watch as with rapid skill the batter is spread over the hotplate, the pancake flipped and folded into a rectangle. The galette is street food, to be eaten piping hot with your fingers. It is one of the many pleasures of being in Brittany.

the loire

Mention the Loire and most people think either wine or châteaux—or both. But here they are not associated together as they are in Bordeaux or Burgundy. The impressive châteaux that dot the landscape were built for a quite different reason. I remember being told as a young girl that Chambord, with its magnificent marble staircase and 400-odd rooms, was built for François I as a hunting lodge (he ended up spending less than a month there). I simply wouldn't believe it.

At the time we were sitting in an old-fashioned restaurant with a view of the castellated 'lodge', with its many wings and delicate turrets, surrounded by elegant parkland. We were also tucking into dishes of *râble de lièvre à la crème*, a whole saddle of hare baked in cream, and médaillons of venison cooked with redcurrants and red wine. My father gently pointed out that there was a reason why the dukes and kings of France chose this area for their hunting lodges—the abundant forests teeming with game. It was just that they built rather more grandiose buildings than one would normally think of as lodges.

The château of Chambord

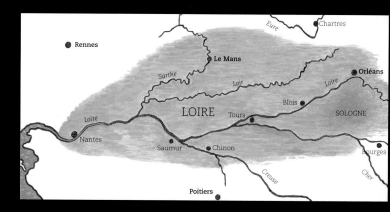

Many of those forests remain today, especially in the Sologne region, often thick with mist in the colder months. Here wild boar and deer are plentiful, as are wild duck and other waterfowl. They are not shot or hunted (chasse à cours, where the curly French horn is used to call the hounds, is still practiced on some private estates) purely for pleasure but also for the table.

There are not only rich dishes that hark back to the traditions of courtly cuisine, but also simple game pâtés and terrines, and plain casseroles and roasts made from the many birds and animals that congregate in the vast wheat fields after the harvest: partridges wrapped in cabbage leaves and braised, quail larded with bacon and cooked over the first of the autumn fires, hare simmered in a civet of its own blood, chunks of rabbit flesh preserved in aspic. It is not a cuisine for the squeamish.

My brother's wedding took place in my sister-in-law's family village in the Loire, not far from Chambord. There are many things I remember from that day—the service in the vast local church, where we stood in the choir stalls while the villagers crept to the very back of the pews, the extraordinary tiered contraption that the photographer produced for the wedding guests to stand on in

The château of Chenonceaux

serried ranks, the reception in the village hall where the sparkling Vouvray flowed and the locals commented on the fact that all the English seemed to be *géants*.

But what really sticks in my mind is the dish of *sandre au beurre blanc* served at the splendid and many-coursed lunch we enjoyed in a nearby restaurant. Sandre, translated as pike-perch but not a fish I have ever seen on sale in the UK, is a favorite river fish of the region, prized for its delicate white flesh. But what really made the dish was the buttery white sauce. The people of the Anjou and of Nantes both like to claim the delicate white sauce of beurre blanc as their own, the Angevins because apparently it can only be made correctly with the local grey shallots. The people of Nantes believe it was made at the nearby château of the Marquess of Goulaine at the turn of the last century.

Like many of the best recipes, the story goes that it came from a mistake created under pressure. The plan had been to serve a sauce béarnaise with the fish but the sous-chef forgot the eggs, so the head chef, one Clémence Lefeuvre Prault, in desperation whisked in more good butter. The Marquess congratulated her on it and later she claimed it as her own at the auberge she opened on the banks of the

Sandre is not the only food provided by the rivers that bisect the Loire landscape. There is the delicious pike, as well as carp, lamprey and eels. Of a dark night wandering beside a romantic waterway, perhaps with a château looming in the background, you will often see the flare of a torch as an eel fisherman goes about his stealthy way, luring his prey. It can seem a strange mixture of grandeur and peasant living, but round about here the locals, however wealthy (and this is one of the richest parts of France), remain inured to their way of life.

But there is a softer side to this region too, among the fruit trees and vineyards of Touraine. There are just as many châteaux, but they are rather more understated, belonging perhaps to minor families of the nobility. The cooking too is simpler, with plenty of vegetable dishes, particularly in the late spring, made from cardoons, artichokes, peas, green and fava beans. In the early autumn, the pride of the orchards are the plums destined to become the prized prunes of Tours but there are also mirabelles and greengages, made into little tarts.

Not all here is delicacy of course. The rillettes de Tours are famous throughout France, although the best of this delicacy of potted pork comes from Vouvray, home to the excellent white wine that is traditionally aged in the limestone caverns above the river from which

soupe au cresson
watercress soup

A delicate pale green, a watercress soup is a thing of beauty—even before you taste it—and is the most elegant of soups. Similar if more strongly flavored soups are also made with the tops of radishes and beetroot.

Serves 6 to 8

3 red-skinned potatoes, around 2 pounds
4 tablespoons unsalted butter
2 bunches of watercress, around ¾ pound
3 cups vegetable or chicken stock
salt
3 cups whole milk
crème fraîche or sour cream

Peel the potatoes and chop into smallish cubes. Melt the butter in a heavy pan over a medium heat and add the potato cubes. Cook 3 minutes then remove from the heat.

Bring a separate pan filled with water to the boil. Add the watercress, stalks included, and blanch 45 seconds. Drain well.

Add the blanched watercress to the potatoes, together with the stock and a good pinch of salt. Bring to the boil, turn down to a simmer and cook 10 minutes. Add the milk, bring back to the boil and again turn down to a simmer. Cook another 5 minutes, then remove from the heat and as soon as it's cool enough liquidize until completely smooth. Check the seasoning for salt and chill.

Just before serving swirl a little crème fraîche into each bowl.

porc aux pruneaux de tours
pork with prunes

There is serious competition as to where the best prunes in France come from—the orchards around Agen or those around Tours? Certainly one of the best savory dishes with prunes comes from the Loire region, and that is at least in part due to the wine it is traditionally cooked with. Vouvray, made principally from the Chenin Blanc grape, was once one of the most prized wines of the Loire Valley but these days it is less popular due to the decline in fashion of sweet wines.

Although dry and medium-dry as well as sparkling wines are made in and around the village of Vouvray, on the right bank of the Loire to the east of Tours, it is most famous for its moelleux (sweet) wines. Of course, you need not use an old Vouvray for this dish, but if you can get hold of a bottle it will add the local flavor.

Serves 4

½ pound good quality dried prunes, unpitted
sufficient fruity white wine, ideally Vouvray, to
  cover the prunes (generous 1 cup)
1½ pounds pork tenderloin
sea salt and freshly ground black pepper
all-purpose flour
3 tablespoons unsalted butter
2 heaped tablespoons crème fraîche or sour cream
2 teaspoons redcurrant jelly

Cover the prunes with the wine and leave to soak, preferably overnight.

When you are ready to cook, cut the tenderloin across into pieces about 1-inch thick. The aim is to have 16 'noisettes'.

Put the prunes and the wine in which they have soaked into a heavy pan and simmer for 20 minutes. Meanwhile, season the pieces of pork well and dust with flour. Preheat the oven to 300°F and put a serving dish in to keep warm. Melt the butter in a heavy frying pan over a medium heat and when it is fizzing add the noisettes of pork. Sauté the pork 2 minutes on either side, until lightly browned, then reduce the heat and leave to cook 4–5 minutes on either side (you may like to cut into one of the noisettes, just to make sure it is cooked through). Transfer to the warmed serving dish, leaving the buttery pan juices behind.

Strain the prunes, reserving the liquor, and arrange them over the pork (at this stage some cooks like to remove the pits, though I leave them in). Cover the serving dish with foil and return to the oven.

Add the soaking liquor from the prunes to the pan juices from the pork and heat gently. Stir in the crème fraîche, a little at a time, and when it is all amalgamated allow to bubble, 3–4 minutes. When the sauce has thickened, remove from the heat and stir in the redcurrant jelly. Add the pork and prunes to the pan, together with any juices, stir all well together, check seasoning, return to the serving dish—and eat.

poisson de rivière au beurre blanc
river fish with white butter sauce

This is the memorable dish from my brother's wedding (see introduction to this chapter, page 74). Beurre blanc is splendid with poached salmon or sea bass as well as sandre and pike.

To make enough sauce for 4

6 shallots, approximately ½ pound
¾ cup cider or white wine vinegar
salt
2 sticks salted butter, cut into pieces

Peel the shallots and chop finely. Put them in a non-reactive pan with the vinegar and a good pinch of salt. Bring to the boil, turn down to the slowest possible simmer, and cook uncovered until all the vinegar has evaporated. This will take around 20 minutes, and it is a good idea to shake the pan from time to time.

Meanwhile, cook the fish as you prefer.

Just before serving, add the butter to the warm shallot and vinegar mixture, swirling the pan around to melt the butter and amalgamate the sauce. Under no circumstances let it boil or the sauce will split. As soon as all the butter has melted, check the seasoning and serve. The sauce should be the consistency of a thick cream.

sauté de pintade aux champignons sauvages
sauté of guinea hen with wild mushrooms

The French verb *sauter* means to jump and that is literally what pieces of meat or vegetables should do when you sauté them. It is a quick method of cooking but it does require constant attention, as you need to keep turning the meat. You can make this recipe with guinea hen, or even chicken breast, off the bone but the meat on the bone will have a far better flavour, as well as retaining moisture.

Serves 4

1 plump guinea hen, cut into eight pieces
    (two wings, two legs and four breast pieces,
    still on the bone)
sea salt and freshly ground black pepper
2 tablespoons butter
2 tablespoons sunflower oil
2 large shallots, peeled and chopped
scant ½ pound wild mushrooms—like chanterelles
1 glass white wine
2 teaspoons chopped fresh tarragon
1 tablespoon crème fraîche or sour cream

Wipe the pieces of guinea hen clean with a cloth and season. In a large heavy-based pan, melt the butter and oil. When they start to fizz, add the guinea hen and sauté, turning to make sure it browns nicely.

Preheat the oven to 350°F and put a serving dish in to warm. When you have cooked the pieces of guinea hen for around 20 minutes, transfer them to the dish in the oven, leaving the fat in the pan. Now you need to move swiftly. Add the shallots to the hot fat and sauté for a few minutes, then add the mushrooms and do the same. Pour in the wine, bring to a bubble and add the tarragon. Bubble for 1 minute, then stir in the crème fraîche. Check the seasoning, then pour over the guinea hen hot from the oven and serve.

navarin printanier
spring lamb stew

A dish which comes straight from the potager or vegetable garden. But this being France there is no vegetarian option; instead the tiny spring vegetables are accompanied by early season lamb.

Serves 4

3 pounds lean lamb
3 tablespoons unsalted butter
salt and freshly ground black pepper
1 tablespoon all-purpose flour
1 tablespoon tomato paste
3 cups vegetable stock
½ pound tiny carrots
½ pound very small turnips
1 pound unpodded peas or ½ pound shelled weight

Cut the lamb into roughly 1-inch pieces. Melt the butter in a heavy pan over a gentle heat and add the lamb. Cook for 2 minutes, turning once or twice, then season well and stir in the flour and tomato paste. Cook a further 3–4 minutes, again turning once or twice. Warm the stock in a separate pan. Pour over the lamb, stirring all the time, bring to a simmer, cover and leave to cook at barely a bubble for 1 hour.

Meanwhile, scrub the carrots and turnips. Providing they are small enough (and they should be truly tiny), they can be left whole, preferably with a little of their green stalk attached. Add them to the lamb, together the peas and a little extra liquid (water is fine) if necessary. Cook until the vegetables are just tender, another 15 minutes, check the seasoning, and serve.

petits pois à la française
peas with lettuce and cream

I like the French habit of serving vegetable dishes all on their own, either before or after the main course. In fact, nothing fills me with more dread than an English 'roast dinner', with six different vegetables piled on the plate beside overcooked meat. This delicate, simple little dish is my favorite way of cooking freshly podded peas, to be served before a roast chicken. Tiny white onions are often added, but I find their flavor overpowers the sweetness of the peas, so I use a shallot instead.

Serves 4 as a first course

2 pounds unpodded weight of fresh peas, shelled
1 shallot, peeled and very finely diced
2 tablespoons unsalted butter
1 butter lettuce, leaves washed and shredded
scant ½ cup crème fraîche or sour cream
salt and freshly ground black pepper

Bring a large pot of unsalted water to the boil and add the podded peas. Bring back to the boil and cook for 5 minutes. Meanwhile, sweat the shallot in the butter. Drain the peas, reserving a tablespoon of the cooking liquor. Add the peas, reserved cooking liquid, shredded lettuce and crème fraîche to the shallots, together with generous seasoning. Cook, stirring, until the lettuce has wilted, 2 minutes, and serve.

civet de lièvre
jugged hare

The wheat fields of the Loire provide the ideal habitat for the hare, which is cooked locally in a positively medieval fashion. Often called *à la royale* and without inclusion of the hare's blood not entitled to the name civet), this is a favorite dish at Christmas time.

The word civet originates from the old French *cive*, meaning a dish cooked with onions. Only in the nineteenth century did the habit of binding the sauce with the blood come into regular use, but what a good idea it was. And although *civet de lièvre à la royale* is now often found on menus, this was originally a dish for poachers—or *braconniers*, as they are evocatively called in French.

Serves 4 to 6

1 large hare, jointed, with its blood and liver
2 tablespoons Armagnac or Cognac
2 large carrots, peeled and chopped
1 bottle of good red wine
1 tablespoon olive oil
2 bay leaves
a sprig each of thyme and rosemary
3 white onions, peeled and chopped into fine
  half moons
3 tablespoons butter
4 slices smoked bacon, diced
salt and freshly ground black pepper
all-purpose flour
2 squares of good quality dark chocolate

Strain the blood from the hare and mix with the Cognac or Armagnac. Set aside together with the hare's liver. Put the joints of hare in an earthenware or other non-reactive bowl and add the carrots, wine, oil and herbs. Leave to marinate, ideally overnight.

When you are ready to cook, set a heavy pan over a medium heat and add the onions, butter and bacon. Cook, stirring regularly, until the onion is soft but not browned, 15 minutes. Meanwhile, remove the pieces of hare from the marinade and pat dry with paper towels. Season well and dust with flour. Add to the pan and brown on both sides. In a separate pan, bring the marinade to the boil. When it is hot, pour over the hare. Cover and leave to simmer over the lowest possible heat for 2 hours, until the hare is very tender.

Just before serving, finely chop the hare's liver. Check the seasoning of the sauce and then stir in the blood and Armagnac or Cognac mixture together with the liver and pieces of chocolate. Heat through but do not allow to boil. Serve piping hot.

The Château of Chambord, 1722,
by Pierre-Denis Martin

game

The family of my sister-in-law Martine have long been farmers in the valley of the Loire. Their farm is largely arable but there are plenty of coverts on their land and they await the annual start of shooting with enthusiasm. Martine was born on the first day of the season, apparently rather to her father's irritation (on the timing, that is, not her birth). He turned up at the hospital with his pockets stuffed full of partridges. So, at least, goes the story. Since her mother still posts the first feathered birds of the year to Martine in her home in Alsace, I am inclined to believe it. Apparently the package is often rather soggy.

Hunting, fishing and shooting form an integral element of life in rural France. There is even a political party, 'La Chasse et la Pêche', whose sole purpose is to protect the rights of the hunters. Sanglier are still hunted with packs of hounds and huntsmen on horseback carrying the classic curly French horn in these parts, although elsewhere rifles are more common. Over in the flat marshy woods of the Sologne to the south of Orléans, duck shoots are especially popular, and the land is full of hides.

tarte aux mirabelles
tart with mirabelles

The lovely golden little plums known as mirabelles are just as popular in the Loire as they are in Alsace. However, the way a mirabelle tart is prepared here as opposed to in the north-east of the country demonstrates the subtle differences in French regional cookery. The Alsatian tart is flat with the fruit dominating, while in the version from the Loire the fruit is buried in the pie crust. It is best to make these little tarts in individual portions and this is a dish that needs to be cooked quickly. It was once described to me as a dessert to be prepared at eleven for lunch at midday, whereas the Alsatian version will taste even better the next day—especially at breakfast.

Serves 4

2 cups all-purpose flour
pinch of salt
¼ cup white sugar, plus an extra 2 tablespoons
   for sprinkling
6 tablespoons unsalted butter, removed from
   the fridge an hour before cooking
2 large eggs, well beaten
1½ pounds mirabelles, washed

Preheat the oven to 425°F. Mix together the flour, salt and ¼ cup of sugar, then with your fingers crumble in the butter, reserving a knob. You can make this in the food-processor but I have always found results best if it is done by hand—and it only takes a couple of minutes, albeit messy ones. When you have a crumble type mixture, add the beaten eggs and as quickly as possible work them into the mixture with your hands. It is important not to overwork the dough.

Ideally you will cook these tarts in 2 or even 4 small individual serving dishes, made from cast iron (forget china quiche dishes) but if you don't have those make sure you use a non-stick metal pan, preferably with a removable base. Grease it well with the remaining knob of butter then spread the pastry around the pan with your fingers, making sure it comes well up (but not over) the sides. Pack in the mirabelles as closely together as possible in one layer and sprinkle with the remaining sugar, then transfer immediately to the hot oven. Cook until the edges of the pastry are lightly browned and the plums a nice golden colour, 40 minutes. Leave to stand 10 minutes and then serve.

chèvre frais au coulis de framboises
fresh goat's cheese with raspberry coulis

Little crémets, a sweetened mixture of cream and egg whites which has been strained through muslin and traditionally set in heart-shaped moulds, are famous in the Anjou region, where they are served with either strawberry or raspberry coulis. A fresh goat's cheese goes just as well.

Serves 4

2 fresh goat's cheeses, halved
1 pound fresh raspberries
about ¼ cup superfine sugar
4 small sprigs of fresh mint

Chill the goat's cheese well and then place in four separate bowls.

Crush the raspberries with a fork and press through a fine sieve to extract the juice. You should end up with roughly 1 cup. Add sugar to taste, but the coulis should remain sharp.

Pour the coulis over the cheese, place a sprig of mint on top of each, and serve.

tarte tatin

Ideally a tarte tatin is made in a beaten copper dish designed especially for the purpose, so that it can go both on top of the cooker and in the oven, but in the past I have successfully used a heavy cast-iron skillet.

Serves 4 to 6

3 pounds tart eating apples
½ cup brown sugar
1 stick unsalted butter
1 quantity of sweet pie crust (see page 32)

Make the pie crust as in the recipe for tarte aux quetsches on page 32. Chill for 30 minutes.

Preheat the oven to 425°F. Peel and core the apples and cut into thick slices. Place the apples, sugar and three quarters of the butter in the chosen cooking pan and cook over a medium heat 10 minutes, until the apples are lightly caramelized.

Meanwhile roll out the dough so that it will fit over the top of the apples in their dish. Tuck the dough over the top (take care not to burn yourself here), dot with the remaining butter and transfer to the oven. Cook until the pastry is browned on top and the apples bubbling underneath, 25–30 minutes (don't worry if a little juice oozes through—this is a positively good sign). Carefully turn the tart upside down onto a serving plate, and serve, perhaps with a little crème fraîche or sour cream.

the tatin sisters

Sometimes a simple culinary mistake can result in great success, as shown by the tale of the Tatin demoiselles, sisters Stephanie and Caroline. Inheriting the family hotel in Lamotte-Beuvron in the Sologne from their father in 1888, they soon became renowned for their cooking and the warmth of their welcome. Caroline worked front of house, soon earning the nickname 'la petite princesse de Sologne', while her somewhat simple elder sister did the cooking. Her specialty was apple tart.

One lunchtime, when a large party of hunters was expected, Stephanie accidentally assembled the tart upside down and put it in the oven with the pie crust on top and the sweetened fruit underneath. The mistake discovered, there was no time to dither, so the tart was unceremoniously turned over and served anyway. It was pronounced delicious and tarte tatin was born.

These days, however, there is concern that the tradition of the true tarte tatin is under threat. The Grand Chapitre, or Great Chapter, of the Confrérie des Lichonneux de Tarte Tatin exists to defend its heritage, travelling 'the four corners of France and the world over' in order to promote the original recipe and 'criticize the heretics'. Shame on you should you choose to make, say, a savory tarte tatin with tomatoes, or a caramelized pineapple one—the correct version depends upon apples.

Still Life of Apples and Biscuits, 1880–82, by Paul Cézanne

le plateau de fromages

No correct French meal is complete without a cheese course, served before the pudding, not after in the Anglo-Saxon style. In smart restaurants the *chariot de fromages* is wheeled round, often with a selection of thirty or forty cheeses, many of them local. The waiter stands poised with his knife, asking you whether you would like a slice of this or that. Etiquette suggests that you should not choose more than four, however tempting.

At the market stall, the cheese seller will generally question you as to when you plan to eat your cheese, whether you want it *bien fait* (which doesn't refer to whether or not it is well made, which naturally it is, but whether you want it ripe)

or to keep for a few days later. The profession of *affineur de fromages*, the individual who is in charge of ripening the cheeses, is a highly respected one. With almost 500 varieties, France boasts that it has the most cheeses of any country in the world.

One perfectly ripe whole cheese such as an unpasteurized Camembert is far better than a dubious selection of over-chilled or under-ripe cheeses. Or you could present a slice of Roquefort or Fourme d'Ambert with some sliced ripe pears and fresh walnuts. I also like to serve a selection of goat's cheeses with fresh figs—arranged on fresh fig leaves if available.

fraises des bois au vin rouge
wild strawberries in red wine

The small strawberries known as *fraises des bois* grow in the wild, though they are now also cultivated. This dish is incredibly simple to prepare and deliciously refreshing on a hot summer's day.

Serves 4

2 punnets of wild strawberries (about 1 pound)
2 tablespoons confectioners' sugar
the juice of ½ orange
a glass of light red wine (ideally a Beaujolais or other Gamay)

Wash the strawberries well, sprinkle with sugar and add a squeeze of fresh orange juice. Divide between four wine glasses, top up with the wine and chill well before serving

le centre

It is perhaps unfair to lump together such regions as Auvergne, Corrèze and the Massif Central under the title of the center of France but not only do they justify the definition geographically, they also do so by the nature of their cooking. For centuries often virtually inaccessible in the winter months (and still sometimes so today, as I have found to my cost), the cuisine is mainly *montagnard*, with potatoes, pork, cheese and butter the most common ingredients.

Historically too they are linked. Gateway to the center is the region of the Bourbonnais, via the merchant city of Bourges, with its magnificent Gothic cathedral. Known under the Romans as Avaricum, Bourges was once the tribal capital of the Gauls. The entire region was bitterly fought over by Julius Caesar and the Gaulish resistance leader Vercingetorix, who is still commemorated

Cheeseseller in the Auvergne

by a statue in the central square of Clermont Ferrand; the eventual surrender of Vercingetorix and his men was a decisive moment in the creation of the Roman Empire.

Not to be missed here in Bourges is the fifteenth-century palace of local man Jacques Coeur, by far the wealthiest businessman of his times, who even lent money to the King. He made his money from trade, in salt and spices among other foodstuffs. Nevertheless, in a lesson to all budding entrepreneurs, he was eventually disgraced and lost all his money. But the people of Bourges continue the wealthy tradition. A few years ago, I did my Christmas food shopping here and rarely have I seen more treats such as foie gras, stuffed capon, marrons glacés and fine wines on offer.

Head a little further south towards the high lands and the cooking remains sophisticated. Nowhere more so than in the spa town of Vichy, made famous by Napoleon III, whose visits during the 1860s first put the spa town on the map as a fashionable place to take the waters. In more recent years the name became associated with the infamous Vichy government of the Second World War, while in a gastronomic sense it is (erroneously) linked to the cold leek and potato soup known as vichyssoise. You can still take a spa treatment followed by an appropriately gourmet menu and sleep in grand fin de siècle buildings. But just beyond lie the extraordinary volcanic structures of the Massif Central, from where the spring waters issue.

t is these salty waters that should be used to cook a dish of authentic carottes Vichy, one of those very precise vegetable dishes at which the French excel. The waters also lend their peculiar taste to the tiny dark green lentilles de Puy, a local delicacy that is appreciated all over France. This was all explained to me when I was in my early twenties by a lady from the region whom I was working with in Paris. At the time I thought it something of an exaggeration but now I appreciate her wisdom. The correct ingredients are important in the simplest of dishes.

From the Bourbonnais and the Massif Central the hills rise rapidly up to Auvergne, a harsh land but one that even in the Middle Ages was supplying its splendid cheeses, such as Tomme, Cantal, Bleu d'Auvergne and its neighbour Fourme d'Ambert and the herb- and garlic-flavored Gaperon, to the wealthier lands to the north. These cheeses are still produced today, with great efforts to keep them as 'fermier' as possible under current legislation. The freshest of Tomme or Cantal (by which I mean just a few days or even hours old, and preferably unpasteurized) is a key ingredient in the famous potato dishes of the region, aligot and truffade.

To accompany those potato dishes are the fresh sausages for which Auvergne also has a reputation, as it does, even more so, for its dried saucissons. In recent years I have visited stalls advertising 'produits auvergnats' in markets across the country, in Paris and Boulogne, Loches in the Loire and Périgueux in the Dordogne, even Antibes on the Côte d'Azur. In each case there was a healthy queue at the stall, while nibbles of this cheese and that saucisson were offered. And it always turned out that the stallholder had indeed travelled from Auvergne to attend that day's market. Such are the advantages of being located in the center of France, but it also shows the pressures that small producers are under to sell their product (even in France, where regional food remains so highly valued). The tradition of taking farm produce to the big city remains as strong as in medieval times, it is just that the distances have grown larger.

A patisserie in Bourges

vichyssoise
chilled leek and potato soup

This famous chilled soup is often regarded as French, but in fact has its origins in the US, where it was created by a Frenchman. Louis Diat came from Vichy and was cooking at the Ritz-Carlton on Madison Avenue in New York in 1917 when, rather unkindly, it is suggested that he found himself short of time to heat the leek and potato soup he had planned for a banquet to celebrate the opening of the rooftop gardens. So he added cream and a sprinkling of chives and brought it out cold, to a triumphant reception. It is a good story—and, of course, so is the soup. I prefer to think that Louis tasted it cold and thought it rather good just as it was, especially on a hot day. Either way, crème glacée vichyssoise was soon to become a classic.

Serves 4 to 6

4 large leeks
3 tablespoons unsalted butter
2 medium-sized potatoes, around 1½ pounds
   when peeled and roughly chopped
5 cups mild vegetable or chicken stock
salt
white pepper (optional)
4 teaspoons crème fraîche or sour cream
2 teaspoons chopped chives

Chop the white parts of the leeks only (ideally you will already have used the green parts to make your stock, together with a white onion, a carrot or two, some sprigs of parsley and leaves of celery and perhaps a few chicken wings). Melt the butter in a heavy casserole and gently stew the leeks until soft, 15 minutes. Now add the chopped potatoes and stir well. Meanwhile heat the stock in another pan. After a further 10 minutes, add the stock to the leek and potato mixture, bring to the boil, turn down to a simmer, cover and cook, 40 minutes.

Remove from the heat and leave to cool to tepid before liquidizing. The soup should be completely smooth. When you have achieved this, check the seasoning and salt to taste, depending upon whether or not the stock was salty. Traditionally pepper is not added to vichyssoise, although if you like you can add a pinch of white pepper. Chill very well and just before serving swirl in the crème fraîche or sour cream (if the crème fraîche is very thick whisk in a little whole milk to loosen it) and sprinkle with the chives.

carottes vichy
carrots vichy style

The waters of Vichy have long been famous and their minerally, salty characteristic give a unique flavor to this simple vegetable dish. The best carrots to use will have just been pulled from the ground, but failing that look out for carrots sold in bunches with their fronds still attached, as this keeps them fresher.

Serves 4 as a side dish

1 pound young carrots
½ teaspoon salt
2 teaspoons brown sugar
3 tablespoons unsalted butter
Vichy or other mineral-rich water
2 teaspoons finely chopped parsley

Wash and scrape the carrots and then cut them on a diagonal at 1/2-inch intervals. Arrange them in a pan so that they just cover the surface, and add the salt, sugar and butter, cut into small pieces. Pour in sufficient Vichy or other mineral water barely to cover them and set over a low heat. Cook uncovered, slowly, shaking the pan occasionally, until the water has all but evaporated, around 20–25 minutes. Sprinkle with parsley and serve.

mineral water

Nowhere in the world are people more passionate about their mineral water than in France. They may offer mineral water menus in New York, but in France everyone has their own favorite source, to which they attribute extraordinary health-giving properties. Sit down in a restaurant and as like as not the first question a waiter will ask you is what water you want (though one of my Parisian friends has expressed concern over the increasing dominance of the Italian San Pellegrino).

It was the Romans who first sought out natural springs as they established their empire across Europe. But, according to legend, it was Hannibal, the general of the Carthaginian army, who discovered the source of Perrier when he rested his troops and their elephants at Les Bouillens in Languedoc-Roussillon, some twenty kilometres from Nîmes.

Not until the eighteenth century did the tradition of 'taking the waters' at a spa become popular in France; one of the first spas was at Contrexéville, source of Contrex water, believed to cure kidney stones. And it was another century before water started to be bottled on a large scale, the first being

Vittel in 1855, closely followed by Perrier in 1863. For another hundred years or so bottled water remained the preserve of the wealthy, until in 1968 Vittel once again took the lead by launching mineral water in a plastic bottle.

There are some 1,200-odd springs in France and their waters are closely regulated. Only two treatments are admissible under French law: the removal of iron and regasification, which must be done with natural gas from the source if the title of mineral water is to be used. Despite its name, spring water is something entirely different.

Perhaps the most famous source in France is that of Vichy in the Auvergne. Known initially as the water of the Célestins after the monks who built a monastery around one of the springs at the beginning of the fifteenth century, by the eighteenth century it was popular in the court of Louis XV and was the very first mineral water to be bottled. Emerging from the rock at a temperature of 71°C, this is one of the most 'minerally' of mineral waters and is certainly an acquired taste, though many swear by it for an upset stomach.

The Pas de Peyrol, Monts du Cantale, Auvergne

lentilles à l'auvergnate
lentils in the auvergne style

The small green lentils grown in the area around the Puy de Dôme, the volcanic plug that is the symbol of the Massif Central, are famous throughout France. They are so highly prized locally that they are served as a dish on their own, with crispy slices of bacon and poached eggs, but to be honest you should have first done a hard day's work in the field (and that's before lunch) to justify such a treat. I prefer them as a side dish for sausage. Any leftovers can be made into lentil salad, dressed with a mustardy vinaigrette.

Serves 4 to 6 as a side dish

generous 1 cup green Puy lentils
1 tablespoon duck or goose fat
1 fat slice of Canadian smoked bacon, chopped, including the fat
2 large carrots, peeled and diced
1 large white onion, peeled and diced
a sprig of thyme
1 bay leaf
2½ cups chicken stock or water (not a bouillon cube)
salt and freshly ground black pepper
a knob of unsalted butter
chopped flat-leaved parsley (optional)

Rinse the lentils thoroughly and pick out any discolored ones. In a heavy pan over a medium heat, add the fat and bacon. As soon as the bacon fat starts to run, add the carrot and onion. Cook, stirring regularly, 10 minutes.

Now add the lentils and stir well to coat in the fat. Pop in the herbs and pour in the stock or water. Bring to the boil, reduce to a simmer, cover and cook, around 25–30 minutes. The exact cooking time will depend upon the freshness of the lentils: halfway through start stirring and tasting to make

perdrix à l'auvergnate
partridges in the auvergne style

Auvergne is good hunting country, for game birds as well as wild boar. This is my favorite way with partridges, flambéed, then stewed in white wine and finished in a buttery sauce. Lentils are an ideal accompaniment.

Serves 4

4 fat young partridge
4 slices smoked bacon, rind removed
4 tablespoons unsalted butter
2 tablespoons Cognac or other brandy
1 cup white wine
2 bay leaves
freshly ground black pepper

Clean the partridge inside and out, removing any gizzards and cutting off the claws if they are still attached. Place a heavy lidded pot in which the birds will fit snugly over a moderate heat. Using scissors, snip the bacon into the pot and add half the butter. Stew gently, stirring from time to time, until the bacon fat has run, 10 minutes. Add the partridge breast side down and cook over a medium heat until lightly browned, 3 minutes. Warm the cognac in a ladle, set light to it and pour it over the birds, shaking the pot to distribute the flames evenly. Add the wine, bay leaves and pepper, bring to the boil, reduce to a simmer, cover and cook, 15 minutes.

Preheat the oven to 300°F and put plates in to warm. Turn the birds over and cook a further 15 minutes breast side up. Turn breast side down again for a final 5 minutes. Remove the birds from the pan and transfer to the serving plates. Bring the sauce to a rolling boil for a few minutes, then remove from the heat and whisk in the remaining butter, cut into pieces. Check the seasoning, pour over the birds and serve straight away.

sure they don't stick or overcook. When you are happy with them, remove from the heat. Season to taste with salt and pepper and stir in the butter.

Leave to stand 5 minutes before serving. A little chopped parsley wouldn't go amiss.

potée auvergnate
auvergne hotpot

There are plenty of more sophisticated versions of this dish, whether involving cabbage rolled around ground pork, or the addition of a boiling sausage or potatoes cooked separately in the stock. In the end, though, it is a pork, cabbage and vegetable stew, the sort that people living off the land make all over the world, from China to South America, especially in their winter months. It relies upon slow cooking and the aroma that permeates the kitchen makes the wait worthwhile. Traditionally the broth, vegetables and meat are served one after the other, though I often serve it in one go. Rye bread is ideal with it and mustard essential.

Serves 6 to 8

1½ pounds or so salt pork, in one thick slice
1 pound or so unsalted bacon, again in one
  thick slice
1 pound carrots, peeled and cut into chunks
1 pound small turnips, peeled and topped
  and tailed
2 large leeks, white parts washed and chopped
1 large white onion
4 cloves
8 peppercorns
a sprig of thyme, a few stalks of parsley and a
  couple of bay leaves
1 Savoy cabbage, around 2 pounds

Soak both the salt pork and the bacon overnight in plenty of water. The next day, put them in a large heavy Dutch oven together with the carrots, whole turnips and leeks, as well as the onion, peeled and studded with the cloves. Add the peppercorns, herbs and sufficient water to cover generously. Bring very slowly to a gentle simmer and cook covered, 2 hours.

Peel the tough outer leaves from the cabbage and cut into eighths, leaving the central core and stalk so that the leaves stay attached. After the stew has been cooking for 2 hours, add the cabbage pieces. Continue to cook as slowly as possible, another 3–4 hours.

Slice the meat and place in large soup bowls. Ladle over some of the broth and vegetables (keep some back for seconds) and serve, making sure everyone has a spoon as well as a knife and fork.

aligot
potato with cheese

A couple of years back we were driving across the hills of the Massif Central, slightly worried about the forecast of impending snow. But we were hungry and a sign to a local restaurant beckoned. The dish of the day was aligot. A huge poached sausage appeared on a mound of the richest potato dish I have ever tasted. Afterwards we had to go for a long walk down one of the Routes de Santiago de Compostela to recuperate. We especially liked the fact that one route was signed as suitable for donkeys and another for those walking on foot. And luckily the snow never came.

Ideally aligot should be prepared with the freshest Tomme cheese of the region, but use older Tomme if need be (or even Cantal), though if you can find an unpasteurized cheese so much the better.

Serves 4

about 2 pounds medium-sized floury potatoes,
  in their skins and well washed
salt
generous ½ cup full-fat crème fraîche or sour cream
1½ sticks unsalted butter
½ garlic clove, peeled
white pepper
¾ pound Tomme cheese, rind removed, cut into
  small cubes

the pilgrim's way and the scallop shell

Bring a large pan of salted water to the boil and cook the potatoes, whole and unpeeled, depending upon their size, until nice and soft, 30–40 minutes. Drain and as soon as they are cool enough to handle, peel them. Mash carefully (a fork is the best bet, and under no circumstances use the food-processor or you will end up with a glutinous mass).

Gently heat the crème fraîche, butter and garlic together, stirring all the time. Meanwhile place an earthenware pot in the oven at a temperature of around 350°F. Still over a gentle heat, whisk the mashed potato, 1 tablespoonful at a time, into the crème fraîche mixture, adding some white pepper halfway through. When the potato is fully amalgamated, start adding the cheese cubes, working as quickly as possible so that the mixture stays light. This is best done with a wooden spoon, which you lift out of the mixture often—the aim is for the cheese to melt into strands.

When all the cheese is added, transfer to the pot and serve straight away. Whether you add grilled sausage or not is up to you; in my opinion, the dish is quite rich enough on its own, and a green salad with walnuts makes it a meal. And any reheated leftovers are a treat the next day with a slice or two of cured ham.

Ever since early medieval times pilgrims have made their way across France, crossed the Pyrenees and travelled on through Spain in order to pray in the magnificent if rather sombre granite cathedral of Santiago de Compostela, where the faithful hold that the apostle St James is buried. Along their route they found many magnificent monuments and churches to encourage them, but there are smaller ones in out-of-the-way places. One day, enjoying lunch on the terrace at our house in the eastern Pyrenees, we picked up the tap tap of a staff and there, walking up the hill, was a barefooted man. He went up to pray in La Bastide's ancient church, where the relief behind the altar displays devils treading on the heads of unbelievers, then continued on his way around Mount Canigou. I rather hoped he had some boots in his rucksack.

The main routes of pilgrimage are traditionally marked by an image of the scallop shell. Regarded in Greek times as a sign of fertility and associated with the goddess Venus, in a splendid mixing of

pagan beliefs and Catholicism the shell, known in Spanish as *concha venera*, has become an emblem for those who reach Santiago de Compostela, or St James of the Field of Stars. This is because a particular kind of large scallop, often described as in the very shape of a hand, is found on the Galician shores, and as early as the twelfth century it became the habit for returning pilgrims to display the empty shells on their hats as a mark of success.

There is even a legend that a prince on horseback on his way to Santiago was overcome by a huge flood; he prayed to St James and was saved, his body covered with scallop shells. And an Italian pilgrim who took a scallop shell back to his native Apulia used it to heal an enormous goitre. By the thirteenth century the monks of Santiago were selling the shells so that the pilgrims didn't have to gather them themselves (anyone decrying the avaricious commercialism of places such as Mont-St-Michel might reflect that it has a long history). All of which is why, in France, the scallop is known as the Coquille St-Jacques—the Shell of St James.

The Supper at Emmaus, 1601, by Michelangelo Caravaggio. Note the scallop shell on the chest of the man on the right

steak au beurre de roquefort
steak with roquefort butter

The well-hung meat of the white Charolais cattle makes for especially tender steaks, which are often served with pats of butter mixed with the blue Roquefort cheese from the limestone plateau further to the south. The idea is that the butter melts over the hot steak, creating its own sauce.

Serves 2

2 tablespoons unsalted butter, removed from the refrigerator at least an hour in advance
scant ¼ pound Roquefort cheese, at room temperature
2 fillet steaks, preferably from Charolais beef
sea salt
freshly ground black pepper

Mash the butter and Roquefort together with a fork. Form into two round pats, wrap in plastic wrap, and chill.

When you are ready to eat, heat a heavy ridged pan for the steak, which you have seasoned. Once the pan is very hot, grill the steak to your satisfaction (personally, I veer towards the very rare side, but it is a matter of personal taste. Always remember to ask your fellow diner, unless you know them intimately.) Put the cold pats of butter and cheese on top of the hot steak and serve straight away.

poires au fourme d'ambert

Fourme d'Ambert is one of France's oldest cheeses, and it is even rumored that the druids of the Gauls were rather fond of it. Easily recognized from the tall cylindrical shape of the entire cheese, it is deeply blue-veined, a result of the traditional maturation in damp cellars where the walls are covered with mold, a process encouraged by piercing the cheeses so that the spores can penetrate.

Once made daily in the *jasseries*, the summer high-pasture barns to the south of the Puy de Dome and across to Cantal which served as both dwelling place and fromagerie, at the beginning of the twentieth century the production became more industrial as it moved down to the plains. However, in the many local markets of the region you can still find high quality farm-made cheeses, often produced with unpasteurized milk for the best flavor.

Fourme d'Ambert is traditionally served with pears, sometimes in elaborate concoctions such as a cheese tart with caramelized pears, especially in restaurants. But I prefer a slice of the cheese and a perfectly ripe pear. (You can if you like halve and peel the pear and cut into a fan shape, but it really isn't necessary.) The cheese also goes well with pears cooked in red wine (see page 137).

soufflé glacé à la verveine
verveine-flavored iced soufflé

An iced soufflé may sound grand but it is nothing more than a puffed-up confection of whipped eggs and cream, which instead of being cooked are frozen to the required consistency (so the usual warnings about raw eggs apply here). Verveine is a strong alcohol peculiar to the Auvergne, traditionally made from an infusion of 32 different plants, but the important point is that the flavor of the ice should be slightly bitter, as is typical of the mountain herbs of the region. To achieve the same effect you could also use genepi, Benedictine, or even (in moderation) absinthe.

Serves 4 to 6

4 large very fresh eggs
⅔ cup confectioners' sugar, sieved
a small pinch of salt
generous ½ cup whipping cream
2 tablespoons verveine or other liqueur
high-quality cocoa powder, for sprinkling

Separate the eggs and beat the whites with the pinch of salt until they stand in soft peaks. Add half the sugar and beat again until the peaks are stiff.

Beat the yolks with the rest of the sugar until they form smooth ribbons, then stir in the liqueur of your choice. Beat the cream until thick. Fold all three together carefully then spoon the mixture into ramekins or (rather more elegantly) coffee cups to about two-thirds of the way up.

Freeze for several hours but don't beat again—there should still be air bubbles on the surface. Dust with the cocoa powder before serving.

clafoutis aux cerises
cherry pudding

The cherries arrive late in this hilly region but driving through in the spring the blossom is stunning. And when the cherries do come (or when they are imported from nearby Limousin) the favorite way to treat them is in a clafoutis, a baked sweet batter pudding that the locals fondly describe as a 'taste of childhood'. Ideally the cherries should be left unpitted so that they keep their texture.

Serves 6

generous 1 cup whole milk
1½ pounds cherries
1½ cups all-purpose flour
½ cup superfine sugar
a pinch of salt
4 tablespoons unsalted butter
4 large eggs, beaten well

Bring the milk to the boil, taking care that it does not boil over. As soon as it starts to fizz up, take it off the heat and leave to cool slightly. Remove the skin. Preheat the oven to 350°F.

Butter a deep ovenproof dish liberally and scatter the cherries over the base, making sure they are evenly distributed. Sift the flour with the sugar and salt into a mixing bowl. Melt the butter and remove any scum. Make a well in the center of the flour and whisk in the beaten eggs then, very slowly, the melted butter, followed by the milk, which should still be warm. Whisk thoroughly so that you have a smooth batter and pour over the cherries.

Bake until the batter rises and the top browns, 40–45 minutes. Leave the oven door slightly open for the last 5 minutes of cooking, so that the batter doesn't sink the minute you take it out of the heat. Serve straight away, sprinkled with confectioners' sugar if you like.

burgundy and the rhône valley

Already enormously wealthy by the fifteenth century, the Duchy of Burgundy was incorporated into France only in 1482 through the Treaty of Arras. Today its inhabitants retain a certain independence and pride in the heritage of the dukedom, still evident in the architecture of towns such as Beaune. But what they are most proud of is their wine, which was once used as a currency for bribery in political and papal circles alike.

The region's capital of Dijon is of course famous for its mustard, vital accompaniment to the Charolais beef which features in perhaps Burgundy's best known dish, boeuf bourguignon. But it is further south and to the west that the real business of Burgundy begins, with names that trip with pleasure from the tongue of the wine lover: Nuits-St-Georges, Gevrey-Chambertin, Rully, Montagny, Marsannay... The wine villages are often small, unprepossessing places, just as the vignerons, unlike their Bordeaux counterparts, mostly live in modest establishments rather than vast châteaux. Do not be fooled: even a small parcel on the Côtes makes these farmers some of the wealthiest in the world in terms of land values per hectare.

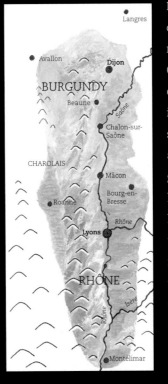

If they are outwardly modest in their display of wealth, the Burgundians are not known for their culinary restraint. On a hot day in the pretty wine town of Rully, I once sat down to what I imagined would be a light lunch of a salade gourmet. Eventually out came a plate composed of: hot and cold foie gras, a pile of garlicky snails, frog's legs, fried duck's gizzards, pressed ham, crayfish, scallops, prawns in their shells, smoked river fish, sliced melon and chicken mousse. There were a few leaves of lettuce on the side. Madame was surprised that I did not wish to follow up with her magnificent platter of local cheeses, arrayed on fresh fig leaves.

The vineyards of Chateauneuf in the Rhône valley

Come the winter months, which are often surprisingly cold, slow-simmered dishes are the favored choice. It is not just mature cockerels that are cooked in red wine—even eggs are poached in a red wine sauce and the wine should be Burgundian in origin, the locals insist (though fortunately not grand cru). There is an entrenched tradition of hunter-gathering (I have heard some very wealthy vignerons describe themselves as peasant farmers) and wild mushrooms, snails, rabbit, partridge and other game birds all feature widely on autumn menus. With a well-chosen bottle on the table, *naturellement*.

Beyond Burgundy, Lyon, gateway to the south, has long been known as the gastronomic capital of France. It is a reputation forged most

Vézélay, northern Burgundy, approaching the famous abbey

marvelously named *cervelle de canut* (literally silkworker's brain), goat's cheese mixed with fresh garlic and herbs. The silkweavers who did so much to create the prosperity of Lyon in the nineteenth century would not have been delighted to have had their brains described in this way, especially as tradition has it that you should buy a 'male' fromage blanc, that is one which is quite hard, and then 'beat it like a woman'. Nor are the Michelin restaurants more restrained. A recent meal at the venerable Léon de Lyon featured slowly stewed pig's cheeks and tail and roast kid with thyme. The Lyonnais are proud to say that they use every bit of the animal. And they know just how to cook it.

The Lyonnais draw from all directions on the food of the lands that surround them, from the cheeses and chickens of the nearby foothills of the Alps and the Jura to the pike and crayfish of the rivers; head south down the Rhône Valley and the food soon acquires a southern flavor. Just a short drive south lies the source of my favorite white wine in the world, the luscious Condrieu, a wine scented with peaches, melons and apricots. From the hearty, meaty dishes of Burgundy and Lyon, the meals turn lighter, with more use of herbs and olive oil. This is, after all, the way to Provence.

Characteristic Burgundian rooftops, near Beaune

recently by Michelin-starred chefs such as Paul Bocuse, as well as those working locally, such as Georges Blanc in Vonne, famous for his dish of poulet de Bresse with crayfish, or Michel Troisgros in Roanne, but goes back much further. Some of the most famous cooks of the last century were women, known as *les mères lyonnaises*, many of them previously cooks in private houses who later started *restaurants familiales*. Best known of all was perhaps la mère Brazier, who opened up shop in 1921 and earned renown for her *quenelles* (delicate dumplings of pike) and *poularde demi-deuil* (chicken half in mourning, so-called because of the black truffles slipped under the skin of the poached bird), but all of them offered well-constructed menus featuring seasonal favorites.

The food of Lyon is robust. Wander around the brasseries and cafés in the center of the old town, alongside the two rivers that dissect the city, and you will see menus offering *pieds et paquets* (trotters and tripe), veal's tongue with *sauce gribiche* or *ravigote*, poached Lyonnais sausage with lentils and Dijon mustard and the

soupe à l'oignon gratinée
french onion soup with cheese

This Lyonnaise brasserie standard has become one of the most recognised of French dishes around the world, if also one of the most traduced. Well known because it is so restorative, especially when served as is traditional in Paris late at night after the theater, and traduced because correctly cooked it takes time (though little effort) to prepare. With onions, stock, bread and cheese, it is another example of how French peasant cooking can turn simple ingredients into something special.

Serves 4

2 pounds large sweet onions—Bermuda are ideal
3 tablespoons unsalted butter
sea salt
about 2 quarts beef stock
8 slices of baguette
½ pound shredded Gruyere or Tomme

Preheat the oven to 350°F. Peel the onions and slice finely into half moons. Melt two thirds of the butter in a heavy pan over a medium heat, add the onions, sprinkle generously with salt and cook, stirring occasionally, until lightly browned, 15 minutes. Meanwhile, heat the stock until simmering. Pour the liquid over the onions, bring back to the boil and transfer the soup to an ovenproof Dutch oven, ideally earthenware, and put uncovered in the oven.

After an hour or so, butter the slices of bread and top with the shredded cheese. Place these in the pot and cook until bubbling hot, a further 15–20 minutes. Serve straight away, from the cooking dish, with pepper on the side for those who wish to add it.

escargots en chaussons
snails in pockets

Yes, the French do eat snails, especially in Burgundy. These days they are mostly farmed, but I once went on a trip with friends who lived to the south of Troyes to gather them. To be honest, we were simply on a walk, but it had just rained and Marie-Pierre could not resist collecting the petit gris, as the edible variety is known. She would feed them on a diet of herbs, she explained, then starve them for several days so that they would purge themselves, and boil them in plenty of salted water.

You can of course buy snails stuffed back into their shells and topped with garlic butter, but served this way they taste of little but garlic. In this dish, however, which I was served as an amuse-gueule, or appetite-whetter, in Beaune, the flavour of the snails comes through.

Serves 8 as an amuse-gueule

1 small jar of ready-prepared snails, ideally containing 24
2 tablespoons butter
4 shallots, peeled and finely chopped
1 fat garlic clove
1 tablespoon finely chopped parsley
2 teaspoons crème fraîche or sour cream
salt and freshly ground black pepper
½ pound bought frozen puff paste, defrosted
¼ pound Roquefort cheese
1 egg yolk, well beaten

Rinse the snails well. Melt the butter in a heavy non-stick pan and add the shallots and garlic. Cook gently, stirring from time to time, until softened, 5 minutes. Now add the snails and cook another 2 minutes, until just warmed through. Remove from the heat, add the parsley, crème fraîche or sour cream and seasoning to taste. Leave to cool.

Preheat the oven to 400°F. Roll out the dough on a floured surface and cut out 8 rounds the size of a large wine glass. Place on foil on a baking sheet and pile the snail mixture into the center. Top each pile of snails with a little Roquefort. Fold over to create half moons, crimp the edges together and brush with the beaten yolk.

Bake until nicely puffed up, 15–20 minutes. Serve piping hot.

the cellars of beaune

As the tourists wander around Beaune in the heart of Burgundy, they may be unaware that they are walking over priceless collections of wines. The Hospices de Beaune, the charitable institution established in 1443 by Nicolas Rolin, Chancellor to the Duke of Burgundy Philippe le Bon, is still a hospital for the poor today. But beneath the steeply pitched and ornately tiled roof of the Hôtel-Dieu

stretch the cellars, housing the wines produced from the sixty-odd hectares of vineyards, mostly first growths, which belong to the Hospices.

The Hospices are not the only organization to boast cellars in the heart of the town. Many of the individual wine houses have their headquarters here and none has a better position than Bouchard Père et Fils, sited in the remnants of the town's original castle, built by Louis XI as a defence against the people of Beaune.

The castle eventually fell into disrepair and after being confiscated at the time of the French Revolution was sold on to the local stonemason. Until, that is, the wine-making Bouchard family took it over. Today the dark, deep cellars beneath the towers, their walls around 20 feet thick, house some 5,000 bottles of wine from the nineteenth century alone. It is an atmospheric place to wander around, peering at labels still intact. I was handed a bottle of 1846 Meursault Charmes to hold tremulously. Apparently the white wine is *incroyable*.

Bouchard pride themselves on their wine-and-food matching, not an easy task when pairing dishes to such fine and venerable wines. In general in Burgundy, the more delicate wines from the Beaune region are recommended with poultry, while duck, lamb and game are more often served with Volnay, Nuits-St-Georges or Gevrey-Chambertin. With a young Meursault you might be served say a langoustine salad or a fish terrine, whereas older whites can handle fish in sauce. As for the cheese course, it is increasingly the trend to serve a white, especially with the local goat's cheeses but also with stronger cheese such as Epoisses and Ami du Chambertin.

oeufs en meurette *eggs poached in red wine*

One night a wine grower found nothing in the larder but some eggs, bacon, butter and, of course, bread and red wine. So he decided to cook them all together; or so legend has it. But whatever its origin, this simple yet luxurious dish has become a Burgundian classic. In restaurants, it is usually offered as a starter, but accompanied by a simple green salad it also makes a splendid supper for two. No need to open the best Burgundy but you will want wine you can drink with it—what else will you do with the rest of the bottle?

Serves 2

3 tablespoons unsalted butter
¼ pound smoked bacon in lardons
4 pink shallots, peeled and finely chopped
2 cups red wine (typically a red Burgundy would be used, but a good quality fruity vin de pays will do the trick)
2 tablespoons white wine vinegar
4 slices of French bread
freshly ground black pepper
4 fresh eggs, preferably free-range

In a heavy Dutch oven, melt half the butter together with the bacon and cook for 5 minutes. Chop the remaining butter into small pieces and chill in the refrigerator. Add the shallots and cook, stirring regularly, until they are very soft, 15 minutes. Pour in the wine and allow to bubble gently, uncovered, until the sauce is reduced by half, 30 minutes.

Meanwhile, add the white wine vinegar to a pan of water and bring to a rolling boil. Toast the bread on both sides and place in two deep bowls.

Check the seasoning of the sauce (you may like to add some pepper at this stage but generally the bacon provides sufficient salt). Carefully poach the eggs by simply breaking them two at a time into the water; provided they are sufficiently fresh the white will coagulate around the yolk and the cooking time will be a matter of a minute or two. Lift the eggs out with a slotted spoon, making sure all the water has drained off, and place each egg on a slice of the toast. Remove the hot sauce from the heat and quickly swirl in the pieces of butter—this gives the sauce a gloss. Pour over the poached eggs and serve immediately.

sauté de cuisses de grenouilles
fried frog's legs

lapin à la moutarde
rabbit in mustard sauce

The French are by no means the only people who are partial to frog's legs. In the former British colony of Montserrat in the Caribbean, frog is described as mountain chicken and served with spicy tomato sauce. In Vietnam and Laos in south-east Asia frog's legs are skewered on sticks and cooked over the barbeque. In most people's minds, though, the French have made them their own. These days most of the frogs destined for the French marketplace are reared outside the country, in Turkey and eastern Europe (the same is true for the crayfish, or *écrevisses*, which once were plentiful in mountain streams), but the dish remains as popular as ever.

Serves 4 as a first course

24 frog's legs
all-purpose flour
salt and freshly ground black pepper
4 tablespoons olive oil
2 garlic cloves, peeled and finely chopped
1 glass of dry white wine
2 handfuls of chopped leaves of flat-leaved parsley

Preheat the oven to 350°F and put a serving dish in to heat. Wash the frog's legs well, pat dry then roll in well-seasoned flour. Heat the oil in a large, heavy pan. Fry the frog's legs in several batches, 3–4 minutes on either side, and transfer to the serving dish.

When all the frog's legs are cooked, add the garlic to the remaining oil and fry, stirring all the time, 2 minutes. Now add the white wine and parsley and bubble a further 2 minutes. Return the frog's legs to the pan, turn in the sauce and serve sizzling hot.

Rabbit is a favorite meat in Burgundy (after, of course, the Charolais beef), possibly because its white lean flesh is a good foil to the more subtle of the local wines. Another widely used ingredient is the mustard of the regional capital, Dijon, now often made with imported mustard seed but given its unique flavor by the other elements added, particularly the local wine vinegar. I have eaten this dish made with tarragon mustard but personally I prefer it with the straightforward variety. It is important that you use farmed rabbit—wild rabbit would be too tough for this treatment. Fresh buttered egg noodles are an excellent accompaniment, with a butter lettuce salad to follow.

Serves 4

4 large or 8 small thighs of farmed rabbit
1 tablespoon Dijon mustard
2 tablespoons olive oil
freshly ground black pepper
generous 1 cup white wine
2 fresh bay leaves
2 tablespoons crème fraîche or sour cream
yolk of 1 large fresh egg, preferably free-range, beaten

Wash the rabbit thighs well and wipe dry. Mix together the Dijon mustard and oil and season with plenty of pepper. Smear this mixture all over the rabbit pieces and leave to stand at least 30 minutes.

Preheat the oven to 400°F. Place the rabbit pieces in a heatproof Dutch oven, earthenware for preference, and when the oven is hot roast 5 minutes. Now add the white wine and bay leaves and continue to cook until tender, basting occasionally (the exact cooking time will depend upon the size and youth of the rabbit—if you are in doubt, taste to check), between 30 and 40 minutes.

Reduce the oven temperature to 300°F, wrap the rabbit pieces in foil and return to the oven to keep warm. Pour the cooking juices into a pan, extracting the bay leaves, and bubble to reduce by half. Remove from the heat and stir in the crème fraîche or sour cream, then return to the heat and cook gently for a few minutes. Remove from the heat again, leave to stand for 1 minute, then stir in the beaten egg yolk.

Put the rabbit back in the pot and pour any juices from the foil into the sauce. Check for seasoning, pour the sauce over the rabbit and serve.

cailles aux raisins
quails cooked with grapes

A vigneron's feast, these little birds were traditionally cooked wrapped in fresh vine leaves over a fire of vine cuttings. The dish used to be a treat in early autumn, when the quails ran from the fields as the harvest was brought in. Nowadays most quail are farmed.

Serves 2 as a one-course meal or 4 as part of a series of courses

3 tablespoons unsalted butter
¼ pound smoked bacon cut into lardons
2 shallots, peeled and finely chopped
4 fat quails
1 ladle of Cognac
¾ cup fruity white wine
scant ½ cup water
freshly ground black pepper
⅓ pound green seedless grapes, halved
4 slices of French bread

Melt the butter with the bacon and shallots in a heavy-based Dutch oven into which the birds will just fit. Cook over a gentle heat, stirring occasionally, until the shallots are softened and the bacon fat has run, 10 minutes. Now turn up the heat to medium and add the birds to brown on both sides.

Meanwhile gently heat the Cognac in the ladle. When the birds are browned (no more than a couple of minutes), set light to the Cognac and pour into the pan, standing well back. As soon as the flames die down, shake the pan and add the wine. Allow to bubble, then add the water and a few good grinds of black pepper (you should not need salt as the bacon is salty but as ever check for seasoning before serving). Bring to a gentle simmer, cover and cook, turning the birds once or twice, 30 minutes.

When the quails are cooked (poke a fork between the leg and breast—the juices should run clear), remove from the pan and keep warm. Bring the sauce to an active bubble and add the grapes. Cook until the grapes are warmed through and just softened, about 5 minutes, while you toast the bread. Put each slice of toast in a large soup plate, set a quail on top and spoon over the sauce and grapes.

le poulet de bresse

'Reine de volailles et volaille des rois'– queen of poultry and poultry of kings—wrote the gourmet Brillat-Savarin in 1825 of the poulet de Bresse, the only chicken in France (indeed, in the world) to have its very own Appellation d'Origine Contrôlée, or AOC, awarded in the 1950s. Henri IV, so the tale goes, stopped off in Bresse after an accident with his carriage and praised the bird he was served for supper so highly that he insisted Bresse chickens were to become part of his regular diet. Certainly from 1591 the bird is cited in the registers of Bourg-en-Bresse.

The poulet de Bresse is recognizable from its steely blue feet, red comb and white plumage and all true birds have a special red, white and blue badge denoting their noble birth. Each year since 1862 in the month of December 'Les Glorieuses de Bresse', a competition for the best chickens, as well as capons, takes place. In order to enter the competition, the birds must be raised along very strict guidelines, from the five weeks they spend as chicks in their poussinières to the amount of space allocated to them when they go outside to graze. Finally they are fattened on grain and milk products. The owner of the overall winning bird receives a vase of Sèvres porcelain, donated by no less a personage than the President of the Republic. The chicken is less fortunate: it has already been butchered.

Poulets de Bresse are popular with chefs the world over but none is more famous for his treatment of the chicken than the local Georges Blanc, whose restaurant at Vonnas is renowned. This is Michelin territory, but there is a cheaper alternative: the brasserie-style Chez Blanc on the main square of Bourg-en-Bresse itself. Once on our way to the Alps we made a special diversion to dine there, choosing the two 'classics of the house'.

First came *cuisses de grenouilles sautées comme en Dombe en deux services*, frog's legs cooked with garlic and parsley and served in two goes so that they would be sizzling hot. Then the breast of Bresse chicken cooked with vinegar and tarragon, though we could also have chosen wing and thigh of chicken with puréed potatoes. The menu points out that the chickens have a particular flavor and texture due to the breed, the terroir and their feed. They are truly exceptional and on our way back north from the Alps we felt the need to visit again—choosing exactly the same meal.

coq au vin
cockerel in red wine

One of the most famous of French dishes—and another of the most traduced. It is claimed by both Burgundians and Auvergnats as their own, but the people of both regions agree on some rules: a mature bird, a good bottle of wine, long slow cooking and the inclusion of smoked bacon, small onions or shallots and mushrooms.

Serves 4

1 cockerel, around 4 pounds, or failing that a
    mature boiling fowl (don't try making this with
    a young chicken, it is not worth the effort),
    jointed
1 bottle good-quality red wine (not necessarily
    Burgundy: a solid Côtes du Rhône or Côtes
    d'Auvergne would both be good choices
bouquet garni of fresh thyme, parsley stalks and
    bay leaves
coarsely ground black pepper
2 tablespoons olive oil
4 tablespoons unsalted butter
½ pound smoked bacon, preferably in lardons or
    otherwise chopped into pieces, blanched for
    1 minute
2 tablespoons Cognac
1 tablespoon all-purpose flour
2 garlic cloves, peeled and crushed
16 small onions or 8 shallots
sea salt
1 teaspoon white sugar
¾ pound small white mushrooms
juice of ½ lemon

Marinate the joints of chicken in an earthenware bowl with the wine, herbs, plenty of pepper and the olive oil. Cover and leave at least 12 hours—overnight is ideal.

When you are ready to cook the coq au vin, lift the pieces of chicken from the marinade and pat dry with paper towels. Strain the marinade, retaining the bouquet garni, and warm in a pan over a gentle heat.

Take one third of the butter and melt over a medium heat in the Dutch oven in which you intend to cook the coq au vin, which should be heavy and have a lid. Preheat the oven to 350°F.

Add the blanched lardons to the melted butter and cook for a few minutes, stirring regularly. Now add the pieces of chicken and fry 5 minutes on either side, until lightly browned. Depending upon the shape of your pot, you may need to do this in two batches.

Gently heat the Cognac in a ladle, set light to it and pour over the chicken, standing well back. When the flames die down, shake the pot and then add the flour and stir well. Cook for another few minutes then pour over the hot marinade, adding the retained bouquet garni and the garlic. Bring to a slow simmer, cover and transfer to the oven.

The chicken needs to cook for 1 hour, which gives you time to prepare the remaining vegetables. Peel the onions or shallots and if you are using the latter divide the bulbs along their natural lines. Heat another third of the butter in a heavy pan and add the shallots, sprinkled with some salt and the sugar. Cook gently, turning regularly, until browned all over, 15 minutes. Set aside.

Wash the mushrooms and pat dry. If they are large you may need to cut them in half vertically. Melt the remaining butter in the same pan in which you cooked the shallots, add the mushrooms, the lemon juice and a sprinkling of salt and cook until the juices run, 5–6 minutes. Set aside, keeping the juices.

After the chicken has cooked for 1 hour, add the browned shallots and stir well. Return to the oven for a further 20 minutes, then add the cooked mushrooms, again stirring well. Cook in the oven another 20 minutes.

You can serve the coq au vin at this stage, traditionally with toasted slices of baguette rubbed with garlic, but it is at its best if cooked a few hours in advance of serving and then reheated. Canny French housewives often add a glass of red wine in the reheating process to 'relax' the sauce—as if the cock hadn't drunk enough already.

boeuf à la mode
beef in jelly

This version of a venerable dish is in the fashion of Chris Hewittson who, together with his partner Monsieur Mic, has provided me with endless memorable meals in their house deep in the hills of the Corbières. He tells an alarming story of the first time he cooked it many years ago, when the gelatine from the calf's foot set around the lid of his slow cooker, so that the next day he could not prise it open. But the point is correct – this dish needs to be cooked as slowly as possible. I for one prefer it served cold, as it traditionally is in the brasseries of Lyons, though it is a recipe for winter rather than summer.

Calves' feet are a bit hard to get hold of these days but a pig's trotter serves the same purpose, which is to set the jelly (another reason to serve it in cool weather – if it gets too hot the jelly may 'turn'). Any leftovers are delicious scattered over a salad and dressed with a mustardy vinaigrette.

Serves 6–8

8 pound joint rolled topside of beef, tied with
   string and enrobed in fat
2 rashers smoked streaky bacon, diced
generous 1 tablespoon butter
1 small glass cognac
¼ pound large white onions, peeled and chopped
¼ pound large carrots, scraped and cut into
   rounds
2 cloves garlic, peeled
1 bottle dry white wine, such as a white
   Côtes du Rhône
salt and freshly ground black pepper
bouquet garni of fresh bayleaf, thyme and
   flat-leaved parsley
half a calf's foot or a pig's trotter, split down
   the middle

Preheat the oven to 250°F.

Choose a heavy-based pot with a lid into which the meat and trotter will fit snugly. Place the pot over a gentle heat. Add the bacon and cook until the fat begins to run. Add the beef and turn in the fat until lightly browned. Carefully heat the cognac in a ladle, set light to it and pour over the beef, shaking the pan to distribute the flames. When the flames die down, add the chopped onions, carrots, garlic and the bouquet garni. Pour in the wine and add some seasoning. Poke in the calf's or pig's trotter, cover the top with foil and put on the lid. Cook in the oven 5–6 hours.

Remove from the oven and leave to cool, then place in the refrigerator overnight. The next day, scoop off the fat, slice the meat thinly and arrange the jelly and vegetables around. Serve with potatoes boiled in their skins and plenty of Dijon mustard.

pêches flambées
flambéed peaches

The Rhône Valley is famous for its peaches, particularly the white variety. They are delicious eaten just as they are, especially on a picnic, but for a more sophisticated dish they are stewed in a light sugar syrup and then flambéed in local kirsch or cherry eau de vie.

Serves 4

8 peaches, preferably white
½ cup white sugar
1¼ cups water
4 tablespoons kirsch

Peel the peaches—if they are perfectly ripe, the skin will come off easily, but if not dip briefly in boiling water, plunge into iced water and then peel.

Make a sugar syrup with the sugar, water and 1 tablespoon kirsch. When the syrup has boiled for a couple of minutes, turn down to a slow simmer and add the peaches. Poach gently 10 minutes, remove from the heat, and leave to cool in the syrup.

Just before serving, place the cold peaches in a heatproof bowl with a little of the syrup and heat the remaining kirsch in a ladle. Set light to the alcohol, pour over the peaches, and take flaming to the table.

cassis

According to Burgundian farmer Guy Didier, growing blackcurrants is like cultivating vines—there are good years and bad years. This is not just to do with the weather. 'If the year ends with a nine you will have a particularly good harvest because that is a year with thirteen moons. And you must always prune when the moon is waning. The plant must suffer to make it produce fruit.'

We were standing in a blackcurrant field high up on the Côtes, the rocky outcrops whose stony soil produces some of the best wines of the region. It was only ten o'clock in the morning but already the pickers' hands, arms and legs were scarred from the thorns and stained a deep berry-red with the juice.

Blackcurrants were prized in eighteenth-century France as a cure-all for ailments as diverse as ill-humor or liver disease but then their popularity waned. In 1840, however, a liqueur maker, Denis La Goute and his distiller Claude Joly, both from Dijon, visited Paris. There they found that in the bars and bistros a jug of ratafia, a fruit liqueur, was placed free of charge on the table alongside the other condiments. This ratafia was to be mixed with the mostly poor quality wines of the time, and although it contained all sorts of fruits its dominant flavor was blackcurrant. On their return to Dijon, Messieurs La Goute and Joly set about making a blackcurrant liqueur. And so, in 1841, crème de cassis was born.

Soon everyone in the Burgundian area was planting blackcurrants. Often they were grown as a border around the vineyards, or rows of vines would alternate with rows of blackcurrants. Blackcurrants, it soon became clear, thrived near wine—they appreciated both the terrain and the know-how of

the peasant farmers—and the bushes became part of the Burgundian landscape.

There was another natural affinity between Burgundy and the blackcurrant: crème de cassis goes particularly well with the local dry white wine, Bourgogne Aligoté, as a local café boy discovered at the turn of the century. For forty-odd years the aperitif was simply called blanc-cassis, as it still is by many locals. Then, at the end of the Second World War, Dijon got a new mayor, the Chanoine Félix Kir. He served the local aperitif of blanc-cassis to everyone from Khrushchev to de Gaulle and the kir was born. One step up is the cardinal—cassis with red wine, named after the cardinal's red cassock.

sorbet de cassis
blackcurrant sorbet

Blackcurrants aren't used just for drinks. I once sa through a tasting menu which used blackcurrants at every course, including as a sauce for a large hunk of Charolais beef cooked rare. What stuck in my mind from the meal was a blackcurrant sorbet of sparkling cleanliness on the palate. If you don't want to make your own sorbet, you can also cook blackcurrants in a light syrup, add a splash of crème de cassis, and pour over vanilla ice cream.

Serves 6

1 pound fresh blackcurrants
2 cups white sugar
3 cups water
2 tablespoons crème de cassis

Wash the blackcurrants well and strip from their stalks. Mix together the sugar and water and boil together in a non-reactive pan to make a sugar syrup, stirring occasionally, 5 minutes. Add the blackcurrants, turn the heat down to low, and simmer 5 minutes. Press through a fine metal sieve, making sure you press down on the fruit with a wooden spoon to get all the juices out. Stir in the crème de cassis and freeze in a plastic container. Stir after 1½ hours, and again every 15 minutes thereafter for another hour or so until set. Take out of the freezer 20 minutes before serving and give it another stir. Scoop into chilled serving dishes.

the alps

Under the rule of the Dukes of Savoy until the mid nineteenth century, much of what is now thought of as the French Alps has a distinctly Italian history. Today, depending upon the season, you can still drive or ski into Italy from Haute Savoie. But that does not mean that the food is dominated by pasta and polenta, though they are popular fuel in the huts on the ski slopes. Cheese, cream and potatoes play the main role, especially in gratins. Gratin dauphinois is a splendid example of how a few potatoes with some best-quality butter and thick cream (cheese is never added in the local version) can be turned into a dish fit for a duke.

The lands now described as the French Alps stretch far to the south (Nice, together with Savoy, was part of the deal reached by Napoleon III with his southern counterparts in 1860 upon the unification of Italy, the last time France extended its territory in Europe) but it is in the high mountain pastures that the gastronomy is defined. This is the land of Beaufort d'été, a cheese specifically made from the milk of cows who have grazed the summer grasses, of Reblochon, which is melted on top of waxy potatoes for a truly

Local mushrooms in the market

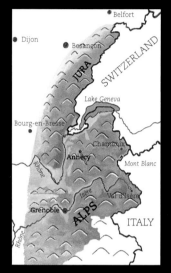

wicked dish, and of Vacherin, a cheese wrapped in the bark of birch trees to stop it from running all over the table, to be eaten with a teaspoon.

To accompany these rich cheese dishes of autumn and winter the choice is not red wine but the fresh whites of the region, such as the skier's favorite, Apremont, which is especially good with cheese fondue. And to follow come fruit tarts made from local berries, the wild bilberry being my choice, or a strong coffee with some of the local berries preserved in eau de vie (or grappa as it is still known in these parts).

When the snow starts to melt, though there is crusty spring snow high up for skiers to enjoy, the fruit trees are in blossom lower down the hills and the food becomes altogether lighter. This is the time of year for the omelette haute-savoyarde, traditionally made with the first bitter herbs plucked from the mountainside, but nowadays just as often made with home-grown herbs such as sorrel, basil, chervil and parsley, or maybe cheese, and possibly even bacon.

Pig, as in any mountain region, plays an important part in the diet. There is nothing like a visit to the charcutier after a hard day on the slopes, though the saucissons, often studded with the walnuts or hazelnuts for which the Dauphiné is especially well known, are sold at markets throughout France. This is sausage rather than pâté country, and the sausage can be very special, its rich fat pink meat speckled with truffles or wild mushrooms. Particular favorites of mine are the *diots*, small smoked sausage which is poached in white wine.

Most prized of all the mushrooms is the spring morel, though the ceps of autumn aren't far behind. I was once taken on a morel hunt behind the ski resort of Val d'Isère, of all places. The snow had barely melted in the forests, yet we walked only a few hundred yards into the woods to find the conical, dimpled little mushrooms popping up. It was a particular privilege; I was sworn not to reveal their location to anyone else. But then mushroom hunting is a national, if highly competitive, pastime in France, and particularly so in the Alps. Here ceps, chanterelles, girolles and trompettes de mort (horns of plenty, in a rather more optimistic English translation) grow freely.

Down from the mountains (though they remain in view), the main towns offer a different level of sophistication. My favorite is Annecy, with its network of canals, its gabled and half-timbered houses and its splendid fish dishes, cooked with particular delicacy. Throughout the region, river and lake fish play an important part in the local cooking.

Until recently the crayfish was especially popular, but just as elsewhere in Europe the native variety is under threat from an invasion of the American signal crayfish, escaped from farms, which eat the smaller and more delicate local shellfish. Brown trout from the mountain streams are also diminishing drastically in numbers. But fortunately pike, used for *quenelles de brochet*, or pike dumplings (much lighter than they sound), are still abundant, and various lake fish find their way into the skillet.

Even the fish tends to get a good spoonful of cream and butter in the cooking. As with most mountain areas, this is dairy country. We may ski down the slopes in winter, but in summer the cows are released from their barns to graze those same hills.

The ski slopes at Megève, Haute Savoie

potage aux champignons
mushroom soup

When I was cooking in the French ski resort of Val d'Isère (for a brief period of time in university holidays, I hasten to add, usually when the chalet girl had broken her leg), this was one of the most popular starters, ideal after a hard day on the slopes. It was a French policeman, who rejoiced in the nickname in this peculiarly English resort of Monsieur Plod, who pointed out to me that if I included some dried wild mushrooms in my soup it would taste less insipid. He was right. And as with all soups the stock should be well reduced.

Serves 4 to 6

4 cups chicken or vegetable stock
2½ cups dried mushrooms, ideally ceps or trompettes de mort, rinsed
3 tablespoons butter
2 large shallots, peeled and finely chopped
½ pound field mushrooms, finely chopped
1 handful each of parsley and celery leaves, finely chopped
2 tablespoons all-purpose flour
salt and freshly ground black pepper
generous ½ cup heavy cream
2 tablespoons shredded cheese such as Tomme, Comté or Beaufort

Heat the stock in a non-reactive pan in which you intend to make the soup and add the dried mushrooms. Leave to steep off the heat, 20 minutes.

Meanwhile, heat half the butter with the shallots over a medium heat and when the butter is fizzing add the field mushrooms and the herbs. Cook, stirring from time to time, 10 minutes.

Pound together the rest of the butter with the flour and add plenty of seasoning. Reheat the stock and add just a little of the liquid to the flour and butter mixture, stirring continuously until you have a smooth cream. Now stir this back into the hot stock, then add the cooked mushroom, shallot and herb mixture. Bring back to the boil, reduce to a slow simmer and cook, 20–25 minutes.

Just before serving, check the seasoning and add the cream. Simmer for another few minutes and serve with shredded cheese and plenty of bread on the side. A glass of eau de vie poured into the soup is also traditional.

tartiflette

This is a truly indulgent dish, which is best appreciated after a strenuous morning on the ski slopes—or at least a brisk winter's morning walk. It is important to use a ripe Reblochon, preferably bought a few days in advance and left to reach maturity out of the refrigerator. For this to happen, it should be unpasteurized. Of course, if you know of a good cheese store you will be able to buy one ripe and ready to eat.

Serves 4

3 pounds medium-sized red potatoes
1 large white onion, peeled and diced
2 thick slices of smoked streaky bacon, diced
2 tablespoons butter
1 garlic clove, peeled and cut in half
sea salt and freshly ground black pepper
1 ripe Reblochon cheese

Preheat the oven to 400°F. Bring a large pan of water to the boil and cook the potatoes whole, in their skins, 15 minutes. Meanwhile, cook the onion and bacon in the butter in a heavy skillet over a medium heat; they should sweat but not brown. Drain the potatoes and as soon as they are cool enough to handle peel them—the quicker the better. Slice thickly across.

Choose an ovenproof earthenware dish and rub it well with the cut halves of garlic. Layer half the sliced potatoes across the base, season, then scatter over the onion and bacon mixture. Add the remaining potatoes and more seasoning. Place the whole Reblochon on top. Bake 10 minutes, then reduce the heat to 350°F for a further 20–25 minutes. The Reblochon should melt within its skin and the fat drip down while the potatoes crisp. All you need is a green salad to go with it.

raclette

f you are serving raclette in any quantity, you really need a raclette dish, where the cheese is individually melted by each diner over the spirit lamp. For two people you can cheat and cook the cheese on a ridged grill pan, spooning it straight onto the hot potatoes, but beyond that it gets complicated. This is a dish where it is best to get people to do their own cooking.

Serves as many as you want it to, depending upon the size of your raclette dish. Four slices of cheese a head is a minimum

small red-skinned potatoes, well washed but still in their skins
sea salt
French-style dill pickles
French-style small white onions
slices of air-dried ham and/or air-dried beef
slices of French-style sausage (it is nice to have a variety)
Raclette cheese, finely sliced

Boil the potatoes in plenty of salted water until tender then drain and transfer to a serving dish. Meanwhile, put all the accompaniments, cheese aside, into serving dishes (traditionally, the onions and pickles are served in small earthenware bowls, and the dried meats on a wooden platter). If you have a raclette dish, get it nice and hot, or do the same for a ridged non-stick grill pan. Cook the cheese, a few slices at a time, spread onto halved hot potatoes and eat with the various side dishes.

gratin dauphinois

My friend Coco, now a farmer but once a patissier and originally from the Savoie region, is quite clear: there is no cheese in gratin dauphinois. His elegant wife Michèle however disagrees—she always adds shredded cheese. But then, as Coco says, she worked in Paris for many years. I err to Coco's point of view. There are other debates. Should you use a mixture of milk and cream, the former first boiled? Should the potatoes be cooked first? To add nutmeg or not? Personally, I go for the simple option. Good butter, cream and potatoes make this most luscious of potato dishes, which is splendid with broiled lamb chops and a green salad.

Serves 4 to 6 as a side dish

8 medium-sized red-skinned potatoes
1 garlic clove, peeled and halved
salt and freshly ground black pepper
1 stick butter
1 cup heavy cream

Preheat the oven to 350°F. Peel the potatoes and slice them across as finely as possible. Rinse them under cold water to remove any excess starch and pat dry. Choose a fairly deep earthenware gratin dish and rub the inside with the cut sides of the garlic clove. Put a layer of the sliced potatoes across the bottom, season well and dot with butter. Repeat the process until all the slices of potato are used up, leaving a little butter to dot on the surface. Pour in the cream, making sure it is evenly distributed. Bake uncovered until the surface is nicely browned and the potatoes soft all the way through (test with a fork), 45–60 minutes—the exact cooking time will depend upon the quality of the potatoes. Serve piping hot.

lunch on the ski slopes

The mountain *réfuge* or hut, reached by an out of the way piste, is one of my favorite places to have lunch in France. Ideally, it will be a sunny day, and you will be able to sit outside, the clips of your ski boots loosened, your face turned towards the sun's rays. The food will be simple and *montagnard*: eggs, cheese, cured meats, potatoes, wild berries.

When I worked in the ski resort of Val d'Isère there was a famous hut situated off-piste at the back of Le Fornet, to which each morning a pisteur skied down with a few dozen eggs on his back for the omelets. And what omelets they were, oozing with the local Tomme cheese and dripping with butter. A simple green salad, a pile of crusty bread, perhaps a myrtille tart to follow. A feast.

But the very best of mountain food involves sharing. Raclette, for example, is an invention of genius. A thick wheel of cheese is heated and placed in a vice on the table so that you can scrape melting strands off the surface onto your potatoes boiled in their skins.

Or there is fondue savoyarde, the white wine- and kirsch-enriched dish of melted cheeses, into which you dip cubes of bread spiked on long forks. The cheese bubbles over its spirit lamp as you try not to lose your bread in the mixture and to transfer it to your mouth without dribbling strands of cheese.

Many of the French ski resorts also boast smart restaurants on the slopes, which you do not even need to ski to. Skidoos are available to transfer the fur-clad ladies. But to me that is missing the point. You want to be eating local mountain food, not sophisticated dishes. Though sometimes the cable car down is an attractive après-lunch option.

fondue savoyarde
cheese fondue

poulet aux morilles
chicken with morels

You don't, happily, need a fondue set to serve a cheese fondue. In any case, those spindly little forks are only designed for you to lose your bread in the cheese mixture. The way I was taught to eat fondue in Savoie was to buy the best cheese, melt it with plenty of good wine, top it up with a little eau de vie, preferably kirsch, and let everyone dive in. In domestic circumstances, I think going for more than four people is pushing it; the cheese must be bubbling hot, straight from the cooker, not set over a little burner. The key is to twiddle your bread in the cheese effectively, as if you were eating pasta—and to do it fast.

Serves 4

equal portions of Beaufort, Comté and Emmental
   cheese, around ½ pound per person in total
1 level teaspoon cornstarch
1 small glass of kirsch
1 garlic clove, peeled and crushed
2/3 bottle good Savoie white wine, such as
   Apremont
a good pinch of white pepper
plenty of slightly stale white baguette, cut into
   mouth-sized cubes, served in a basket

Remove any rind from the cheeses and shred the cheese finely, in the French style of thin strands. Beat the cornstarch carefully into the kirsch, making sure there are no lumps. In either a fondue pot or a heavy-based pan very slowly melt the cheese with the garlic clove and the wine, stirring continuously so that it does not stick or burn. When the cheese mixture is smooth, stir in the blended kirsch and cornstarch, a little at a time, until the cheese thickens. Season with the white pepper (some also add a pinch of nutmeg but I find it unnecessary) and serve bubbling hot, bread of course on the side.

The morel mushroom is unusual in that it grows in springtime rather than autumn. Normally found at altitude, it is much prized, not least because it dries well (though a plate of fresh morels fried in butter with garlic and parsley is a particular treat). It goes especially well with the chicken of Bresse, reared at the gateway to the Alps.

Serves 4

1½ cups dried morels
4 chicken breasts, preferably from a grain-fed
   and free-range bird, skin on (you could also
   use breasts with the wing bone still in)
sea salt and freshly ground black pepper
2 tablespoons unsalted butter
2 teaspoons extra virgin olive oil
¾ cup dry white wine (ideally the yellow wine
   from the Jura, but a fruity white wine will do)
2 tablespoons crème fraîche or sour cream
2 teaspoons redcurrant jelly
a few sprigs of fresh redcurrants (optional)

Soak the morels for 2 hours in just enough boiling water to cover them, until they swell. Remove the morels from the liquor and drain the latter through a fine sieve to remove any grit. Reserve both morels and liquor.

Preheat the oven to 300°F and put serving plates in to warm. Season the chicken breasts well. Melt the butter and oil together over a medium heat in a heavy skillet, large enough to take all the chicken. Fry the chicken breasts until nicely browned, 5 minutes on either side. Drain off any fat.

Now add the morel soaking liquor, the morels themselves and the wine to the pan. Simmer uncovered until the chicken is cooked through, 10 minutes. Transfer the chicken to the serving plates, then stir the crème fraîche or sour cream and the redcurrant jelly into the pan. Bring back to a swift bubble, cook for 2 minutes, pour over the chicken breasts and serve topped with the fresh redcurrants if you have them.

griottes flambées
sour cherries flamed in alcohol

Splendid poured over vanilla ice cream, this dish is usually made with the local sour cherries which are preserved in red wine or eau de vie, but you can make your own version with fresh cherries.

Serves 4

½ pound black cherries, preferably the sour variety
zest of ½ lemon, unwaxed if possible, cut into
   thin strips
¼ cup brown sugar
scant ½ cup light red wine, ideally a Gamay
1 tablespoon redcurrant jelly
2 tablespoons kirsch

Remove any stalks from the cherries and wash the fruit well. Put the lemon zest, sugar, wine and redcurrant jelly all together in a non-reactive pan and bring to the boil, stirring. Simmer for a few minutes then add the cherries. Simmer uncovered until almost all the liquid has bubbled off, about 5 minutes. Meanwhile, heat the kirsch in a ladle. Set light to it, pour flaming over the cherries and serve immediately.

omelette soufflée
a souffléed omelet

A sweet puffed-up omelet is the simplest of puddings for supper, though you should never try to make one for more than three people at the most. Served straight from oven to table, it relies for its success on a very hot oven and speed.

Sometimes in the Alps a filling of black cherry jam is added but I find that an unnecessary embellishment. If you don't want to use alcohol, you could try a little orange zest and a touch of vanilla.

Serves 2–3

4 large very fresh eggs
pinch of salt
⅔ cup confectioners' sugar
2 tablespoons unsalted butter
½ teaspoon all-purpose flour
2 tablespoons Cointreau or Grand Marnier

Preheat the oven to 425°F. Separate the eggs carefully. Whisk the whites with the salt and when they are halfway to forming peaks add a third of the sugar. Continue to whisk until they form soft peaks but don't make the mixture too stiff.

Briefly beat the egg yolks with the rest of the sugar until the mixture forms soft ribbons. Stir in the alcohol and flour and stop beating after this point. Put a heat-resistant metal pan or soufflé dish in the preheated oven with the knob of butter.

Meanwhile gently fold together the egg white and yolk mixtures. When the butter is melted (a matter of a minute or two assuming the oven is hot enough) give the pan a quick swirl to coat, spoon in the omelet mixture, then return absolutely immediately to the hot oven. Cook until nicely risen and browned on the surface, 10–12 minutes, and serve straight away from the pan, dusting with a little more confectioners' sugar if you like.

aquitaine and poitou-charentes

The once vast province of Aquitaine (at its height it extended north of Poitiers and east well beyond Gascony, encompassing what is now called Limousin and Poitou-Charentes) must count as one of the best dowries ever: it was gained by the twenty-year-old Henry II of England upon his marriage to the considerably older and rather indomitable Eleanor in the twelfth century. France did not regain this wealthy region until well into the fifteenth century. But if Bordeaux and its surrounds have long had an English association, it was not until the claret shippers of the eighteenth century that it was truly enforced on the culinary front. Even today, the favored dish in many Bordeaux châteaux is beef from Limousin, though it is usually cooked over the *sarments*, or vine clippings, rather than roasted.

The export market (and British tastes in particular) also encouraged the cultivation of sweet wines, especially those of Monbazillac and Sauternes, made possible by the autumn mists in the vineyards to the south of Bordeaux which encouraged the development of noble rot on the grapes. Still the favored aperitif of the region, they are

The house of Hine, Jarnac

served with everything from the melons of Charente to the north to the foie gras of Périgord to the north-east. And for the digestif at the end of the meal the choice is between Cognac and Armagnac, both also widely used for preserving fruits.

Some of the more famous food products of the area have only recently been revived: for example the *agneau de Pauillac*, milk-fed lamb, which has its origin in the habit of using the ewes to graze the grass between the vines, before the transhumance that took them south to the pasture lands of the Pyrenees. The young spring lambs, however, tended to nibble the tender vine shoots, so they were left behind in the barn, feeding on only their mothers' milk.

The result was tender, pale lamb which was prized as a delicacy. This was an expensive process and some time in the middle of the twentieth century the tradition was lost. But now the *agneau de Pauillac* is once again celebrated, a fact I can attest to as one of the judges of local cooks at Pauillac's *fête d'agneau*. The fact that we awarded first prize to a dish of the lamb cooked with mint caused dark mutterings—typical of the English. In fact, the inspiration for the dish turned out to be Moroccan.

Pauillac is surrounded by some of the grandest châteaux in Bordeaux, but it is also home to many peasant farmers whose small plots of land are interspersed between expensive vineyards. And one of the best ways of seeing some of the more exclusive châteaux

I was invited on a truffle hunt. Before we set out to comb the chestnut woods, we first tucked into a thick soup and were invited to 'faire le chabrot'—pour a glass of red wine into the bowl of soup before finishing it. This is wine country and it is that rather than the finesse of the food that defines it, although the ingredients themselves are of the finest quality.

St-Cirq-Lapopie, Lot

Morning view over the Dordogne from Domme

is from the Gironde estuary, which cuts right through the region, giving the term right and left bank wines. In spring elvers swim up the estuary, and eel is a local favorite, though most popular of all is the very unattractive lamprey, which is traditionally cooked in chocolate sauce. One morning I had the pleasure of going out with a local fisherman to land sandre, and as he threw out his lines I gazed on the honey-colored stone of Château Margaux. It was a magical moment.

The pine forests of the Landes, a favorite for mushroom hunters, are to the south. Also south of the estuary lies Arcachon and to the north the Ile d'Oléron, the only two places in France where oysters still reproduce naturally. Both products find their way into Bordelais cuisine, the mushrooms for the classic *cèpes à la bordelaise*, cooked with garlic and parsley, the oysters served with cooked sausage as a starter. Further south and inland come Périgord and Dordogne, without whose foie gras and truffles the châtelaines of Bordeaux would struggle to compose their menus during the annual en primeur wine tastings.

These wooded valleys and hilltop villages have in recent years seen a new English invasion of second-home owners and permanent settlers but local culinary tradition persists, as I discovered when

salade de périgueux
a salad from périgueux

The Dordogne, the Lot and Corrèze are all famous for their walnut orchards, where the walnut of Périgord grows, which has its own Appellation d'Origine Contrôlée. In September the markets are full of the so-called wet walnuts, fresh nuts picked off the tree to be eaten straight away. But the bulk of the crop is gathered in in early October, when the walnuts fall to the ground and are dried under hot air to preserve them. Those, anyway, that aren't used to make walnut oil, one of the most distinctive flavors of the region. The salad is especially delicious paired with another local speciality, foie gras. Walnut bread makes a fine accompaniment.

Serves 4 as a first course

generous 1 pound green beans, topped and tailed
sea salt
2 tablespoons walnut oil
freshly ground black pepper
juice of 1 lemon
⅓ cup fresh walnuts, shelled and crumbled
¼ pound conserved foie gras (the mi-cuit version is best for this dish)

Wash the beans well. Bring a large pan of water to the boil with plenty of salt and boil the beans 6–10 minutes—they should still be green and fairly crisp. The exact time will depend upon the freshness of the beans so taste regularly.

As soon as the beans are cooked to your satisfaction, drain them and dress immediately with the walnut oil, pepper and lemon juice, even if you are serving them later. When you come to assemble the salad, scatter over the walnuts and thin slivers of the foie gras.

soupe glacée de melon
iced melon soup

A few summers ago we were driving through the western edges of the Charente when we came across a roadside stall. It sold nothing but melons, for that, as the stallholder informed me, was the 'fruit of the season—and of the Charente'. Later in the season, she explained further, she would turn to gourds and pumpkins. The small orange-fleshed melons are often served just cut in half, with a splash of the local sweet wine in the cavity, but that night at dinner we had an exquisite melon soup, with slivers of jambon de Bayonne scattered over the surface and small glasses of chilled sweet Monbazillac on the side. The weather was very hot, the soup was icy cold. It was memorable.

Serves 4

3 very ripe French melons
several pinches of salt
freshly ground black pepper
1 small glass of sweet white wine such as Monbazillac, Sauternes or Barsac
iced water
some shreds of air-dried ham

Cut the melons in half and scoop out the seeds. Remove the flesh and put in a bowl, making sure you catch any juices. Season with the salt and a little pepper and pour in the wine. Leave to stand for 15 minutes. Liquidize, adding just sufficient iced water to get a pouring consistency (the exact amount will depend upon the ripeness of the melons, but usually 2 tablespoons is about right). Chill very well before serving scattered with the shreds of ham.

aillade

This powerful sauce bears some similarity to the walnut pesto of Liguria in Italy, but there is one key difference: walnut rather than olive oil is used. Further south in Languedoc a mixture of the two is often substituted, which makes the flavor slightly less strong. Just as I use a mixture of olive and sunflower oil in my mayonnaise, this is the approach I prefer, but it is up to you.

Aillade is usually served with broiled duck breasts or slices of goose, but it also goes very well with broiled vegetables.

Serves 4 to 6

6 fat garlic cloves
½ teaspoon sea salt
⅓ cup peeled walnut halves
iced water
a handful of flat-leaved parsley leaves, finely chopped
generous ½ cup walnut oil or half-and-half walnut and olive oil
½ lemon

Most of this sauce can be made in the food-processor, but for best results I find it is a good idea first to pound the garlic with the salt in a pestle and mortar. Then transfer the mixture to the processor and add the walnuts and 2 teaspoons iced water. Whiz until smooth, then add the parsley and whiz again. Add the walnut oil or mixture of oils drop by drop at first, as if making mayonnaise; as the mixture starts to amalgamate you can increase the flow. Do not keep the processor running contin-uously but instead process in short bursts—the sauce should be slightly knobbly in texture. Finish with a squeeze of lemon.

the marché au gras

It may translate literally as a 'fat market' but the marché au gras gets its name from its specific purpose: to sell the products of geese and duck which have been 'gavé', or force-fed, in the last few weeks of their lives to produce foie gras. One of the largest takes place on Wednesdays and Saturdays in the attractive medieval town of Périgueux from November to mid March. Nowadays, with freeze-drying techniques, even 'fresh' as well as conserved foie gras is available all year round, but the traditional marché au gras only took place in the winter months, when the geese had been fattened. They still reach their climax in the weeks leading up to Christmas, when the market in Périgueux in particular becomes highly competitive.

The day of the judging of the best foie gras in the market in the Place Saint-Louis is a highly serious affair, though once the awards have been made the place goes into party atmosphere, with bands and of course a sit-down lunch. I visited on a non-prize-giving day, but there were plenty of other pleasures to be had. You should not miss the 'demoiselles', the grilled carcasses of the birds. Then there are *magrets de canard*, or duck breasts, to be bought, which must come from a bird produced for foie gras. And there are also big fat black Périgord truffles for sale, at a price.

There is much debate about the production of foie gras. Certainly, the livers of factory-produced birds, which are now commonplace in supermarkets, should be avoided. Largely reared in eastern Europe, the birds are subjected to atrocious conditions, and their livers taste like it. At the other extreme, the tradition of the farmer's wife rearing a few geese and feeding them herself after the vendange, or wine harvest, has largely disappeared. But there is a halfway house.

At the Manoir de Hautegente in the middle of one of the most beautiful parts of the Dordogne, where Patrick Hamelin's family have lived for over three centuries (apart from an unfortunate period when the house was burned down during the Second World War), the geese and ducks waddle happily by the river. The Hamelins produce large quantities of foie gras for the international market (Patrick's wife is French Canadian) and have strict standards.

The birds (mainly ducks, which the Dordogne is most famous for) are reared locally, fed in the last four to six weeks of their lives on the best quality corn, killed at 6 a.m. and are ready for packing at the Manoir by 9 a.m. 'They are so fresh,' says Marie-José, 'that the livers are often still warm and still have corn in them.' Which is just how the French housewives did it. But they did not make foie gras spring rolls, as we ate that night.

cèpes à la bordelaise
mushrooms with garlic and parsley

The pine forests of the Landes are particularly famous for their ceps (King Boletus) and the Bordelais have made them their own with this recipe which is now the favorite way of cooking ceps all over the country. Cooking the mushrooms twice may seem fussy but it really is worth the trouble.

Serves 2 as a light supper dish or 4 as a first course

4 large wild cep (King Boletus) mushrooms
2 tablespoons olive oil
salt and freshly ground black pepper
a large knob of butter
1 shallot, peeled and finely chopped
1 garlic clove, peeled and finely chopped
1 tablespoon toasted white breadcrumbs
1 tablespoon chopped flat-leaved parsley
juice of 1/2 lemon

Wipe the mushrooms with a clean damp cloth, making sure you remove any earth, especially from the stalks—but do not wash, or the mushrooms will become waterlogged. Slice the mushrooms down through the stalk into 4 or 5 pieces.

Heat the oil in a non-stick pan and sauté the mushrooms for a few minutes over a high heat, turning several times. Now remove, pat dry with paper towels and season well. Melt the butter in the same pan, which you have wiped dry, and when it is fizzing add the mushrooms, together with the chopped shallot and garlic. Sauté for another few minutes, then stir in the breadcrumbs and parsley. Add the lemon juice and serve piping hot, possibly with a little air-cured ham and some bread fried in goose fat.

lapin aux pruneaux
rabbit with prunes

Rabbits are widely farmed in France (my neighbor keeps his in a tumbledown barn and we regularly drop off leftover salad for the animals to nibble on) and the resulting meat is much more tender than the wild variety. The meat can be a little bland, though, so fresh herbs and plump prunes as well as plenty of wine are added to rabbit stew to make a more sumptuous dish.

Serves 4

1 large farmed rabbit, jointed into 6 pieces
1 large white onion, peeled and chopped
1 large carrot, peeled and chopped
a bottle of robust red wine
a few peppercorns and juniper berries
a sprig of fresh rosemary
1 fresh bay leaf
1 garlic clove, peeled and crushed
2 tablespoons olive oil
salt and freshly ground black pepper
all-purpose flour
3 tablespoons butter
⅓ pound prunes, preferably from Agen, of the
 ready-to-eat variety
3 tablespoons crème fraîche or sour cream

Put the joints of rabbit into a large earthenware or other non-reactive dish and marinate overnight with the onion, carrot, wine, peppercorns and juniper berries, rosemary and bay leaf, the garlic clove and 1 tablespoon oil. When you are ready to cook, remove the joints of rabbit from the marinade and pat dry. Season well and sprinkle with flour. Heat half the butter and remaining oil in a casserole and fry the rabbit until nicely browned, 4–5 minutes on either side. Remove the rabbit from the pan and set aside.

Now add the onion and carrot from the marinade (reserve the liquor) and fry 10 minutes in the rest of the butter, stirring regularly. Meanwhile, heat the liquor from the marinade in a separate pan until warm but not boiling. Return the rabbit to the pan and pour over the hot marinade, including the garlic, herbs and berries. Simmer until the rabbit is tender, about 30 minutes, then add the prunes.

Preheat the oven to 350°F and put in a serving dish to warm up. Cook the rabbit mixture a further 15 minutes or so. Remove the rabbit and prunes from the pan and keep warm in the serving dish. Stir the crème fraîche or sour cream into the pan juices, simmer briefly, taste and adjust the seasoning if necessary. Pour over the rabbit and prunes and serve straight away.

salade de pigeon aux girolles, figues et noix
squab salad with girolles, figs and walnuts

The lovely little girolle, its flower-shaped top the yellow of a fresh egg yolk, is one of the wild mushrooms most often seen in French markets. I suspect its popularity is because it is so versatile in the kitchen. It makes an excellent omelet and is a very good side dish for a roast, especially of veal. In this autumnal salad of classic ingredients from the Dordogne, it adds both color and earthiness.

Serves 4 as a first course

2 fat squab breasts
2 tablespoons walnut oil
2 teaspoons red wine vinegar
salt and freshly ground pepper
½ pound girolle mushrooms
2 tablespoons olive oil
8 dried figs, cut into quarters
⅔ cup crushed shelled walnuts
a mix of bitter salad leaves

Marinate the squab breasts for 1 hour or so in the oil and vinegar with some seasoning. Wipe the mushrooms clean with a damp cloth. Preheat the oven to 300°F and put a dish in to warm.

Just before serving, heat a ridged grill pan. Remove the squab breasts from the marinade and cook them 4–5 minutes on either side. Transfer to the dish in the oven to keep warm. Sauté the mushrooms in the olive oil, stirring constantly, until tender—a matter of a few minutes. Arrange the salad leaves on four plates and scatter over the walnuts, figs and hot mushrooms. Cut the squab breasts into bite-sized pieces and sprinkle them over the salad. Finally, warm the marinade, pour over the salad, and serve straight away.

mouclade

This is a dish from Vendée, although I first tasted it in another area of sea-flats, the Camargue. It was a bright white-hot July day and the marshland shimmered in the sun. We pulled into a roadside café, thankful for the shade and cool, and ordered the dish of the day—mouclade. It was correctly made with saffron rather than the curry powder which is more typical these days, and served in a vast earthenware pot.

Serves 4

4½ pounds mussels, scrubbed
1 shallot, peeled and finely chopped
1 large white onion, peeled and finely chopped
1 fat garlic clove, peeled and finely chopped
2 tablespoons unsalted butter
1 tablespoon olive oil
1 tablespoon Cognac or other brandy
generous ½ cup fruity white wine
½ teaspoon saffron strands
a good pinch of curry powder
freshly ground black pepper
scant ½ cup heavy cream

Check the mussels over, discarding any with broken shells or that don't close when tapped. Debeard them; that is, pull out the strands that stick out of the side. Put a large lidded pan over a medium heat, and cook the mussels, covered, in their own juices for 5–6 minutes, shaking the pan from time to time. Leave to cool.

In a heavy skillet, sweat the shallot, onion and garlic together with the butter stirring occasionally, until thoroughly softened, around 20 minutes.

Pour the Cognac into the onion, shallot and garlic mixture and stir well for 1 minute or so until evaporated. Now pour in the wine and add the saffron and curry powder and plenty of pepper. Allow to bubble until reduced by half. Meanwhile, strain the liquor from the mussels, through paper towels if it seems very gritty. Add the mussel liquor to the onion pan and allow to simmer.

Preheat the oven to 350°F. Now comes the boring part. Take a large earthenware or other heatproof serving dish. Break each mussel open, discarding the upper shell and laying the deeper shell in the dish. If some mussels have come out of their shells during cooking, then simply put two into one shell.

When all the mussels are neatly arranged, return your attention the sauce. Check the seasoning (you will not need salt as the mussel liquor is salty) and stir in the cream. Bubble briefly and then pour over the half mussel shells. Put in the preheated oven for 5 minutes before serving.

les huîtres aux saucisses
oysters with sausage

The Bordelais have a peculiar but highly successful habit of serving small, slightly spicy grilled sausage with their oysters. The trick is to eat the chilled, slippery oyster first and follow it up with a mouthful of hot sausage. I recommend squeezing the lemon over the sausage as well as the oyster.

Serves 4

24 medium-sized Pacific oysters
12 small spicy sausages
4 lemons, quartered

Open the oysters as close as possible to the time of eating and place on a bed of crushed ice. Broil the sausage (in the south-west of France they are often barbequed over vine twigs) and serve straight away with plenty of bread and butter and the quartered lemons.

the oysters of the bassin de marennes oléron

Oysters have been gathered from the shallow basins around Arcachon, the Ile d'Oléron and the increasingly fashionable holiday resort of the Ile de Ré since Roman times, as archaeologists have proved from the middens. But it is a little known fact that all live oysters reared in France come originally from these parts. Or so Sylvianne Normandin explained to me from one of the brightly colored *cabanes*, or huts, typical of the Ile d'Oléron, a marshy island now linked to the mainland by bridge.

The flat oysters indigenous to the area were wiped out by disease in the 1820s. Portuguese oysters were then introduced, only to succumb again in the early 1970s. Oysters from Japan came next and so far have survived well. So much so that only in this part of France do these hermaphrodites reproduce naturally. The tiny oysters, smaller than a fingernail, are then sold on to other oyster farms elsewhere in the country for rearing.

Raising an oyster is a complicated and lengthy business. Sylvianne explained that during their progression to the plateau de fruits de mer each oyster will be handled on average thirty-one times. But the only intervention in the reproduction process is to put rods in the water (historically roof tiles were used) for the larvae to attach themselves to. The oysters release a milk of eggs (hence the expression a milky oyster) and male and female mix to make an egg, from which a larva is released. This floats for some eight to ten days in the water before fastening itself to the collecting rods. It is then left for eight to ten months to feed naturally from the tidal waters.

At this point the oysters are growing too close together so they are moved to wider rods and put back in the water. Another ten months or so pass

before they are lifted onto the flat-bottomed estuary boats typical of the region, removed from the rods and placed in cages at the opening of the sweet waters of the estuary, usually in June.

The shellfish are then left to feed for another six months until the New Year, before the first triage, or grading of the oysters. They are now transferred back into deeper waters, so that they can feed more plentifully as the tidal waters flow over them. By the following September they are ready to return for

Dockside on the Ile de Ré

another triage and then they are placed for some weeks in the *claires d'affinage*, the ancient salt basins on the island from which they get their name. The most special oysters of all go green from an alga in the water which gives them a peculiar color and flavor. But then they are all special. It is, as Sylvianne remarks, a hard life as an oyster cultivator. Soon her son will take over the business, though she is worried about what her husband will do when he no longer goes out on the boats. 'It has been our life,' she says.

a day at the vendange

As a teenager I had joined in the vendange in the south of France but this was something quite different. I was spending a day as one of the 500-odd grape-pickers at Château Mouton-Rothschild in the vineyards near Pauillac, to the north of Bordeaux. Many would be working for several weeks, often having taken their annual holiday from their jobs to do so. Whole families, spanning several generations, were following their tradition of joining in the grape harvest.

When picking you need to select your grapes carefully, discarding any with signs of rot. Snip each bunch, carefully place it in your trug, and when it is full wait until the hod carrier appears down the serried ranks of vines for you to tip in your load. This then goes to the tractor, where the first of several triages, or selections for quality, takes place (the grapes will be picked over twice more before they are pressed). It is repetitive work that strains knees and back. But there are rewards.

Many Bordeaux châteaux no longer feed their vendangeurs but Mouton Rothschild keeps to the old tradition. As the Baronesse Philippine told me: 'Lunch is an essential part of the day. It is at least some recompense for ruining your hands and fingernails, but that is a badge of honor.' Taken back at the château, this is a four-course affair with a centerpiece of classic French dishes such as boeuf en daube, cassoulet or pot au feu, with of course more red wine, and in the evenings the pickers are supplied with a picnic hamper for their supper. The day I was there it included magret de canard and a bottle of wine. I was grateful though that, unlike most of the pickers, I was not camping out in a tent; a hot bath was much needed to soothe my aching joints.

le parfait d'armagnac aux pruneaux
frozen armagnac and prune mousse

Prunes often have something of a dreary reputation but in France they are a prized delicacy. Those from Agen are often sold bottled in the local Armagnac, which is also used to make a rich dessert.

Serves 6 to 8

1 pound best quality pre-soaked dried prunes, ideally from Agen (although the Californian variety makes a good substitute), pitted
a few strips of lemon zest, preferably from an unwaxed lemon
4 tablespoons Armagnac
2 cups thick heavy cream
whites of 2 large eggs
2 tablespoons superfine sugar
a pinch of salt

Soak the prunes with the lemon zest and Armagnac 1 hour or so. Remove the lemon zest and in the food-processor whizz the prunes and Armagnac to a purée. Whisk the egg whites with the pinch of salt until stiff, then add the sugar. Whisk the cream until it has a floppy consistency. Carefully fold the prune purée into the cream and then, with a wooden spoon, fold in the stiffened egg whites. Spoon into individual serving pots and place in the freezer for no more than 2 hours—this is not an ice cream.

poires au vin rouge
pears in red wine

st-émilions au chocolat
chocolate st-emilions

I have been cooking this dish for so long and have eaten it in so many parts of France that to choose a region to place it in seems slightly invidious. The spices used vary locally (some, for example, add nutmeg or mace, others leave out the peppercorns). The important point is to use good wine—this is no dish for using up the dregs.

Serves 4

4 slightly under-ripe pears (Bartletts are the best variety but you could also use Conference or Doyenne de Comice)
3 tablespoons brown sugar
red wine (you must use a good quality, robust wine)
1 cinnamon stick
2 cloves
4 peppercorns
several pieces of orange zest

Peel the pears, leaving the stalks on, and pack them into a non-reactive pan into which they fit snugly. Sprinkle over the sugar and pour in just enough red wine to cover. Add the cinnamon stick, cloves, peppercorns and orange zest. Bring the wine to the boil, cover and simmer for 20–25 minutes, turning the pears several times during the process (the exact time will depend upon the size and ripeness of the pears—test with a fork). Leave the fruit to cool in the liquor. Just before serving, boil down the spiced red wine to the required consistency (I like it fairly runny) and strain (though you could leave the cinnamon stick for decoration), then pour over the pears.

The golden stone medieval town of St-Emilion, set on a limestone plateau on the right bank and still with its thirteenth-century ramparts from which you can overlook the valley of the River Dordogne, is famous for its first growth wines—and its macaroons. The recipe, so the story goes, was first invented by the Ursuline nuns in 1620. The very precise but of course secret recipe was lost for a time but then rediscovered after the Revolution by one Veuve, or Widow, Goudichaud. She made her name with them but after her demise the famous recipe was once again misplaced. Until, that is, the local Blanchez family, clearing out their attic, came across it in 1930. They were quick to seize the potential and there is still a Madame Blanchez making and selling macaroons in St-Emilion today, though now there is plenty of competition.

The macaroons (see recipe page 149) are served with a glass of champagne as an aperitif, with red wine to dunk them in, or at the end of the meal with coffee. But they are at their very best in adding a layer of crunch and an almond flavor to this ridiculously rich chocolate dessert, which gets its name from the town.

Makes 6 little pots

½ pound dark chocolate, high in cocoa solids
scant 1 cup whole milk
1 stick unsalted butter, removed from the refrigerator 30 minutes before you want to make the puddings
½ cup superfine sugar
yolk of 1 large egg, preferably free-range
2 tablespoons Cognac, Marc or Armagnac
¼ pound macaroons

Break the chocolate into pieces. Put the milk in a non-reactive pan and add the chocolate. Heat gently, stirring with a wooden spoon, until all the chocolate has melted, and the sauce has the consistency of thick cream. Under no circumstances allow it to boil. Leave to cool slightly.

Cream together the butter and sugar until smooth (you can do this in the food-processor or with a wooden spoon). Add the egg yolk and cream together again. Finally, add the alcohol and stir well.

Stir the butter and sugar mixture into the chocolate milk until well amalgamated. Crush the macaroons (this is easiest with a clean dishcloth and a rolling pin or other such wooden implement). Sprinkle a layer of crushed macaroon at the bottom of each little pot, followed by some of the chocolate mixture. Continue to layer macaroon and chocolate, ending with chocolate.

Put in the refrigerator for at least 4 hours in order to set. It is a good idea to remove the pots about 15 minutes before serving.

the basque country

Politically speaking there is no such defined entity as the Pays Basque or French Basque Country; the land that abuts the Pyrenees to the south of the River Adour, once part of Aquitaine, is now simply within the department of the Pyrénées Atlantique. But from a culinary point of view, as you approach the rolling green hills that rise towards the Spanish border, everything changes. This is the land of red peppers and the vibrant colored piment of Espelette, of cured hams and salted cod, of slow-cooked bean dishes, which are quite different from the cassoulet of neighbouring Languedoc, and of the famous poule au pot, the chicken that Henry of Navarre declared all his citizens should have the right to enjoy on Sundays.

Known on both sides of the border as Euskal-herri, it is also a land of proudly independent people, who retain their own language (even the road signs are in Basque, or Euskara, as well as French) and very definitely their own unique culture. Voltaire may have called them a 'petit peuple' but that is certainly not the way they see themselves.

On feast days, the Basques dress up in their traditional clothes, of which the women's headdresses are the best known. They play instruments that resemble the bagpipes, compete in the fast and furious ball game of pelota, sing traditional folk songs, and tell tales. It is a land that, as travel writer Jan Morris noted, likes to wreath itself in mystery. 'Mystery,' she wrote, 'offers to the Basque people a powerful fascination.' Basque mountaineers say that on stormy nights in the Pyrenees the ghostly echoes of a horn can be heard—the horn of Roland, blown as he lay dying in the pass of Roncesvalles. The Song of Roland is, of course, one of the earliest of French epic poems.

Much of this legend and myth, however, has its roots in memories of a far-flung homeland. The Basques travelled the world as fishermen, often spending many months at sea in their search for cod in particular, as well as on whaling ships. Many settled abroad, reflecting the former poverty of the region, but these days they are returning in their droves to buy up the red-roofed farmhouses that nestle in the valleys within sight of the snow-capped mountains and the pretty, gaily colored seaside houses in the former fishing port of St-Jean-de-Luz. And as the wealth of the region increases, so too does the quality of the restaurants. Just as in the Basque Country over the border in Spain, this region of France has in recent years become a favored spot for gourmets.

But then the local ingredients are so good that often the restaurateurs do not have to work too hard. The seaside towns have a wealth of expensive restaurants serving the freshest of fish, but the real gourmets head inland. At a recent dinner in Bayonne, the elegant city on the banks of the Adour which was once a great port, I was served a starter of nothing more than the eponymous ham, thinly sliced. The meal continued with a thick slice of cod

Opposite: St-Jean-de-Pied-de-Port

with red peppers, followed by perfectly cooked lamb from the high pastures (the Basques are credited with being the first to train sheepdogs to control their flocks). It finished with an incredibly rich, slightly bitter, chocolate mousse. Ham apart, chocolate is another ingredient for which Bayonne is famous.

At the end of the fifteenth century many Jews fleeing from the Spanish and Portuguese Inquisition settled over the border in France, establishing a large community in Bayonne. As traders, they later encouraged the importation of cocoa beans from the New World, and by the eighteenth century Bayonne was famous for its hot chocolate drinks, which was how the bitter chocolate was first served, melted and flavored with cinnamon. The Académie du Chocolat still celebrates this heritage at the Feast of Ascension but all year round the town is renowned for its chocolate truffles.

The region is also known for its gâteau basque, to which I was introduced by the brothers Jean and Michel Minhondo, who live and work in Irissary, near St-Jean-Pied-de-Port. Pâtissiers and boulangers by family tradition, they have made it their responsibility to preserve the tradition of the gâteau basque, which their father before them used to bake. The classic gâteau is made with a rich buttery pastry which encases a thick custard or crème patissière, although there are variations including dark cherry jam or prunes.

The Minhondo brothers have, as heads of the Gâteau Basque Association, recently applied to the European Commission for a Label Rouge for a correctly made cake, which will stress the need for the authentic version to use farm butter, fresh milk and eggs and good quality flour and sugar. It is one of the many things that I love about France in general: the fact that people care enough to seek to protect the proper recipe for a cake.

oillade
garlic soup

Cooked garlic loses its pungency and acquires sweetness in the same way as onions. In this simple soup, thickened with egg yolks, the two are combined.

Serves 4

1 large white onion, peeled and finely sliced
1 fat head of garlic, cloves separated, peeled and sliced, except for 1 clove which you reserve whole
1 tablespoon goose fat or, failing that, olive oil
4 cups concentrated chicken or beef stock
4 rounds of slightly stale French bread, thinly cut
sea salt and freshly ground black pepper
2 egg yolks

Put the onion, sliced garlic and goose fat or oil into a heavy lidded pan over a gentle heat. Cover and cook, shaking the pan occasionally, 20 minutes; the garlic and onion should soften but on no account brown. Meanwhile, bring the stock to the boil.

When the onion and garlic are nicely soft, pour over the hot stock. At this stage you can either transfer the soup to an earthenware Dutch oven in the oven, heated to 350°F, or continue to cook the soup in the pan on top of the stove. Either way the soup should cook slowly, around 40 minutes covered on the hob or 1 hour or so uncovered in the oven. At this stage, remove from the heat, let it cool a little and then liquidize. The result will be quite thin.

When you are ready to serve the soup, brush the slices of stale bread with the cut side of the remaining garlic clove and place each in a warmed soup bowl. Check the seasoning of the soup and if it has been standing a while reheat to just below boiling. Whisk the egg yolks into the soup to thicken it, ladle over the bread and serve. Be warned that once you have whisked in the egg yolks the soup cannot be reheated.

salade de morue aux poivrons
salt cod salad with peppers

Salt cod, once a food for the poor, has become a delicacy due to dwindling cod stocks, and these days tails of salt cod fetch high prices in the shops of St-Jean-de-Luz and Biarritz. This salad is a popular restaurant dish.

Serves 4

1 piece skinned salt cod fillet, around 1 pound
4 large red peppers
2 fat garlic cloves, peeled and finely chopped
a good handful of flat-leaved parsley, leaves roughly chopped
extra virgin olive oil
sweet paprika
1 lemon

Rinse the salt cod well, then soak overnight in plenty of water. The next day, bring it to the boil in a fresh pan of water and as soon as it comes to the boil turn off the heat. Leave to cool in the liquor.

Broil the peppers under a very hot broiler, turning regularly, until they are nicely blackened all over. This should take around 20 minutes. To peel easily, put them in a sealed plastic bag for 10 minutes then scrape off all the blackened skin. Cut the flesh into strips, discarding the seeds, and arrange on a plate.

Drain the salt cod and carefully flake over the strips of peppers; scatter with the garlic and parsley. Sprinkle liberally with the oil and paprika and serve, with thick wedges of lemon on the side.

jambon de bayonne avec sa pipérade
bayonne ham with eggs and peppers

Traditionally ham fat is used for this classic Basque dish but olive oil is a good substitute. I throw in the fat from the slices of ham to add flavoring. Ideally, the dish should be made with the long, thin green peppers for which the Basque Country is famous but if you can't get hold of these use a mixture of red and green bell peppers for sweetness. The eggs should be the freshest you can lay your hands on.

Serves 4

3 tablespoons olive oil

4 thin slices of Bayonne ham, fat removed

2 large Bermuda onions, peeled and sliced into fine half moons

1½ pounds long green peppers, or a mix of red and green peppers (see above), peeled, deseeded and cut into long strips

3 garlic cloves, peeled and crushed

1½ pounds large ripe tomatoes, roughly chopped

8 large eggs

a pinch of red paprika

salt and freshly ground black pepper

1 tablespoon finely chopped flat-leaved parsley

Heat the oil in a heavy non-stick pan over a medium heat, together with the fat from the ham. Add the onion and stew gently until soft, 10 minutes, then add the strips of pepper and the crushed garlic. Cook for a further 15 minutes, until everything is very soft, then fish out the ham fat. Add the tomatoes and cook, stirring once or twice until the tomatoes are broken down but the skin is still intact with the flesh, 5 minutes. Meanwhile, beat the eggs and season with paprika, salt, pepper and parsley. Pour the eggs into the pan and stir continuously until lightly scrambled. Serve topped with a slice of ham, together with lots of bread and a green salad to follow. And some red wine.

jambon de bayonne

Michel Guérard, he of nouvelle cuisine fame, called it 'the cathedral of hams' and it was clear what he meant. I was standing in a large, high-roofed barn and suspended by metal chains from the rafters were hams of extraordinary size, twirling gently in the breeze that came from 'the four winds' through the fly-meshed windows on all sides. Just opposite was a view of the castle of Guiche, rebuilt in the fourteenth century after it had been torched in 1257 by the Bayonnais, though now once again in ruins. 'Of course, jambon de Bayonne has been made for more than a thousand years,' said my hostess, Madame de Montauzer. 'But only now are we seeking to return to the old standards.'

Henri IV of Navarre was extremely fond of his Bayonne ham and it is through the connection with Eleanor of Aquitaine that it is believed to have got its name. The ham, which under recently reinstated regulations must be made from pigs raised in the region, was very popular in medieval times in the north of Europe and the hams were shipped from the then port of Bayonne. After, that is, they had arrived by barge from river towns such as Guiche, or the capital of Bayonne ham, Orthez.

The Montauzers played a vital role in restoring the historic reputation of Bayonne ham by insisting on quality. A family business set up just after the Second World War, they buy all their pigs from a producer in St-Jean-Pied-de-Port, a scenic village in the foothills of the Pyrenees. The pigs grow slowly, fed only on cereals, and become very large indeed, as is evident from the size of the hams. When their time comes, the entire carcasses are delivered to the Montauzers for butchering. Then comes the salting process, using *le sel dit de*

Bayonne, the salt said to be of Bayonne, but which in fact comes from Briscous les Salines, a little to the east of the city.

The hams are salted for a period of time dependent upon their weight and the opinion of those in charge of the salting process—the *salaissioniers*. Then they are moved to the *chambre de repos*, or resting place. Just before sale, usually after seven to nine months, the hams are rubbed with *piment espelette*, a pimento pepper which gets its name from a local village.

But the hams in the 'cathedral' are even more special. These are from pigs that have lived longer, typically nine months to a year, and are seasoned for at least fifteen months. And they finish their time spinning in the wind, before making it to tables in prized restaurants.

lotte à la basquaise
monkfish in the basque style

A la basquaise almost always means with peppers but the variety is important. Sometimes sweet red peppers are needed but with meaty monkfish the long, thin green peppers are better.

Serves 4

2 pounds monkfish or goosefish tail
⅓ cup olive oil
3 white onions, around ¾ pound, peeled and sliced
  into fine half moons
1 cup canned tomatoes
sea salt and freshly ground black pepper
a good pinch of white sugar
2 green peppers
5 garlic cloves

Skin the fish if necessary and cut the fillets from the central bone, then across into slices about 1 inch thick.

Put half the olive oil in a heavy skillet with a lid over a low heat. Add the sliced onions, cover and cook, shaking the pan regularly around 30 minutes.

When the onions are very soft, add the tomatoes, some seasoning and the sugar, pushing down on the tomatoes with the back of a wooden spoon to break them up. Cover again and leave on a low heat, a further 15 minutes.

Preheat the oven to 300°F and put a heavy serving dish in to warm. Remove the heads of the peppers, cut the flesh in half, remove the seeds, and dice the flesh. Peel the garlic cloves and slice finely across. In a separate pan, cook the peppers in 2 tablespoons oil together with one of the sliced garlic cloves for a few minutes, stirring continuously. Remove the garlic and peppers with a slotted spoon and set aside.

Add the rest of the oil to the pan in which you have just cooked the peppers. When it is hot, add the medallions of fish. Sear on either side, then reduce the heat, add plenty of seasoning, and the sliced garlic. Cook for 7–8 minutes, turning the pieces of fish halfway through.

Transfer the tomato sauce to the serving dish. Remove the pieces of monkfish and slices of garlic from the oil with a slotted spoon and place on top of the sauce. Scatter the cooked pepper over the top. Return to the oven for 5 minutes before serving.

River-front houses in Bayonne

poulet basquaise
chicken in the basque style

Onions, peppers, paprika, cured ham, chicken: a dish to make a Basque happy. Plain boiled long-grain rice is the classic accompaniment.

Serves 4

4 chicken thighs and legs
salt and freshly ground black pepper
3 tablespoons olive oil
4 long green peppers, around 1¼ pounds, deseeded and cut into long, thin strips
1 large Bermuda onion, peeled and chopped into fine half moons
1 slice of cured ham, preferably from Bayonne, cut into strips
2 garlic cloves, peeled and crushed
1 large glass of white wine
6 ounce can tomato paste
scant ½ cup water
1 teaspoon red paprika
1 small dried red chilli, crumbled
1 tablespoon finely chopped flat-leaved parsley

Season the chicken pieces well. Heat the oil in a heavy pan over a medium heat and fry the chicken until lightly browned, 5 minutes on either side. Remove the chicken pieces from the pan, add the pepper and onion and reduce the heat. Cook gently for 10 minutes, stirring occasionally, and then add the ham and the garlic. Cook for a further 10 minutes, stirring from time to time, then pour in the wine. Allow to bubble for 1 minute. Stir the tomato paste into the water and add to the pan, along with the paprika and red chilli. Bring to the boil, turn down to a simmer and slip in the chicken pieces. Cook uncovered, turning the chicken once or twice, until it is cooked through and the sauce nicely reduced, 25–30 minutes. Leave to stand 10 minutes before serving, scattered with the parsley.

la poule au pot—and other sunday lunch specials

French royalty seemed to like making pronouncements on how their people should eat. Think of Marie-Antoinette. Henri IV of Navarre, which he ruled from 1562 to his death and who was King of France from 1589 to 1610, expressed the wish that 'every laborer of my kingdom should be able to put a chicken in his pot each Sunday.' The difference was that he and his courtiers made efforts to make it happen.

This was a king who concentrated on agriculture, who encouraged the plantation of orchards, who rebuilt roads destroyed by forty years of civil war and lined them with fruit trees, who encouraged the cultivation of mulberry trees, leading to the growth of the silk industry, who built up the export of wheat, especially to Spain. He built canals, colleges and châteaux. He largely acted as a peacemonger across Europe. All French school-children are taught about good King Henry. But it is for his pronouncement on the poule au pot that he is remembered.

The pot simmering with the contents of Sunday lunch remains an integral part of French life, at least in the countryside. I love to wander round our village on a Sunday morning, especially in winter, sniffing not the crisp mountain air but the cooking smells. It is a punctual affair: come midday, the men gossiping in the village square disappear inside for lunch.

Each region has its specialty, be it entitled *garbure, potée, daube* or *pot au feu*. Usually there will be a mixture of meats, and even poule au pot is often cooked with beef, while the simmered chicken is stuffed with breadcrumbs mixed with ham and the chicken's liver. The vegetables will also vary by region, but the important point is that there

should be enough of them to make this is a complete dish—and to have leftovers for soup the next day.

Some of these dishes have even created others: *hachis parmentier*, for example, the French version of shepherd's pie which is a Paris bistro classic and gets its name from the man who brought the potato to France, should be made with the leftovers from pot au feu. After all, if you go to the trouble of making these family dishes, you want to eke them out over a few meals.

The Hunt Lunch, 1737, by Jean François de Troy

truites au lard
trout with bacon

la garbure béarnaise
vegetable and meat stew

I am no fisherwoman but freshly caught brown trout are worth learning to fly-fish for. Of course, there is the cheat's method: in restaurants in northern France, especially on the German border, there are pools stocked with trout, ready for the fish to be cooked *au bleu*, that is, fished out of the water, knocked on the head and promptly poached in an aromatic liquor. For farmed trout, however, I prefer the Basque approach, where the fish is fried with ham and finished with vinegar. This is a recipe I was first taught by a man of Basque heritage who lived in the foothills of the Argentine Andes—and yes, he did catch the trout himself.

Serves 2

2 trout
sea salt and freshly ground black pepper
a little all-purpose flour
2 teaspoons goose or duck fat or olive oil
1 medium-sized red potato, peeled and finely diced
1 thick slice ham, with plenty of fat, diced
1 garlic clove, peeled
1 teaspoon sweet paprika
1 tablespoon white wine vinegar

Wash the trout well inside and out and season, including the cavity. Chop off the tail in a V shape and the head as well if your pan is small or you are squeamish. Dust the fish lightly with the flour.

Melt the fat in a heavy, non-stick pan. When it is spitting add the potato, ham and garlic. Cook, stirring, until the ham fat runs, 2 minutes. Sprinkle the paprika over the potatoes, stir well and add the trout. Fry 5–6 minutes on either side. Tip the fish and vegetables onto the plate, deglaze with the vinegar, scraping well to get any residue, pour over the fish and serve straight away—in the pan if at a campfire.

A garbure (the name is said to come from the Basque *garbe*, meaning a bunch or sheaf) is a dish to simmer on the stove, to come back to time and time again, as it improves with keeping; true peasant cooking. The classic way to eat garbure is to serve the broth first over bread followed by the meats and vegetables, but I prefer to dish it all up together and allow the diners to choose which sequence they wish to eat in. And I draw the line at the habit of floating a few tablespoons of goose fat on top of the dish just before eating—I don't do enough work in the fields to justify that.

Serves 6 to 8

2 pound piece of gammon or country ham or other
  cured pork
½ pound dried white haricot beans
3 turnips, around 1 pound in total
3 large carrots, around 1 pound in total
2 large potatoes, generous 1 pound in total
1 large Bermuda onion
2 cloves
bouquet garni of parsley stalks, fresh thyme
  and 2 bay leaves, tied together
2 large leeks, green parts removed
1 small or ½ large green cabbage, around
  2 pounds
2 thighs of confit de canard
1 teaspoon sweet red pepper
a pinch of red chilli
2 fat garlic cloves, peeled and chopped
freshly ground black pepper
1-day-old French bread

Soak both the ham and the beans overnight in plenty of water, in separate pots. The next day, discard the soaking water and place both in a large heavy pot, big enough to take all the ingredients. Add 3 quarts water and bring to the boil. Turn down to a simmer and remove any scum.

Peel the turnips, carrots and potatoes and cut into generously sized bites—you don't want the vegetables too small or they will fall apart during cooking. Add them to the pan, together with the whole peeled onion studded with the cloves, and the bouquet garni. Roughly slice the white part of the leeks and also add. Simmer, covered, 30 minutes or so (the garbure is not a dish for precise timing, thankfully). Meanwhile, remove the tough outer leaves and the ribs of the cabbage and slice the rest of it into fairly thin shreds. Add these to the cooking pot. Simmer gently for another hour, then add the preserved duck, together with 1 tablespoon or so of its fat, the sweet red pepper, chilli, garlic and plenty of pepper. (At this stage you might also like to check whether salt is needed, which I rarely use given the saltiness of the ham.) Simmer, covered, for a further 40 minutes or so.

Ideally, leave to cool overnight. When ready to serve, preheat the oven to 400°F. Slowly reheat the garbure on the stove. Thinly slice some stale baguette and layer an earthenware dish with it. Spoon in sufficient broth to cover the bread and cook in the oven until the bread has absorbed the liquid and is lightly browned (around 20 minutes). Slice the meats, which should be falling apart, and place on a warmed serving dish. Serve the meats, broth, vegetables and stock-soaked bread in separate dishes, with mustard on the side.

truffes au chocolat
chocolate truffles

les macarons
macaroons

Bayonne is famous for its chocolate truffles, which get their name from their rough-edged shape, resembling the sought-after tuber. The Jewish community is supposed to have introduced this tradition, selling the chocolate-based sweets to be passed round during the long masses of Lent. Today Bayonne boasts several very smart chocolatiers, and their truffles are highly prized, but they are also easy to make at home, provided you use the best quality chocolate.

St Emilion may claim the little almond cookies known as macaroons as its own, but they are popular throughout the southwest of France and especially right down by the Spanish borders. My home-made variety is far from the perfectly formed, very crisp, flaked almond-topped and confectioners'-sugar-dusted cookie on offer in local patisseries, but then you do get the advantage of eating the macaroons still warm from the oven—and they are ludicrously simply to bake.

Makes 20 to 24 truffles

1 cup heavy cream
2 tablespoons superfine sugar
scant ½ pound dark chocolate with at least
  70 per cent cocoa solids
2 tablespoons unsalted butter
1 tablespoon Cointreau or Armagnac (optional)
good quality cocoa powder

Scald the cream with the sugar by just bringing to the boil and then removing from the heat immediately. Whisk in the chocolate piece by piece until you have a smooth emulsion. Allow to cool slightly then whisk in the butter, again in pieces, followed by the alcohol if you are using it. Chill the mixture in the freezer 20 minutes.

Now stir the mixture well and, using either two teaspoons if you are dexterous or your fingers if you don't mind getting messy, fashion the truffles into small balls. Place on parchment paper or foil on a baking sheet and put in the refrigerator for 30 minutes or so. Roll well in the cocoa powder and leave in the refrigerator at least overnight before serving.

Makes 16 to 20 macaroons

1 cup ground almonds
⅔ cup confectioners' sugar
1 tablespoon good-quality apricot jam, strained
the yolk of 1 large egg, beaten

Preheat the oven to 325°F.

Mix the ingredients together to make a smooth paste, adding a few drops of iced water if necessary. Dip your hands in iced water and, working as quickly as possible, fashion into a long roll. Wrap in plastic wrap and chill for at least a couple of hours before baking.

You do not have to cook the macaroons all at once. Simply line a tray with buttered parchment paper, and slice off a few discs at ½ inch intervals at a time. Bake until just browned, 8–10 minutes, and leave to cool for 10 minutes before eating. The remaining mixture, wrapped in clingfilm, will keep for several days in the refrigerator.

languedoc-roussillon

The boats of Collioure

For today's holidaymaker the region of Languedoc-Roussillon is easily defined: it is that long stretch of Mediterranean coast that extends from the Camargue to the Spanish border. Besides the sandy beaches lie salt lagoons where oysters flourish and fatten, fishing ports where anchovies, squid and sardines are landed in quantity, orchards on the flatlands near the coast where the first cherries of France grow, followed by peaches, nectarines and apricots. And of course there are huge vineyards, many first planted in the nineteenth century to satisfy the thirst of the French army. Today, although quality has improved dramatically on some properties, much of the European 'wine lake' still comes from this region.

But step back a little from the coast and you will find a different character to the region. For the backdrop to the coastal plains so beloved of the sun-seekers is a rocky, harsh environment, where small wine growers and shepherds still eke out a living. From the limestone plateaux of the Causses and the high pastures of the Cévennes to the foothills of the Pyrenees only sheep thrive on the pasturelands. In the north of the region their milk is used to make the famous blue cheese Roquefort, aged in the traditional manner in caves in order to produce the mold, while on the Spanish borders the ancient practice of transhumance, moving sheep to the upper pasture for the herb-scented summer grasses, remains an annual occurrence.

Then cross the mountains and you will find a third level to the region. Just like Bologna in Italy, another famous university town and one also characterized by its red buildings of the local sandstone, Toulouse has been called the 'fat city'. For here, for centuries merchants have accumulated their wealth. The result shows in the gastronomy and in particular cassoulet, that rich mix

of white beans, preserved goose or duck and Toulouse sausage, which the city's next-door neighbour of Castelnaudary also lays claim to.

In short, the cooking of Languedoc-Roussillon is a mix of terroirs, where not just the wine but the food is defined by the local geography. But it also reflects a long history of invasion and immigration. The Greeks, the Phoenicians and the Romans all settled here. Later came the Moors from Spain, moving as far north as Narbonne; they may have left many centuries ago but in recent decades the people of North Africa have returned and settled, and in the south of the region méchoui (roast lamb) and paella are popular local summer dishes in the markets and at village festivities.

Languedoc-Roussillon has always been border territory, as evidenced by the number of castles scattered across the foothills (we are not talking elegant eighteenth-century châteaux here, but much earlier and bleaker fortresses, built for war not luxury). There are few more dramatic than the castles of the heretic Cathars, in particular Peyrepertuse and Quéribus in Corbières. But if this strange medieval sect prided themselves on their abstention from meat, it was no lasting legacy. For away from the beaches, meat remains the food of choice, at least in the harsher months. Autumn signals the start of the game season, with *civet de sanglier*, or wild boar stew, being a favorite. Capons and guinea fowl are reared for Christmas. And in spring there is the first lamb, broiled over vine clippings and given a Mediterranean touch with the addition of aioli, garlic mayonnaise.

But this is food for feast days. The everyday diet is much more likely to be vegetables, especially in summer, and the attitude of the peasant farmer still prevails. Where I live, on the foothills of Mount

Canigou, my neighbors make vast quantities of tomato paste from the summer glut, make home-canned green beans for the winter months and preserve the wild mushrooms, which abound in the woods, in olive oil for later in the season. Further inland just about every bit of the pig is preserved in fat, preferably with plenty of beans. There are also treats to be nurtured, especially for the sweet of tooth. In Toulouse violets are candied, and shipped all over France. Soft fruits are canned in alcohol or sweet wine, in anticipation of Christmas, and chestnuts and figs preserved in sugar syrup.

Over the passes from here are the mountainous lands that border Spain and Andorra, lands of goats and sheep and therefore cheese. On the high pastures there are pale-skinned cattle too, reared for their milk rather than their flesh. The houses are high-roofed, usually with slate, and there are piles of wood stocked outside. Many of the farms still have the traditional stables for the animals below the living quarters. Those who live here dream of balmy winter nights by the sea.

The vast area of Languedoc-Roussillon is a land of contrasts, harsh in places, rich in others, offering a sweet Mediterranean way of life by the coast, all of which is reflected in the great variety of food on offer, depending upon season as well as geography.

La Plage Rouge, Collioure, summer 1905, by Henri Matisse

the sardinade

la salade de pêches blanches et tomates
white peach and tomato salad

One of the very first local celebrations that I attended after we moved into our little house in the Pyrenees was the sardinade, or sardine feast. We may be high up on the slopes of the Catalans' sacred Mount Canigou, but we can also catch a glimpse of the Mediterranean. More importantly, Collioure, famous for its anchovies and sardines, is just an hour and a half's drive away.

We arrived promptly in the small village of Calmeilles at midday to find boxes and boxes of the sparkling silvery fish piled up beside the braise set up in a cork forest above the church. A slow-burning fire of vine clippings had been prepared and vast metal double grills, so heavy that it took four men to lift each one, were already warming over the embers. First, though, it was time for the inevitable *apéro*. Pastis for the boys, Muscat for the ladies is the local rule.

Then, while we all took our seats under the cork trees, the sardines went on the grill, sprinkled with nothing more than sea salt. A few minutes on one side, a quick heave-ho to turn the grills over, wait until the skin crisps up, and the fish were shaken into wooden boxes to be delivered direct to the table. Jugs of rosé and red, baskets of chopped baguette and bowls of tomato and onion salad were already waiting. There were knives and forks but the preferred approach was fingers. Later these could be rinsed in the spring water flowing from the source just below us.

The boxes of sardines kept on coming. I stopped at about twenty fish; the gentleman next to me told me that fifty would have been a more acceptable quantity. I didn't count how many he put away. Of course, there was cheese and dessert to follow, accompanied by more of the local Muscat chilled in the well. The women drank coffee, the men peeled off to play pétanque. English author Peter Mayle may have been accused of writing about a fantasy land but it really does still happen like this in the south of France.

Since the advent of irrigation, this region now produces vast quantities of peaches, and none is more delicious than the white varieties, their flesh sometimes delicately tinged with pink. I was introduced to this salad by a local friend; another friend living in Corbières suggested the addition of the mint and quite right he was too. The dish's success does depend upon perfectly ripe fruit, both tomatoes and peaches; no chilled supermarket crops here.

Serves 4

4 large ripe white peaches
2 large beefsteak tomatoes
salt and freshly ground black pepper
2 tablespoons extra virgin olive oil
several sprigs each of basil and mint

Peel the peaches—if they are perfectly ripe the skin will come away easily. If not, dip them in boiling water for a couple of seconds, plunge into a bowl of iced water and then peel. Cut them in half, remove the pits and then slice the flesh horizontally into thin slices, making sure to catch any juices.

Wash the tomatoes and slice across very thinly, discarding any core. Arrange the tomato slices over a large serving plate and put the peach slices on top, together with any extra juice. Season well and leave to stand for 15 minutes. Just before serving, drizzle over the oil and tear the leaves of the herbs to scatter over the salad (though if you have tiny leaves of basil and mint, leave them whole).

salade de chèvre chaud au miel et noix
hot goat's cheese salad with honey and walnuts

Goat's cheese salads are served in brasseries and bistros all over France and no wonder—this is a simple-to-prepare dish that just works. Towards the center and north the cheese used will normally be the harder *crottins*, with their almost lemony rind, but in the south the softer freshly made goat's cheeses come into their own. My local goat's cheese maker, the rather funky Laurence, advises serving her soft cheeses cooked on rounds of baguette, piled onto soft sweet lettuce, dressed with local herb-scented honey and sprinkled with fresh walnuts and mountain herbs. I cannot think of a better autumn lunch.

Serves 4

4 slices of baguette
4 small soft fresh goat's cheeses or 2 slightly larger
    ones, cut in half horizontally
1 large butter lettuce
salt and freshly ground black pepper
2 teaspoons clear honey, preferably herb-
    scented (I use miel des garrigues)
2 teaspoons shallot or red wine vinegar
4 tablespoons extra virgin olive oil
⅓ cup crumbled fresh walnuts
a few sprigs of thyme

Preheat the oven to 400°F. Place the slices of bread on a baking sheet covered with foil and top with the goat's cheese. Bake in the oven until the edges of the bread are browned and the cheese just melting— around 8 minutes, but watch it like a hawk to make sure it doesn't burn.

Wash and dry the lettuce well and divide between four plates. Make a dressing with the seasoning, honey, vinegar and oil (the easiest way to do this is to put everything in a sealed jam jar and shake well).

Arrange the toast and goat's cheese on top of the salad leaves, scatter over the walnuts, dribble over the dressing, including over the cheese, pull the thyme leaves off their stalks, sprinkle over the cheese and serve straight away.

cassola de langoustines
langoustines with red peppers and garlic

As you head south in this region it becomes harder and harder to distinguish between Spanish and French Catalan cooking. This dish definitely turns its head towards Spain—hence the name cassola, referring to the type of round earthenware dish typically used in the region. It is an essential implement in my kitchen, whether used for shellfish in the summer or cassoulet in the winter.

Serves 4

2 large red peppers
2 long pink shallots
4 fat garlic cloves
3 tablespoons olive oil
¼ pound smoked Canadian bacon
　 cut into lardons or small thick pieces
a small bunch of flat-leaved parsley
1 small dried red chilli
3 tablespoons tomato paste
1 large glass of fruity white wine
4 thin slices of pain de campagne
generous 1 pound whole cooked langoustines or
　 any large shrimp in their shells
freshly ground black pepper

Core the peppers, discarding all the seeds, and cut the flesh into squares about 1 inch wide. Peel the shallots and chop finely. Peel the garlic cloves and chop 3 of them finely.

Traditionally this dish is made in an earthenware pot, but a large, heavy-based Dutch oven will do fine. Gently heat the olive oil and add the peppers, shallots, bacon and chopped garlic. Fry for 10 minutes, stirring regularly, until all is softened. Meanwhile, pick the parsley leaves off the stalks and chop around two-thirds of the leaves finely, reserving the rest.

Stir half the parsley into the softened pepper mixture and crumble in the chilli. Add the tomato paste and cook, stirring all the time, 1 minute, then pour in the white wine. Add an equal quantity of water, turn up the heat to medium and let bubble gently, uncovered, 15 minutes.

Toast the bread on both sides under the broiler. Cut the remaining garlic clove in half and rub over one side of the toasted bread then drizzle with olive oil.

Place the slices of bread in the cassola or in the base of four individual soup bowls.

Add the langoustines to the pepper sauce and stir well. Allow to bubble for a few minutes, stirring occasionally, until the langoustines are heated through and have 'taken' the sauce. Spoon over the slices of bread. Scatter with the rest of the parsley leaves, give a few grinds of black pepper and serve straight away—with plenty of napkins.

the anchovies of collioure

salade mimosa
mimosa salad

The Roque family have been salting the anchovies of Collioure since the nineteenth century but theirs is part of a much longer history. The records show that since the early Middle Ages these tiny silvery fish were caught in the waters off the pretty fishing port, with its medieval castle on an almost perfectly formed bay. In the 1930s there were some thirty anchovy companies operating in the town, but now only two large ones remain. The fishing fleet of 120 or so boats that famous artists such as Matisse and Derain painted is long gone. But Guy Roque and his family are determined to maintain the tradition.

As he explains: 'Salted anchovies were a dish of the poor, just like salt cod. But now they have become a *plat de luxe*—a luxury item.'

The reason, of course, is a paucity of supply. While the Roques prefer to get their fish locally, they are sometimes forced to the Atlantic seaboard and even as far afield as Argentina. At least the salt always comes from the region, along the coast at the famous salt pans on the edge of the Camargue at Aigues Mortes, and is delivered in the traditional wooden boxes. The Roques get through 100 tonnes a year and 200 tonnes of anchovies, all of which must be delivered fresh, as freezing destroys the texture.

When I went on a tour of the anchovy processing plant, I understood why few companies persist in producing this delicacy. The fish are salted whole for a first time, in a proportion of almost half salt to fish, and then kept in barrels in the cold for up to a month. Thereafter they are gutted and their heads removed, a process that no machine could perform, and then re-salted, although this time with much less salt, depending upon their size and even the weather. Only after at least another three months, under a heavy weight, are they ready for packaging or marinating.

I watched as the packers carefully arranged the fish in their glass jars by hand, delicately placing them in a *couronne*, or crown shape. Monsieur Roque explained that under the reign of Louis XI Collioure was exempt from salt tax so that the locals could continue to enjoy their anchovies. 'It is the savoir faire that makes our anchovies special,' he went on. 'To be honest, if my family hadn't wanted me to I wouldn't have carried on. But my daughter and sons are all involved in the business.' And as I sat by the beach, eating my anchovy salad dressed with the local Banyuls vinegar, I gave thanks for that.

This salad apparently gets its name from the bright yellow egg yolks, their color echoing the startling hue of the mimosa flower which studs the deep green foliage in the mountains in February. Mimosa flowers are usually grown and picked by small cherry producers who also keep a few acres of vines, thus ensuring something to sell at market across most of the year. Banyuls vinegar is made from the sweet wine produced from vines grown on terraces which tumble down to the Mediterranean; if you can't get it use another sweet dark vinegar such as balsamic.

Serves 4

16 salted anchovies from Collioure or 16 anchovy fillets
2 large red peppers
4 hard-cooked eggs, peeled and quartered
2 fat garlic cloves
a small bunch of flat-leaved parsley
Banyuls or sherry vinegar
extra virgin olive oil
freshly ground black pepper

If you have salted anchovies, soak them in plenty of water for 30 minutes, then fillet them. Heat the broiler to maximum and grill the peppers until the skin is blackened all over, turning them regularly. Place in a sealed plastic bag for 10 minutes, then peel (the blackened skin will come away easily), discarding the core and seeds. Cut the flesh into long, thin strips.

On four plates arrange alternate strips of pepper and anchovy, interspersed with the quarters of egg. Finely chop the garlic and parsley and mix together. Sprinkle the resulting 'persillade' over the salad and dress with a sprinkling each of the vinegar and oil. Grind over some pepper and serve with French bread.

magret de canard aux cerises
duck breast with cherries

Roussillon, and particularly one of its southernmost towns, Céret (which just happens to be my local market town), is famous for its cherries, though less so for its ducks, which generally come from the Languedoc area north of Toulouse. However, the two do make a very happy marriage. Magrets are from ducks fattened for the production of foie gras, and the slight sharpness of the cherries cuts through their richness. Locally, the cherry producers also recommend serving their fruit with fresh escalopes of foie gras—but I like it with rosy-pink slices of duck breast.

Serves 4

2 fat magrets de canard, around 1 pound each
   (or 4 ordinary duck breasts)
sea salt
1 pound fresh red cherries
2 teaspoons clear honey, for preference thyme-
   or herb-scented
juice of 1 orange, plus 4 slivers of zest
¾ cup red wine
a sprig of thyme
freshly ground black pepper

Heat a heavy ridged grill pan over a medium heat. Score the fat of the magret at ½ inch intervals across, cutting just down to the pink flesh. Salt well and leave to stand for 10 minutes while the grill pan heats up.

Place the magrets fat side down on the grill pan. As soon as the fat starts to run, pour around 1 tablespoon into a separate pan and drain off the rest into a bowl (it is worth keeping the fat for the best of roast potatoes). Return the magrets to the heat. Set the pan with the hot duck fat over a gentle heat and add the cherries, turning to coat them in

the cherries of céret

the fat. Cook for several minutes, then add the honey, the orange juice and zest slivers, the red wine, the sprig of thyme and a few grinds of pepper. Bring to the boil, reduce to a simmer and cook for 10 minutes. If you like, this can be done in advance.

Now turn your attention back to the magrets, which by this time should have been cooking for around 12 minutes. Turn them over so that they are flesh side down—the fat should be nicely browned by this stage—and again drain off any excess fat. Cook a further 5 minutes (more if you like your duck well done but my preference for this dish is for the duck to be 'rosé') then flip back onto the fat side for another few minutes to crisp up the fat. Remove from the heat and leave to stand for 5 minutes. Note that if you are using the thinner duck breasts rather than magrets the cooking time should be reduced.

If necessary, reheat the cherry sauce and in either case fish out the sprig of thyme. Slice the magrets across through the scores on the fat and arrange in a fan on four plates. Spoon the cherries and the sauce to the side, making sure each plate has a sliver of the orange peel, and serve.

My local market town of Céret, right on the Spanish border south of Perpignan, proudly boasts that it produces the first cherries in France—and most years it is right. Those first cherries are sent by tradition to no less a person than the Président de la République for his delectation, with luck in the last days of April, assuming the climate has been kind.

From then on picking begins in earnest, in time for the cherry festival in early June. Old-fashioned producers can still be seen in the orchards, shod in their clogs for comfort, gathering up the cherries in their aprons—although to be honest these days plastic buckets are a more common sight among the larger farmers. But the tradition of cherry production is deeply engrained here, for many of the smaller producers inherited their orchards from preceding generations.

Not so, however, my own producer, who sold me the trees for my orchard and prunes the ancient (but very productive) cherry tree in my back garden. Born in a *mas* or farmhouse just across the valley from me, Monsieur Rigail had to buy back the land which his father had sold, land which had been in his family for four generations. He has planted more than 15 varieties of cherries, as well as peaches, apricots and nectarines, from which his wife makes very special jams.

Since we are on the slopes of the sacred Catalan peak of Mount Canigou, the altitude means that he cannot lay claim to the first cherries, but he wouldn't have it any other way. 'I am ill if I don't wake up and see the mountain each morning,' he explained. 'I went to Paris once and I took with

me a rock from Canigou just in case anything happened to me.' His sign at the local markets he sells his produce at throughout the summer reads 'Paysan, Catalan, et fier de la terre'—roughly translated 'a peasant, Catalan and proud of my land'.

le beurre de montpellier
montpellier butter

les côtes d'agneau grillées avec aïoli
broiled lamb chops with garlic mayonnaise

There are different butters from all over France: the butter known as *maître d'*, which is simply chopped parsley and seasoned butter, or *beurre d'anchois*, anchovy butter, both of which find their way onto steaks, are just two examples. But the absolute classic, named after its town of origin, is the *beurre de Montpellier*.

It is believed to have its origins in the sixteenth century, when Montpellier was renowned all over France as a gastronomic capital, and contains an extraordinary variety of ingredients, some quite frankly interchangeable. The important points are that the butter should be a vibrant green and is ideally made in a pestle and mortar; you can use a food-processor but it will bruise the leaves and herbs. The good news is that the pestle and mortar version keeps much better in the fridge. It is at its best served on poached or broiled fish.

Serves 8 to 10

a selection of the leaves of: watercress, sorrel, baby spinach, flat-leaved parsley, chervil, and tarragon to taste, total weight around ½ pound
2 tablespoons capers
4 fillets of anchovy
4 small dill pickles
2 hard-cooked egg yolks
2 sticks good quality unsalted butter, softened
juice of ½ lemon
freshly ground black pepper

Remove any stalks from the leaves and wash them well. Rinse the capers, anchovies and dill pickles. Pound the lot together with the egg yolks in a large pestle and mortar until you have a dry mixture. Add the butter, lemon juice and pepper and pound until smooth. Transfer to a small pot and chill until needed.

Aïoli (or all y oli as it is more properly known in Catalan; that is, garlic and oil) is traditionally made without eggs, but for practical purposes a little cheating is necessary. No matter, the resulting thick garlicky emulsion is an essential element of the local cooking, served as a side dish for everything from Catalan sausage to large Mediterranean shrimp. Until I moved here, however, I had never thought to combine it with lamb chops. Now, whenever I arrive in the Pyrenees in the spring months, my first move is to buy some of the exquisite local lamb, grill it, preferably over vine trimmings but certainly on a barbecue scented with herbs, and serve it up with aïoli. The only other accompaniment should be a tomato and onion salad and some crusty French bread. A simple feast.

Serves 4

8 lamb chops or 2 small trimmed racks of lamb, cut into 8 sections
sea salt and freshly ground black pepper
a few sprigs of rosemary, lavender and thyme
6 fat garlic cloves, peeled
yolks of 3 large fresh free-range eggs
extra virgin olive oil
juice of 1/2 lemon

It is important to season the chops well in advance, making sure that there is plenty of salt on the fat, and to bring them to room temperature before barbequing. It is also vital that the coals are only glowing or the fat will burn—so the barbeque needs to be lit well in advance. Alternatively you can just broil the chops but they will lack something of that special flavor. Just before cooking throw on the herbs so that the chops cook in their aroma.

Classically the aïoli is made in a pestle and mortar but a food-processor will do the job admirably. What is essential is that all the ingredients are at room temperature before you start—cold egg yolks will usually make the sauce curdle. Either crush or whizz the garlic with plenty of salt until you have a paste. Now add the egg yolks and pound or purée again. When you have a smooth mixture start adding the oil, literally drop by drop at the beginning, either whisking in or giving short blasts on the processor. As the mixture starts to thicken, you can begin to add the oil in a steady stream. Exact quantities will depend upon the garlic, the eggs and the temperature—some even say the cycle of the moon—but a generous 1 cup of olive oil would be a good estimate. You might also choose to make the aïoli with half olive oil and half sunflower oil for a less bitter taste. The aim is to end up with a stiff emulsion, which you serve alongside the broiled lamb chops. Finish the aïoli with a few drops of lemon juice.

cassoulet

Cassoulet gets its name from the *cassole*, the earthenware pot it is traditionally cooked in, which is claimed by a small village called Issel, some 5 miles from Castelnaudary, south of Toulouse. The original cassoulet was simply a one-pot dish of mixed vegetables and meats but it acquired its particular characteristic in the sixteenth century from the introduction of the white bean known as lingot, brought back from the Americas. There is intense competition between the neighbouring towns of

Castelnaudary, Toulouse and Carcassonne for the 'vrai' cassoulet. The famous chef Montagné put it well when he wrote in 1928: 'Cassoulet is the God of the cuisine of the occitane. A God in three persons: God the Father which is the cassoulet of Castelnaudary, God the Son which is the cassoulet of Carcassonne and the Holy Ghost, which is that of Toulouse.'

When in France I buy my cassoulet ready prepared from a farmer who rears his own ducks and geese.

When making my own, I prefer to use confit de canard rather than goose in my cassoulet, and also include Toulouse sausage, but most people have their own version. What is important is to use a deep, wide earthenware dish and to stir the crust that forms on top of the beans back in on several occasions (classically this should happen seven times, but that is going a bit far in my opinion). And you really can't cheat and use ready-cooked beans, as the texture is all wrong. In a cassoulet, the beans are all.

The medieval fortifications of Carcassonne

cassoulet de seiches
cassoulet of cuttlefish

Serves 6 to 8

generous 1 pound dried weight of white haricot
beans, soaked overnight in plenty of water

1 large onion, peeled

4 cloves

8 peppercorns

bouquet garni of fresh thyme, bay leaf and parsley,
tied together with string

2 garlic cloves, peeled

½ pound pork belly

4 pieces of confit de canard

2 tablespoons tomato paste

4 Toulouse sausage

6 tablespoons white bread crumbs, preferably from
a stale baguette

Put the soaked and drained beans in a large heavy pot and cover with 2 quarts water. Add the onion, studded with the cloves, the peppercorns, bouquet garni, garlic cloves and the piece of pork belly. Bring to the boil 5 minutes, remove any scum from the surface then turn down to a simmer. Cover and cook, about 1½ hours. The exact cooking time will depend upon the freshness of the beans but they should remain distinctly firm to the tooth.

Meanwhile, gently heat the pieces of duck in a heavy pan just so that they release their fat, which you should reserve. Do not allow to brown.

Preheat the oven to 325°F and put your earthenware pot in to warm. Drain the beans, reserving a little of their liquor. Discard the onion and the bouquet garni. Mix a little of the warm bean liquor with the tomato paste. Pour a ladleful of duck fat over the base of the pot then cover with one third of the beans. Add the pieces of duck and the slice of pork belly from the boiled beans. Add another third of beans then tuck in the sausage. Cover with the remainder of the beans and pour over the tomato mixture.

Transfer to the oven. After 1 hour or so, stir the top in for the first time. Repeat this process several times over the next 1½ hours. Thirty minutes before serving, increase the heat to 350°F and cover the surface of the cassoulet with the bread crumbs. Return to the oven and cook until bubbling and the bread crumbs lightly browned. Serve straight away, with mustard and a bitter green salad.

This unusual dish is a specialty of the fishing port of Sète. In the traditional version the cuttlefish are first stuffed with a mixture of pork, bread and egg, but I prefer this simple approach. You could also use squid, though the texture will be different.

Serves 4

1 pound small cuttlefish, cleaned of their ink,
flesh and tentacles chopped

olive oil

2 shallots, peeled and finely chopped

2 fat garlic cloves, peeled and finely chopped

sea salt and freshly ground black pepper

1 teaspoon sweet paprika

good pinch of chilli powder

⅔ cup dry white wine

2 cups canned plum tomatoes

a sprig of thyme

1 bay leaf

2 cups canned precooked white haricot beans

Wash the cuttlefish well. Cover the base of a heavy pan with oil and add the shallots and garlic. Fry gently until soft, 5 minutes, then turn up the heat and add the pieces of cuttlefish, plenty of seasoning, the paprika and chilli. Fry, stirring, 5 minutes, then pour in the white wine. Allow to bubble then add the tomatoes and their juice, breaking the flesh up with the back of a wooden spoon, the thyme and the bay leaf. Simmer uncovered 20 minutes then add the beans, drained and well rinsed. Simmer until the sauce is thick and the cuttlefish tender, 20 minutes or so, and serve with plenty of crusty bread to mop up the juices.

civet de sanglier
wild boar stew

Daniel, our local mayor in the Pyrenees, leads the hunt. This means that he puts his dogs into the undergrowth to chase out the wild boars while the 'guns' stand in a ring on their *pointes*, or allocated spots, in order to take a rifle shot at a beast as it emerges. It is, as one can imagine, a slightly risky process, but Daniel is very careful to make sure that they only shoot mature boar and certainly not the protected species of antelope known as izzard. And preferably not each other either.

On the days when a boar is shot, it is taken straight back to the garage beneath the town hall and butchered there and then. The cuts of boar are divided up among the hunters by lottery, although the man who shot it is always given first choice (and yes, it is always a man). Then the hunters sit down to a rather splendid lunch of charcuterie followed by boar (from the hunt the week before)—sometimes ribs cooked over vine clippings, sometimes the belly casseroled in red wine.

Serves 6

3–4 pounds wild boar
1 bottle rough red wine
1 tablespoon brandy
3 tablespoons olive oil
2 or 3 carrots, scraped and roughly chopped
1 or 2 onions, peeled and sliced
3 garlic cloves, peeled
2 sprigs each of rosemary and thyme
2 bay leaves
a few black peppercorns and juniper berries
2 tablespoons butter
4–5 slices smoked bacon, cut into small pieces
1 tablespoon all-purpose flour
sea salt

There are two key points to the cooking of wild boar: plenty of marinating and then plenty of long, slow cooking. Chop the meat into large pieces, place in a non-reactive pan and add all the wine, brandy, oil, carrots and onions, garlic, herbs, peppercorns and juniper berries. Leave to marinate, at least overnight.

The next day, melt the butter in a heavy lidded pan, and add the bacon. While the bacon fat melts, strain the marinade from the boar, and pick out the meat. Add the vegetables and garlic to the pan with the butter and bacon and cook slowly 15 minutes, stirring occasionally. Pat the meat dry and sprinkle with seasoned flour (not too much salt—remember the bacon). Now increase the heat and add the meat. Fry briefly for a few minutes on either side, until browned. Meanwhile, warm the marinade.

Pour the hot marinade into the mixture and add boiling water if necessary barely to cover the meat. Add the lid and either simmer as gently as possible on top of the stove or transfer to a medium-low oven, preheated to 300°F. Cook until the meat is very tender, 3–4 hours. Check the seasoning before serving.

les abricots de roussillon au muscat
roussillon apricots poached in muscat wine

Roussillon is famed for its apricots, which have a particularly beautiful blush tinge to them as well as an exquisite flavor. The area also produces a sweet white wine made from Muscat grapes, the preferred local aperitif, most famously from the vineyards around Rivesaltes, near Perpignan. Lightly poached in the wine, the apricots acquire extra sweetness, especially if they are slightly under-ripe, while the infusion of rosemary adds a touch of the flavor of the *garrigue*, as the herb-covered hillsides are known.

Serves 4

16 apricots
½ bottle Muscat wine, preferably Muscat de
    Rivesaltes or another sweet wine from the south
    of France
a sprig of rosemary

The apricots should not be over-ripe. If they are the Roussillon variety they will boast a delicate pink blush over their orange skin. Put them in a heavy casserole in which they fit snugly and pour over the Muscat—they should be just covered. Bring to the boil as slowly as possible and as soon as the liquid bubbles remove from the heat and tuck in the sprig of rosemary to infuse. Leave the apricots to cool in the liquid and when it is completely cold chill well. Serve the apricots in the poaching liquid.

Provence is a country to which I am always returning, next week, next year, any day now, as soon as I can get on to a train.' So wrote Elizabeth David in French Provincial Cooking in the 1950s, going on to quote Ford Maddox Ford that 'somewhere between Vienne and Valence, below Lyon on the Rhône, the sun is shining'. And so it is still, but on increasingly developed hillsides. The provençale dream as famously described by Peter Mayle is under threat from hotel and villa estates, with their accompanying golf courses, swimming pools and tennis courts.

And yet—the essence of Provence can still be found, and sometimes in surprising places. The market in Antibes is one. Just a few hundred yards away from the ridiculously grandiose yachts in the harbor lies a covered market used by locals. Here you can buy the *poissons de roche* needed for a fish soup, so fresh they are literally still twitching. Steaks of swordfish are sliced straight from the body of the fish, while its proud head, spear still intact, stares silently skywards. The octopus are wriggling when they are weighed and put into plastic bags. There are long sheets of pressed

The Olive Pickers, 1888–89, by Vincent van Gogh

and dried red peppers to add color, and vast bunches of basil to scent the air. And then there are the fruit and vegetable stalls.

The food of Provence is characterized not by elaborate fish stews or by elegant cuts of meat but by its seasonal vegetable dishes. Give a local a vegetable, be it a marrow or a tomato, an eggplant or a mushroom, even a zucchini flower, and they will stuff it to make it go further. But the flavors of the stuffing, whether rice and herbs and Parmesan, or spiced minced meat, means British writer Shirley Conran's famous comment of 'life is too short to stuff a mushroom' is easily forgotten. And in any case, sensible provençale housewives buy their stuffed vegetables ready to bake from the market or at the traiteur.

The further east you travel in Provence, the more obvious the Italian influence on the food becomes. Polenta, fresh pasta, gnocchi and the local form of pizza, pissaladière, are all on offer. It is not just a question of geographical proximity; the historic provençale association with Italy goes back to Roman times. And just as in Italy you need to head away from the coast to find true local food, so these days to understand Provence you need to head inland towards the mountains. Get away from the beachside sprawl and you soon find yourself in a land of scrub herbs interspersed with olive trees and vines, lavender fields and sunflowers, with fortified villages on hilltops and distant views of Mont Ventoux, nightmare of cyclists on the Tour de France.

Whatever Ford Madox Ford thought, Provence is not all about sunshine. In winter it can be a cold, unforgiving place, especially when the Mistral blows. That is when the locals huddle round their firesides and eat daubes and civets, the stews of beef and game designed to keep out the cold. The effort of canning the tomatoes, peppers and beans in oil during the summer glut, of preserving the fruit in eau de vie or sugar syrup, is now rewarded.

And soon enough the spring sunshine will come and it is time to reopen the shutters and start revisiting the local markets for which Provence is renowned. One of my favorites is in the hilltop town of Banon, near where my father and stepmother have had a house for some years. The local cheese sold wrapped in chestnut leaves alone makes it worth a visit. Try it with lavender-scented syrup to remind you that the heat of summer is once more on its way.

Lavender fields of Drome, Provence

soupe au pistou
pistou soup

Italy has pesto and Provence has pistou. There is lively debate as to who had it first, but the difference is clear: there are no pine nuts in the French version. But, just as in Italy, you will find pistou spooned over pasta and stirred into soups. I hardly dare to write it, but soupe au pistou is remarkably like a minestrone. It is at its best made in late spring, when the vegetables and the basil are at their sweetest.

Serves 4 to 6

2 small young leeks
5 fat garlic cloves
extra virgin olive oil
6 plum tomatoes
salt
white sugar
tops of several leaves of Swiss chard, if available,
    shredded
½ pound green beans, topped, tailed and cut into
    bite-sized lengths
bouquet garni of parsley, sage and basil
1 cup cooked borlotti or white haricot beans
2 medium-sized zucchini, diced
a good bunch of fresh basil
a good hunk (around ⅓ pound) of fresh Parmesan,
    shredded
¼ pound vermicelli

Finely chop the white part of the leeks, discarding the green tops. Peel 2 of the garlic cloves and chop finely. Heat 2 tablespoons oil in a large heavy pan big enough to make the soup in. Add the leeks and chopped garlic and sweat gently for 10 minutes, stirring occasionally. It is important that the leeks and garlic do not brown.

While they are cooking, pour boiling water over the tomatoes, leave for 45 seconds, then remove and peel as soon as they are cool enough to handle. Cut in half, remove the seeds and roughly dice the flesh. (In almost all other instances I would use canned tomatoes, but for this soup, which relies on fresh ingredients, this really is a necessary step.)

Add the tomatoes to the leek and garlic mix, together with a good pinch each of salt and sugar. Cook, stirring several times, until the tomatoes have begun to break down, 5 minutes. Remove from the heat.

Bring 1¼ quarts lightly salted water to the boil and blanch the Swiss chard tops, if you have them, for 1 minute. Lift out with a slotted spoon and then cook the green beans in the same liquor with the bouquet garni for 2 minutes. Add the liquor, green beans, bouquet garni, Swiss chard tops, diced zucchini and borlotti or haricot beans to the leek and tomato mixture, bring back to the boil and reduce to a simmer.

Cook for 10 minutes, during which time you can make the pistou. Traditionally this is done in a pestle and mortar but a food-processor does perfectly well, as long as you remember the sauce should be quite chunky. Crush the remaining garlic cloves with a generous pinch of salt then whizz in the basil leaves, stripped from the stalk, and the Parmesan. Drizzle in just enough oil to make an emulsion—6 tablespoons as an estimate.

Bring the soup back to the boil and add the vermicelli. Cook for 5 minutes, until the pasta is just cooked. Remove from the heat, check seasoning, and leave to cool for 10 minutes before stirring in the pistou. A sprinkle of Parmesan and a few basil leaves floating in the soup do no harm.

pan bagnat
salade niçoise in a roll

Pan bagnat literally means 'wet bread' and was originally a salade niçoise to which stale country bread was added to make the meal go further. Wise and parsimonious grandmothers also realized that the way the bread soaked up the olive oil and tomato juices added to the salad's deliciousness. These days pan bagnat more typically comes in the form of a roll, but it should still be prepared in advance, making it ideal picnic food for the beach.

It's important to note that either anchovy fillets or canned tuna are used—never both. Personally I prefer anchovies, but it's a matter of taste. When in season, small green fava beans or the sliced hearts of the small artichokes known as violettes are also sometimes added—always raw, never cooked.

For 4 rolls

4 very ripe large beefsteak tomatoes
sea salt
1 red onion
1 green or red pepper (green is traditional but some prefer the sweeter taste of a ripe red pepper)
2 hard-cooked eggs
4 large round rolls, such as ciabatta
4 crisp lettuce leaves
8 anchovy fillets or ¼ pound canned tuna, drained of oil
12 small Niçoises black olives, pits removed
some fresh basil leaves (optional)
freshly ground black pepper
extra virgin olive oil

Cut the tomatoes across into thin slices and sprinkle liberally with salt (if you aren't sure of their ripeness you could also sprinkle over a little white sugar). Peel and finely slice the onion. Cut the pepper in half, remove the seeds, and slice the flesh finely. Cut the eggs into slices.

Slice the rolls in half and arrange all the ingredients inside, adding a good sprinkling of black pepper and a generous slug of the oil. Press the top of the rolls down and wrap tightly in plastic wrap or foil. Leave for a few hours before eating, so that all the flavours mingle.

tapenade
olive paste

I have never seen a market in Provence without an olive stall. Usually the range on offer reaches many tens of varieties and each olive is intended for a particular purpose. So there are black olives to add to your daube, green ones stuffed with anchovies or almonds for nibbling with your *apéro*, the tiny Nyons black olives or the fat green new season's lucques to go with your charcuterie. And then there is tapenade, the crushed olive paste which is often made to the stallholder's particular taste. Recipes vary (capers, anchovies and preserved tuna can all be added, though not all together) but salt, garlic and olive oil are essentials. It is easy to make at home and worth making in quantity as it keeps well—if you can resist eating it all at once, that is. There is nothing better to spread on toast to accompany a glass of rosé or a pastis on a warm summer's evening.

Serves 6 to 8

about ¼ pound capers, preferably those packed in salt
2 garlic cloves, peeled
6 anchovy fillets, well rinsed
scant 2 cups small black olives, preferably Niçoises, pitted
a good pinch of dried thyme
freshly ground black pepper
½ cup extra virgin olive oil

If you have salted capers, soak them in plenty of water for 1 hour, changing the water halfway through. If you are using capers in vinegar, rinse them very well under running water. Pat dry in paper towels.

Pound the garlic and anchovies in a pestle and mortar. In the food-processor, blend the capers with the olives. Stir in the garlic, thyme and plenty of pepper and then add just enough of the oil to make a paste. To store, put in a sealed jar and top with a layer of olive oil.

socca in nice market

'Socca, socca, caouda que bullie,' used to cry the street vendors as they wandered around Nice, pushing their barrows with charcoal stoves laden with thin metal trays filled with the chickpea bread that remains the favorite merenda, or mid-morning street food, of the town. The message was to get your socca while it was hot and it went out to workers on building sites and market traders, who would send their 'bouchou', or errand boy, to pick up the portions of salty, oily socca, to be eaten immediately with the fingers.

The good news is that in the famous market of the Cours Saleya, in Vieux Nice just off the Promenade des Anglais, you can still find an authentic version. Head for a stall in the middle of the market, where Madame Thérèse holds court. You will recognize her from her long dark hair, gypsy clothes and bright red lipstick. She may be the only socca seller in the market these days but she provides quite enough pure theater all on her own.

Socca is poor people's food, made of nothing more than chickpea flour, olive oil and salt, designed to fill the stomach cheaply. But as with so much provençale cooking, the result is unutterably delicious. Madame keeps her socca warm over an oil drum filled with glowing charcoal but it hardly has time to get cool. I took my seat at one of the trestle tables in the market, covered with a tarpaulin for shade, and watched as tray after tray of the thin bread was brought out from the kitchens behind, the bearer running at Madame's command. Each thin circular metal tray was placed over the brazier until small dark brown spots formed on the surface of the socca.

A queue had formed for take-aways but Madame was not to be hurried. Do you prefer it crispy or soft? she asked each customer she didn't know (the cognoscenti would say soft, from the middle). With salt and pepper? Each tray of socca was cut into generous slices, which she folded and placed on paper then liberally sprinkled with seasoning and oil. The key is to eat it as quickly as possible, even if you do risk burning your fingers and lips. And as I observed from my fellow snackers, a glass of rosé to accompany it doesn't go amiss, though locals generally prefer a rough red.

pissaladière

Like socca, pissaladière is served cut in squares from vast baking trays. Like pizza, it is also traditionally cooked in a wood-fired oven. However, unlike socca, a delicious if not exactly authentic version can be made at home. The key is in the long, slow cooking of sweet white onions.

Serves 6

3 cups white bread flour
white sugar
1 heaped teaspoon active dry yeast
sea salt
1 large egg, beaten
olive oil
3 pounds mild white onions
2 garlic cloves, peeled and lightly crushed
a sprig of thyme and a bay leaf, tied together
8 anchovy fillets
16 small black olives

First make the bready dough, as it needs time to rise. Add 1 teaspoon salt to the flour and place in a low oven (225°F) for 10 minutes (this helps it to rise). Meanwhile, whisk the yeast and 1 teaspoon sugar into scant 1 cup warm water until frothy. Spread the warmed flour onto a clean surface, make a well in the center and add the yeast and beaten egg with a dribble of olive oil. With floured hands quickly work all together—it will be sticky at first but will soon become smooth. Knead it for another few minutes, cover with a clean cloth and leave in a warm place for at least 1 hour. You can of course do all this in the food-processor but in my experience the results are not as good—nor as satisfying.

beignets de fleurs de courgettes
zucchini flower fritters

Meanwhile, peel the onions and slice them as finely as possible into half moons. Choose a big heavy pan with a lid, set over a gentle heat, and add 2 tablespoons oil. Add the sliced onions, minced whole cloves of garlic and herbs, together with a sprinkle each of salt and sugar. Cover and cook as gently as possible, shaking occasionally. The aim is to soften the onions without them browning. The whole process should take around 45 minutes.

Preheat the oven to maximum (usually 475°F). Oil a 10 inch non-stick oven tray, ideally rectangular in shape. Punch the dough down and with your fingers spread it as thinly as possible over the tray, right up to the sides. You may well find you have too much. Pile in the onion mixture, removing the garlic and herbs, and arrange the anchovies in a lattice shape across the surface. Put the olives at the cross-over point of the anchovies. Bake the pissaladière for between 10 and 15 minutes, depending upon the efficiency of your oven. Take it out and leave to rest for 10 minutes before serving—it is at its best served warm.

Provence has always been a favorite of American visitors. The renowned American cookery writer, the late Julia Child, whom I was privileged to meet when she was well into her nineties, told me that she was never happier than when she was cooking at her house, La Pitchouline in the hinterland of Antibes—though by the time I talked to her she could no longer travel there, to her sadness. Her kitchen, however, has been kept exactly as she left it.

The house now belongs to another American, Kathy Alex, who runs cookery classes here. After a morning's work in the kitchen we wandered outside to sit under the mulberry tree, which Julia always said told a person's character, to be served these crisp little fritters, which are perfect to get the appetite going. In southern markets the flowers are sold in bundles (they are also delicious in risotto) but elsewhere you will probably have to grow your own zucchini to get them. A simple sauce of chopped fresh tomato and basil goes well with the fritters.

Serves 4 or 8

1 cup all-purpose flour
sea salt
2 large fresh eggs, yolks and whites separated
2 teaspoons extra virgin olive oil
generous ½ cup whole milk
olive oil for frying
16 zucchini flowers, preferably attached to
  very thin stalks

Sift the flour into a bowl and season well with salt. Beat the egg yolks. Make a well in the center of the flour and add the yolks and the extra virgin olive oil. Beat all together then very slowly add the milk,

beating all the time, until you have a smooth batter. Leave to stand for 30 minutes.

When you are nearly ready to cook the fritters, beat the egg whites with a pinch of salt until stiff and gently fold into the batter. Pour the oil into a deep frying pan to a depth of approximately ½ inch and heat gently. When the oil is hot (test with a cube of bread—it should brown gently) dip the zucchini flowers in the batter and fry in several batches. They take only a few minutes and should be turned halfway through cooking; they are ready when the batter is puffed up and browned. Drain on paper towels and serve straight away.

courgettes farcies
stuffed zucchini

Vegetable stalls in early summer markets in Provence are stacked high with the small round green and white striped zucchini which are the preferred variety for stuffing; for the lazy the mobile traiteur stall next door will have them ready prepared, needing only to be heated through. As the former (and somewhat disgraced) Mayor of Nice, the late Jacques Médecin, points out in *Cuisine Niçoise*, the round variety has a particular advantage as 'its halves sit obediently flat in the baking dish'. But the recipe can also be used with the easier-to-find long zucchini.

Serves 4

salt
1 or 2 large zucchini (around 1½ pounds) or
   4 small round ones
⅓ cup Camargue or long grain rice
1 small white onion, peeled
⅓ pound ground pork
¼ cup finely grated Parmesan
1 egg, beaten
a small bunch of fresh basil, leaves torn
freshly ground black pepper
1 garlic clove, peeled and chopped
1 cup fresh bread crumbs
olive oil for drizzling

Bring a large pan of salted water to the boil and boil the zucchini—10 minutes for a large one or 5 minutes if you have small round ones. Drain well, leave to stand for 15 minutes, then squeeze dry. If you have a large zucchini chop it across into 8 pieces then use a sharp knife to scoop out the seeds and discard. If you have small zucchini cut them in half across and again scoop out the seeds and discard.

Bring another pan of water to the boil and cook the rice with the onion until it is *al dente*, or soft to the tooth in Italian, which after all was for a long time the language in Nice. The exact cooking time will depend upon the type of rice, but typically between 10 and 15 minutes. Drain well and discard the onion.

Preheat the oven to 400°F. When the rice has cooled, mix it into the pork together with the Parmesan, egg, basil leaves, plenty of pepper and the garlic. Arrange the slices or halves of zucchini in a well-oiled earthenware pan and press in the stuffing, leaving it well mounded.

Sprinkle over the bread crumbs and dribble over some olive oil. Bake uncovered in the oven until the stuffing is cooked through and the breadcrumbs nicely browned (45 minutes, but check occasionally to see they are not burning). The stuffed vegetables can be served straight away but the Nicois prefer them tiède, or warm—or better still the next day, with a warm fresh tomato sauce.

ratatouille

My neighbour Louis has a terraced vegetable garden just below our house. It is a thing of beauty, the neatly serried ranks of vegetables surrounded by gladioli, and in summer he is at work in it at an early hour every day, before the sun gets too hot, picking baskets of vegetables for his wife to take home and can. But there always comes a point of irritation, when the summer glut becomes just too much even for the ineffably patient Madame Louis, and she goes on strike. I am afraid I look forward to this stage, because that is when he will give me enough vegetables to make ratatouille, a dish which as a true *montagnard* Catalan he regards with suspicion. After all, it comes from Nice.

In a classic ratatouille, the vegetables are cooked individually, so that they retain their flavors and textures, rather than becoming the indeterminate mixture of vegetables that are often given the name. Ironically, though, it is a name that derives from the French verb *trouiller*, meaning to mix together. Make plenty and you will find it worth the effort; it tastes even better the next day.

Serves 6 to 8 (with room for leftovers)

2 pounds plump eggplants
2 pounds zucchini
1 pound green peppers
1 pound red peppers
3 pounds very ripe tomatoes
2 pounds large, white, mild onions, peeled and
   finely sliced
10 fat garlic cloves, peeled and finely chopped
a good bunch of basil
a good bunch of flat-leaved parsley
some sprigs of thyme
salt and freshly ground black pepper
plenty of olive oil

rougets à la niçoise
red mullet in the style of nice

Slice the eggplants and the zucchini across at a thickness of around ½ inch. Place them in two colanders and sprinkle liberally with salt. Leave for 20 minutes then rinse and blot them on paper towels.

Meanwhile, halve the peppers and remove the seeds. Slice them into long thin strips. Pour boiling water over the tomatoes, leave for 45 seconds then remove and peel as soon as they are cool enough to handle. Cut them in half, remove the seeds and juice, and chop the flesh roughly.

Now you can either heat four separate Dutch ovens to cook the vegetables individually or (my preference) cook them one after the other in the same pot. Heat about 4 tablespoons oil over a low heat and first stew the eggplants, turning once or twice. Remove them and set aside, add some more oil as necessary and do the same with the zucchini. Repeat the process with the peppers and onions. Exact cooking times are impossible to give—each vegetable should become tender but not brown nor be in any danger of falling apart, especially in the case of the zucchini. Just take your time, tasting occasionally, and remember that this is a dish designed to be cooked in a cool shady kitchen on a hot summer's day in the south of France.

When all the vegetables apart from the tomatoes are cooked, crush the garlic with the herbs to a fine paste. Mix this with the diced tomatoes. Return all the cooked vegetables to the pot, discarding any excess oil, add the tomato mixture, season, cover and cook over a low heat, 30 minutes or so. Leave to cool; ratatouille is best served warm, preferably the next day, when the flavors have mingled.

The red mullet is also known in this region as *la bécasse de mer*, or woodcock of the sea, not just because it is as delicious as that small bird but also because both are traditionally cooked with their liver still in place. It does give the fish a gamey flavor, which some find too powerful. For myself, I remove the liver.

Serves 4

8 small red mullet, scaled and gutted
all-purpose flour
salt and freshly ground black pepper
olive oil for frying
1 sweet white onion, peeled and finely chopped
4 garlic cloves, peeled and crushed
1 pound ripe plum tomatoes, peeled and chopped
2 good pinches of saffron
8 anchovy fillets
2 lemons, preferably unwaxed, finely sliced into 16
16 small black olives
1 tablespoon capers, well rinsed
extra virgin olive oil

Dust the fish with seasoned flour. Heat the oil to a depth of ½ inch in a non-stick pan and when it is hot quickly fry the fish for no more than 2 minutes on either side, until nicely browned (do this in two batches). Lift out with a slotted spoon and drain on paper towels.

Preheat the oven to 350°F. Arrange the fish in an ovenproof earthenware dish and scatter around the onion, garlic and tomato. Steep the saffron in a little warm water for a few minutes then pour this over the fish. Place an anchovy fillet on each fish and cover with a couple of slices of lemon. Sprinkle the olives and capers over the tomato mixture.

Bake uncovered, 20 minutes. Just before serving sprinkle over a little good olive oil. You need nothing more than bread to accompany this dish.

View over Villefranche-sur-Mer

crevettes au pastis
shrimp with pastis

trouchia
swiss chard omelet

When I was in my late teens, my father regularly used to rent a house in the hills above the sea near Cavalière, not far from St-Tropez. Even then, in the late 1970s, the coast road was heaving with traffic in the summer months, and we mostly spent our time at the villa. But excursions to the fish market were vital and this is one of the first dishes I learned to cook. The fennel was plucked from the hillside as we drove home, the pastis brought out for apéritifs and a generous slug added to the pan.

Serves 4

3 tablespoons olive oil
16 large uncooked shrimp, in their shells
3 garlic cloves, peeled and sliced into fine slivers
1 head of fennel seeds
coarse sea salt and freshly ground black pepper
2 tablespoons pastis

Set a large heavy pan over a medium heat. Add the oil and when it is almost spitting throw in the shrimp together with the garlic, fennel seeds and plenty of seasoning. Cook, stirring all the time to prevent the garlic from burning; around 6–8 minutes, the exact cooking time will depend upon the size of the shrimp, but you can tell when they are done as they will turn a deep rosy pink. Add the pastis and cook for a further 1 minute until all the alcohol fumes have burned off. Serve straight away, to be eaten with fingers and plenty of crusty bread.

Rather like the Italian frittata, trouchia is a solid omelet which is served warm or cold and is another favorite picnic food. The pan you use is important. It needs to be very heavy, ideally cast iron with a handle, so that the trouchia does not cook too quickly. The trick is to get the Swiss chard to cook before the eggs set fully.

A similar dish is tian, named after the sloping-sided pot in which it is baked, the difference being that the tian is served hot from the oven. It is especially good with spinach and fillets of anchovies or sardines.

A chopped tomato, red onion and basil salad is a good accompaniment.

Serves 6

¾ pound Swiss chard leaves, washed and finely chopped into strips
3 tablespoons chopped flat-leaved parsley
2 tablespoons chopped chervil
a good handful of torn basil leaves
8 large eggs
salt and freshly ground black pepper
¾ cup shredded Parmesan
olive oil

Mix together the Swiss chard leaves and the herbs. Beat the eggs lightly, season well, and fold in the chard and herbs together with the Parmesan. Mix all very thoroughly.

Cover the base of a non-stick pan with oil and place over a low heat. Add the egg mixture and cover with a heatproof plate which fits snugly over the surface of the pan. Cook 20 minutes.

The next part of the operation calls for some dexterity. Drain off any excess oil, then grasp the plate firmly in one hand, using an oven cloth, and with the other turn the pan over. Your trouchia should slide out onto the plate, nicely browned on one side. Add a little more oil to the pan and slip the trouchia back in, uncooked side down. Cook for a further 10–15 minutes then slide out onto a separate plate. Pat dry with paper towels to remove any excess oil and leave to cool.

loup de mer en papillote
sea bass in paper parcels

The sea bass has a particular affinity with fennel and is often barbequed over a fire onto which dried fennel stalks have been thrown to scent the smoke. Barbequing fish is however a tricky task (will it stick? is it cooked? has it burned? being three of the most pressing questions). Cooking the fish in parchment paper parcels with a mixture of aromatics means that all these concerns can be avoided. Take the fish directly to the table in its parcel—the aroma as you open up the paper is irresistible. And a tip for determined barbequers is to wrap fish in damp newspaper before placing over the warm coals—especially good for sardines.

Serves 2—but for 4, 6 or 8 just increase the number of paper parcels

1 sea bass, around 1½ pounds, scaled and gutted
sea salt
1 large or 2 small fennel bulbs
½ a lemon, preferably unwaxed
2 plum tomatoes
extra virgin olive oil
freshly ground black pepper
a good handful of basil leaves

Preheat the oven to 425°F. Wash the fish inside and out, sprinkle thoroughly with salt, then rinse again (this helps to remove any traces of gut taint). Chop off the fronds of the fennel and stuff inside the cavity of the fish, together with a couple of slices of the lemon. Roughly chop the remainder of the fennel, discarding the stalks and the core. Also chop the tomatoes into chunks.

Cut a piece of parchment paper big enough to wrap generously around the fish, sprinkle the surface with a little oil and place the fennel and half the tomatoes on the oiled paper. Lay the fish on top, sprinkle with more oil and a generous seasoning of pepper, the basil leaves and then the remaining tomatoes.

Seal the paper parcel well and place on a foil-covered baking sheet to catch any juices that might run before putting in the oven. Bake 30 minutes and take straight to the table.

coquilles st-jacques à la provençale
scallops in the provençale style

In the north, scallops are served with buttery sauces, classically beurre blanc sharpened with shallots and vinegar, but down in Provence they add their own flavors of olive oil, garlic and parsley. I was first served this dish with a touch of pastis used to flambé the shellfish but found the anise flavor overpowering on the delicate scallop, though I love it with shrimp. The substitution of Cognac is mixing regions but it works.

Serves 4 as a first course or 2 as a main dish

8 large scallops, with their corals and shells
sea salt and freshly ground black pepper
all-purpose flour
3 tablespoons extra virgin olive oil
3 fat garlic cloves, peeled and finely chopped
2 tablespoons Cognac
a small bunch of flat-leaved parsley, leaves finely chopped

Wash the scallops well and scrub the shells thoroughly. Remove the corals and set aside. Slice each scallop in half horizontally then pat dry with paper towels. Season a little flour well and lightly dust over the white of the scallops on both sides.

Place the cleaned shells in a medium oven (350°F) to heat, just as you would some plates. Heat the oil in a heavy skillet over a high heat. When the oil is hot, add the garlic and as soon as it begins to sizzle add the whites of the scallops. Cook for 1 minute then add the corals and turn the white parts to cook for a further 1 minute. Stand back and pour in the Cognac. Allow it to sizzle for 1 minute to burn off the alcohol, then remove from the heat and stir in the parsley. Spoon the scallops into the warmed shells and serve.

boeuf en daube
stewed beef

Slowly cooked beef, flavored with garlic, orange peel, herbs and black olives and redolent of wine, best served with fresh egg tagliatelle or polenta.

Serves 6

3 pounds chuck steak; in France the cut known as paleron is typically used)

4 thick slices of pancetta or smoked bacon

2 tablespoons olive oil

3 white onions, peeled and quartered

4 garlic cloves, peeled and lightly crushed

3 large carrots, peeled and cut into thick slices

1 stick of celery, roughly chopped

4 sprigs each of fresh rosemary, thyme and flat-leaved parsley

2 fresh bay leaves

8 fresh plum tomatoes or 1 cup canned plum tomatoes

2 strips of orange zest

sea salt

freshly ground black pepper

a good pinch of allspice

1/2 bottle robust red wine

1 tablespoon small black olives, pits removed

Chop the meat into large chunks, removing any excess fat. Dice the pancetta or bacon, including the fat. Add half the pancetta or bacon to the heavy Dutch oven in which you plan to cook the daube and add the oil. Cook gently for 5 minutes so that the fat runs, then turn up the heat to medium and add half the meat. Cook for a few minutes, turning regularly, until browned then remove with a slotted spoon and set aside. Add the remaining meat and repeat the process.

Now add the onion, garlic, carrot and celery, and reduce to a gentle heat. Stir occasionally. While they are cooking, tie the herbs into a bundle, leaving a long length of string so you can pull them out at the end. If you are using fresh plum tomatoes, pour boiling water over them and leave for 45 seconds then remove and peel as soon as they are cool enough to handle. Chop the flesh roughly. If you are using canned tomatoes, drain them.

When the vegetables have cooked for around 10 minutes, return the meat to the pot. Tuck in the herbs and the orange zest, add the tomatoes, a little salt (remembering that both the bacon and olives are salty) and a few good grinds of pepper and the allspice. Cook for 5 minutes, stirring regularly, until the tomatoes have broken down, then pour in the wine. Bring to the boil and add just enough boiling water to cover the meat.

Cover and reduce the heat (or transfer to a slow oven, 300°F) so that the mixture is barely bubbling. It should cook as slowly as possible for at least 4 hours. After about 3 hours, check the seasoning and add the olives and if necessary a little more water to top up the liquid. Daube is at its best cooked the night before and gently reheated.

biscottins à la fleur d'oranger
orange-flower water cookies

Orange blossom is one of my favorite memories of the south of France and the clever parfumiers of Provence long ago learned to distil its olfactory essence. In Arab style, the water is often used to scent salads, and also to flavor these little cookies, which are made without eggs or fat and should be served with a strong, short shot of coffee.

Makes 16 to 20 cookies

2 large eggs, beaten
½ cup plus 1 tablespoon superfine sugar
2 tablespoons orange-flower water
2 cups plus 2 tablespoons all-purpose flour
a pinch of salt

Preheat the oven to 425°F. Whisk together the eggs and sugar until light and creamy. Add the orange-flower water. Sift the flour with the salt then slowly stir into the egg and sugar mixture, stirring all the time, with a wooden spoon. You will end up with a sticky dough. Chill your hands in iced water, dry well and dust with flour, then roll out the dough into a long oblong around ½ inch thick by 2 inches wide. With a sharp knife, cut across at roughly ½ inch intervals. Butter a baking tray and lay the cookies on top. Bake until they just begin to turn color, 10–15 minutes. Put on a wire rack to cool.

the thirteen desserts of christmas

Planning for Christmas in Languedoc-Roussillon on the foothills of the Pyrenees had started in October. Not on my part, but that of my green-fingered neighbor who, although a confirmed communist and atheist, was most concerned that we should prepare the necessary thirteen Christmas desserts. A tradition originally from Provence but which has now spread all along the south coast, these are intended to symbolize Christ and the twelve apostles and are served after Midnight Mass on Christmas Eve (the main meal is also eaten on the night of the Réveillon, or Christmas Eve).

Alongside the traditional four dried fruits to represent each of the mendicants, gardener Louis insisted that while the orchards were still laden with produce we should store apples in the cellar, make sure we had our order in for Muscat grapes shrivelled on the vine, and can peeled clementines in Armagnac to rack up alongside the cherries we had already preserved in local eau de vie. And we should of course be gathering chestnuts to can in salted water to cook alongside winter cabbage with the roast.

All through the glut of autumn special delicacies are stored away *derrière les fagots*—behind the kindling wood and vine clippings—to be brought out as treats, especially at Christmas.

And so for our thirteen desserts we served:

Pompe à l'huile, a round sweet bread made with olive oil and scented with orange-flower water

The four beggars: dried raisins (Dominicans), figs (Franciscans), walnuts (Augustins) and almonds (the barefooted Carmelites), each one said to represent a monastic order according to their habit

The six preserved fruits: quince paste, clementines in Armagnac, air-dried rings of apple, grapes which were left to shrivel on the vine, cherries from our orchard preserved in eau de vie, and bought-in dates, said to symbolize Christ who came from the East

Calissons, made from almonds and preserved melons, and crystallized fruits from Aix-en-Provence and Avignon respectively

corsica

One of the pleasures of writing a book such as this is that you get the opportunity to fill in gaps in your culinary knowledge and so it was with great delight that I flew to Corsica. My parents had been there several times but had never had the decency to take me along with them to what has been variously dubbed as 'the island of beauty' and 'the mountain of the sea'. I am always dubious of such descriptions, designed to attract tourists, but in the case of Corsica it proved to be true. With mountains tumbling straight down to the Mediterranean, mountain villages perched on hillside ridges, vast Italianate-style villas and vertiginous coastal roads, the island exceeded my expectations.

Yet what also quickly became clear is that this is a harsh land and one in which it has always been difficult to make a living. More than two million tourists visit Corsica every year, but the local population is only just over 10 per cent of that figure. Some of the 'tourists', of course, are Corsican-born individuals returning to visit their families. The local joke is that you cannot go anywhere in the former French colonies without finding a policeman of Corsican descent. What is not so funny is that many were driven overseas in the first place by the devastation the World Wars caused to the male population. With no fathers to support them, many local boys chose the option of the Foreign Legion, married overseas and never returned, except for holidays.

They certainly missed Corsica though—or so an elderly fisherman in Ajaccio's port, whose own father had been driven abroad, pointed out to me. The fisherman had just been diving on a freezing cold morning for one of the local specialties, sea urchins, and was on his way to deliver them to the five stalls set up in front of the fish market. He wouldn't, he explained, have it any other way, though he acknowledged that in winter it was a chilly job.

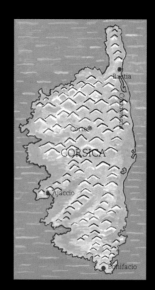

So too for the father and son team of Paul and Joseph Sabiane, whom I met milking their ewes early one frosty Sunday morning in the university town of Corte, in the center of the island. One of the most important elements in Corsican cooking is the soft cheese known as brocciu (brousse in French), which is made from the whey of either goat's or sheep's milk. Brocciu finds its way into dishes ranging from cannelloni (the Italian influence on the cooking is important, reflecting the long Genoese period of rule), via stuffed artichokes and sardines, to baby kid and on to desserts scented with lemon zest. But the best way of all is to eat it still warm on the morning it is made, dribbled with local honey from bees who have feasted on the herbs of the maquis.

The scent of the maquis defines much of Corsican cooking in the spring and summer months. Whole kid and lamb are roasted over herb-scented wood fires for feast days. The townspeople spend weekends roaming over the steep hillsides to pick young tender spring leaves for omelets, fritters, tarts, or simply salads. Herbs are used to stuff the expensive fish such as sea bass, John Dory and bream with which the summer markets are full, reflecting the wealth of the incoming flux of villa owners and tourists. But it is in the cold of the autumn and winter months that the true cooking comes to the fore.

These are the seasons not only when the brocciu is made but when the pork products come into their own. Hams and sausage that have hung in cool cellars all through the hot summer can now be

The Genoese watchtower, built 1549, at Porto

brought out, as the next batch of pigs are slaughtered. The chestnut harvest has been gathered in and the next season's chestnut flour milled. There are bitter leaves to be harvested, slowly simmering bean stews to be made, thick soups to savor, pasta dishes sauced with game to indulge in. And happily the favorite pastime of catching thrushes and blackbirds for pâtés and grillades has now been banned.

Time and again I was told that the winter months were, from a gastronomic point of view at least, the best time to visit the island. I found myself in agreement as we drove over a snowy pass on the way to the former capital of Corte. Now in bright sunshine, the day before it had been blocked, and abandoned cars still littered the road. Somehow the idea of sausage cooked over an open wooden

café appeared. And inside was a roaring fire with sausage cooking over it. We stayed a while.

Corsican food represents a hotchpotch of the various influences on this much invaded but still fiercely independent island, which at times can seem a lot further from France than the mere geographical distance across the sea. Even within the island's bounds, there are significant differences between the food of, say, Corte, Ajaccio and Bastia. In the nineteenth-century home of the Simonini family, who can date their genealogy back to the Dukes of Padua, I was given a long explanation of how local hams were cured differently, reflecting not just tradition, but also altitude, climate, the type of pig, and involving varying periods of smoking, spicing and salting. Corsicans are proud of their individual culinary tradition, and with good reason. At its truest, cooked in the home, it is peasant food of the highest order, even if you are

soupe de marrons
chestnut soup

Made in Corsica in the autumn with freshly picked chestnuts that have been roasted over a wood fire and then puréed, this soup still works well using a can of unsweetened chestnut purée (you can also use vacuum-packed nuts). Chestnuts cooked in milk were a traditional peasant supper but in this refined version the nuts are cooked in stock.

Serves 4 to 6

1 white onion, peeled and finely chopped
2 sticks of celery, preferably including leaves,
   finely chopped
2 tablespoons butter
2 slices smoked Canadian bacon, cut into
   small pieces or lardons
1 pound canned chestnut puree
4 cups concentrated stock (game is ideal)
freshly ground black pepper
2 tablespoons crème fraîche or sour cream
a handful of flat-leaved parsley leaves,
   finely chopped

Sweat the onion and celery, including the leaves, with the butter and bacon for about 20 minutes, stirring from time to time until the vegetables are soft. Stir in the chestnut puree, breaking it up with the back of a wooden spoon, and when it is nicely mixed in slowly add the stock, stirring all the time to make sure there are no lumps. Bring to the boil and simmer for 15 minutes.

Meanwhile, preheat the oven to 300°F and put soup plates in to warm. Liquidize the soup until smooth and add some pepper. Ladle into the warmed soup plates, add a spoonful of crème fraîche or sour cream to each bowl, sprinkle with a little chopped parsley and serve.

a corsican chestnut festival

The chestnut occupies a special place in the cuisine of Corsica. The *castignaccia*, or chestnut orchards, once covered a large part of the island and today the trees still give much color to the beautiful autumn Corsican landscape. It is estimated that there remain some 75,000 acres of chestnut groves, although only around 5,000 acres are actively managed as farms.

Every December in the small village of Bocognano, in the hills behind Ajaccio, a competition for the best chestnut flour takes place. Today chestnut flour is an expensive luxury product but it was once the staple, used to make pulenda, a kind of polenta. First cooked in a copper pot over a wood fire, with constant stirring, the pulenda is then spread out onto a hot tray and sliced. Typically it is served with the sausage known as figatellu, which has first been cooked over a wood fire.

Making pulenda is hard work, so the harvest of the trees has now been put to other uses too. At the chestnut festival I discovered marrons glacés, chestnut breads and cakes, chestnut-studded sausage, chestnut chocolates, chestnut syrup— and even, rather extraordinarily, chestnut whisky, brewed by an enterprising young man from chestnut beer.

Nor do the chestnuts feed only humans. In the winter months the pigs for which Corsica is famous are released into the chestnut groves to feed on the fallen nuts. It is this that gives the resulting pork products their unique flavor, explained Paul Marcaggi, who comes from Bocognano, where he keeps his herd. His proud boast is that he is the only person in Ajaccio who still keeps his own pigs, cures the hams and sausage, and carves the ham by hand. Such is the demand for his product that he will only do this on Friday and Saturday mornings—otherwise he would run out of hams before the cured meat had matured sufficiently. I can testify to the succulent texture and nutty flavor of the twenty-four-month cure.

omelette au brocciu et menthe
omelet with soft cheese and mint

An easy-to-make omelet with simple flavors—the mint makes all the difference. The texture should tend to firm rather than the *baveuse* or slightly frothy consistency of, say, cheese omelet; this resembles an Italian frittata.

Serves 2 to 3

6 large fresh eggs
sea salt and freshly ground black pepper
½ pound brocciu, brousse or other soft
  whey cheese
8 sprigs of fresh mint, leaves finely chopped
3 tablespoons unsalted butter
2 teaspoons olive oil

Beat the eggs with plenty of seasoning then whisk in the cheese and mint leaves. Heat the butter and oil in a heavy pan. When it is fizzing add the egg mixture, stirring just once. Cook over a medium heat for around 10 minutes, and serve as soon as the eggs are set. The omelet is also good cold.

fèves au lard
fava beans with bacon

I remember that the first time my French sister-in-law served me a dish of tiny fava beans with not just the pods but the outer white skins peeled off I thought her quite mad. Who would bother with such a task? But then I had never liked fava beans—until then. This is one of the ways they serve them in Corsica, with the excellent local ham, tiny onions and the wild mint from the mountains. They stand as a dish all on their own.

Serves 4

4 pounds fava beans in their pods
16 small white onions
a pinch of brown sugar
sea salt
4 teaspoons olive oil
4 slices of good quality air-dried ham, cut into
  pieces, fat included
freshly ground black pepper
a few sprigs of mint, leaves chopped

Pod the beans as you bring a pan of water to the boil. Boil the beans for 1 minute then drain and leave to cool. As soon as you are able to handle them, slip off their outer white robes, leaving just the green insides.

Peel the little onions, sprinkle them with salt and sugar, and in either a heavy pan on top of the stove or an earthenware dish in an oven preheated to 350°F, brown them in the oil, stirring or shaking from time to time, about 20 minutes. When they are soft, add the pieces of ham. Cook for a further 5 minutes then add the peeled beans and some pepper. Cook for no more than 2 minutes, then serve, sprinkled with the mint.

fritelles d'herbes
herb fritters

In springtime the Corsican hills are covered in wild herbs and, just as with wild mushrooms, everyone has their favorite picking spot, usually a heavily guarded secret. The herbs are used in all manner of dishes, from the simple to the complicated, such as stuffed sheep's stomach, which bears a strong resemblance to haggis. Favorite, though, are these little fritters, which are served as a welcoming snack with an aperitif when friends visit the household. After weddings, it is also traditional to hand out fritelles of brocciu as a sign of friendship as the guests leave.

Makes about 20 fritters

1¼ cups all-purpose flour
a good pinch of salt
1 large egg, separated
2 teaspoons olive oil
around ¾ cup cold water
groundnut oil for deep frying
a good mixture of fresh herbs and bitter green
  leaves, chopped, such as wild mint, marjoram,
  thyme, parsley, borage, Swiss chard, dandelion

Sift the flour with the salt and make a well in the centre. Add the beaten egg yolk and the oil, and carefully stir in with a wooden spoon. Add the water in a slow stream until you have a smooth but thick batter (you may find you do not need all the water, depending upon the flour). Cover with a clean dishcloth and leave to stand 2 hours.

When you are ready to cook, heat plenty of oil, ideally in a deep fryer. Whisk the egg white to soft peaks and carefully fold into the batter with the herbs. Fry the fritters in batches, a tablespoon for each fritter, llifting out with a slotted spoon and draining on paper towels. Serve piping hot.

les sardines au four avec brocciu et herbes
sardines baked with brocciu and herbs

It sounds a strange combination but it is one that works—sardines roasted with cheese and herbs.

Serves 4

16 sardines (around 1 pound in total), preferably fairly small, gutted and heads removed
green leaves of 4 stalks of young Swiss chard, white part removed
1 tablespoon chopped flat-leaved parsley
1 tablespoon chopped mint
2 tablespoons brocciu, brousse or other white curd cheese
sea salt and freshly ground black pepper
4 tablespoons bread crumbs
2 tablespoons extra virgin olive oil

Preheat the oven to 425°F. Wash the sardines well, especially inside. Lay them side by side in an earthenware or other ovenproof dish in which they fit snugly. Finely shred the Swiss chard leaves and blanch in boiling water for 1 minute, then drain and refresh with cold water. Squeeze out any excess water then mix with the parsley and mint. Mash into the brocciu and add plenty of seasoning. Spread over the sardines then sprinkle with the bread crumbs. Finally drizzle the oil over the surface.

Bake in the oven until the surface is brown and bubbling, 15–20 minutes, and serve straight away.

thon rôti
roasted tuna

Just as elsewhere in the Mediterranean (and Sicily in particular) catching tuna by the traditional method of traps was once an important element of the Corsican fishing industry. Although catches have declined dramatically, due in part to the introduction of drift netting, tuna is still a popular fish in the market-places in summer, when it is sold cut straight from the body of the fish in thick slices on the bone, to be roasted in olive oil with the new season's garlic. It is the custom to roast the fish in a whole piece and then carve and skin it but it is more practical to use ready-cut (and easier-to-source) slices.

Serves 4

4 tablespoons extra virgin olive oil
4 thick-cut slices of tuna
sea salt and freshly ground black pepper
4 garlic cloves
4 tablespoons bread crumbs

Preheat the oven to 425°F. Pour half the oil in a heavy ovenproof dish into which the tuna will just fit. Wash the fish, pat dry and season well. Peel the garlic and slice finely lengthwise. Arrange the fish in the dish and sprinkle the garlic over the surface of each slice. Scatter 1 tablespoon bread crumbs on top of each slice of garlic-covered fish, trying to prevent any getting down into the dish itself. Drizzle the remaining oil over the bread crumbs.

Roast in the oven 10–12 minutes, depending upon the thickness of the fish and how you like your tuna, and remembering that tuna carries on cooking off the heat. Baste with the oil halfway through. I err on the less side, as there is a risk that the bread crumbs will burn, and overcooked tuna has a tendency to dryness. Typically this dish is served lukewarm, having been left to rest for 10 minutes or so.

étouffée de cabri
kid stew

For centuries kid has been the most popular meat on the island for feast days and is the dish traditionally served at Christmas, when a whole kid is roasted over a wood fire. For slightly older animals, however, this is an excellent way of cooking a meat which in my view is much under-rated. The dish is usually served with pulenda made with chestnut flour, though soft (rather than broiled) Italian polenta is a good substitute. Any leftovers make an excellent pasta sauce, served with macaroni.

Serves 4 to 6

3 pounds kid, either shoulder or leg, cut into pieces on the bone
2 tablespoons pork fat or lard (you can also use olive oil)
6 fat garlic cloves, peeled and finely chopped
1/2 bottle strong red wine
sea salt and freshly ground black pepper
bouquet garni made up of 1 bay leaf, a few sprigs of thyme and some mint, tied together

Briefly brown the kid in the fat and remove with a slotted spoon. Add the garlic to the fat, stir briefly, and add the wine. Bring to the boil and reduce for 5 minutes. Now return the kid to the pot, together with any juices, some seasoning and the herbs. Turn down to the slowest possible simmer, cover and cook slowly until the meat is very tender, about 2–2½ hours.

veau aux olives
veal with green olives

Another dish for high days and holidays, this is made for large parties with a whole shoulder of veal, though it adapts well to smaller portions. Veal in Corsica grazes beside its mother on the high pastures and the herbs of the maquis; the meat has a pink color and a determined flavor, bearing no relation to the white, insipid meat of the crated calf, which I for one would never buy. Corsican veal is hard to find off the island, but there is plenty of outdoor-reared veal available. It is a little understood fact that the purchase of veal from outdoor-reared calves prolongs their life rather than shortens it: bull calves not destined for the veal market are often slaughtered at birth.

The ancient olive trees that fill the valleys of the region known as la Balagne produce an especially prized crop, used not just for oil. This dish requires young green olives.

Serves 4 to 6

½ pound piece of unsmoked bacon
1 cup good quality green olives, preferably preserved in oil rather than vinegar, unpitted
1½ pounds stewing veal, off the bone
2 tablespoons olive oil
1 large white onion, peeled and finely chopped
6 round shallots, peeled and separated into their individual bulbs
3 garlic cloves, peeled and finely sliced
3 large carrots, peeled and sliced across at ½ inch intervals
sea salt and freshly ground black pepper
½ bottle fruity white wine
a little stock or water
2 fresh bay leaves, a sprig or two of parsley, some thyme, a small sprig of rosemary, tied together with string if you like (I often leave the herbs in when I serve but the string allows you to remove them easily)

Blanch the piece of bacon for 2 minutes in a pot of boiling water, then drain. Do the same for the olives, to remove excessive saltiness. Cut the veal into large bite-sized pieces. Trim the piece of bacon of any excess fat and cut into smaller pieces, removing any bone.

Heat the oil over a medium heat in a large Dutch oven. Add the veal and fry briefly for 2–3 minutes, stirring all the time, until just browned on all sides. Remove the meat with a slotted spoon and set aside.

Add the bacon, onion, shallots, garlic and carrots to the oil. Reduce the heat to low and cook gently for 20 minutes or so, stirring from time to time, until the vegetables are softened. Return the meat to the pan, together with any juices that have run, and some seasoning, remembering that the bacon may still be salty. Pour in the wine, together with just enough stock or water to cover the meat, and tuck in the herbs. Bring to the boil, reduce to a simmer, cover and cook slowly 1 hour or so.

Now add the blanched olives (if you are cooking the dish in advance, leave this until around 20 minutes before serving), adjust the seasoning, and remove the herbs if you wish. Simmer uncovered for a further 15 minutes, leave to stand 5 minutes or so, and serve.

fiadone
corsican cheesecake

A cheesecake scented with lemon zest and aquavita (eau de vie), this soft and wobbly cheesecake without pastry was originally a speciality of Corte but has now become a favorite throughout the island.

Serves 6 to 8

scant 2 pounds fresh whey cheese such as
   brocciu or brousse
4 tablespoons superfine sugar
5 eggs, separated (the eggs should be of the
   freshest, as they are served uncooked)
zest of 1 unwaxed lemon, grated
1 small glass of eau de vie
a pinch of salt

Mash the cheese with the sugar, egg yolks, lemon zest and eau de vie. Whisk the egg whites with a pinch of salt until very stiff then incorporate into the cheese mixture. Pour into an oiled cake dish and chill well before serving.

the french west indies and the île de la réunion

The French know where to take their winter holidays—they head off to those sunny parts of France that just happen to be in the Caribbean, the Indian Ocean, or even, as in the case of French Guiana, on the South American mainland. In the Caribbean alone they have the choice of Martinique, capital of the French Caribbean during much of the seventeenth and eighteenth centuries, Guadeloupe and its off-lying islands of Marie Galante and Les Saintes, the tiny and exclusive Saint Barthélemy, and Saint Martin, still shared with the Netherlands and especially famous for its restaurants, which attract visitors by speed- and flying-boat over the water from nearby Anguilla. Or there is the Ile de la Réunion, to the east of Madagascar.

All these islands were fiercely fought over for many centuries, and it is something of a surprise to find them today, as French departments, part of the European Union. But the French have always guarded them fiercely, as the British navy found to their cost. Marie Galante and the Iles Saintes attracted immigrant farmers and fishermen from Normandy, Brittany and Charente in particular during the seventeenth century. Guadeloupe's sugar production was considered sufficiently important that under the Treaty of Paris of 1763 France abandoned territorial claims in Canada in return for British recognition of French ownership of the island. As for Martinique, it yielded further treasures: it was the birthplace of one Joséphine Tascher de la Pagerie, who was to go on to become first wife of Napoleon and Empress of France.

Go into a supermarket on these French islands and you will find some surprising goods on offer. Would you really want to eat a cassoulet under the tropical sun? Apparently so, judging from the selection of tins on offer. Foie gras and fine wines are both widely available. I ate a memorable starter of fresh foie gras served on fried

mango in Fort-de-France, Martinique, which at the turn of the last century replaced Saint Pierre as capital after the eruption of the Mont Pelée volcano, which killed all but one of the town's 30,000 inhabitants (one drunken prisoner, Louis Cyparis, survived because he was incarcerated in the dungeons).

For it is when French culinary skill is applied to the local ingredients that you eat best of all. Local ways of cooking white fish include delicately poaching it in a liquid similar to that used on the mainland (known locally as the métropole) for the classic court-bouillon. The local lobster or crawfish is cracked open and broiled and served not with a heavy-handed garlic butter but instead a spiced vinaigrette, though it must be said this goes under the less than elegant name of *sauce chien*. In a beautifully preserved colonial house high in the mountains of Basse Terre on Guadeloupe, the choice of dishes of the day was the crayfish that are found in the mountainous streams, flambéed in wood-aged rum, or magret de canard with a coffee sauce (the coffee grown here is some of the best as well as most expensive in the world, after Jamaica's Blue Mountain). Dessert was liquorice ice cream with a vanilla cream flecked with the black seeds.

Particularly important is the confident uses of spices, influenced by the Creole and Indian populations. After the eventual abolition of slavery in the mid nineteenth century, many Indians from the former French colony of Pondicherry moved to the Caribbean to provide extra labor, as did their Sri Lankan neighbors, who have left their legacy in the bright yellow-colored Colombo spice mix which is found in every marketplace. Turmeric, known as *safran d'Inde*, white and black pepper, cayenne (the capital of Guiana is Cayenne), cinnamon, cloves, cardamom, all thrive in the plantations amid the tropical rainforests, as of course do bananas and coconuts.

For me, though, it is breakfast that sets the gastronomic tone in the French parts of the tropics. Freshly baked croissants and pains au chocolat or aux raisins, unsalted butter imported from Normandy and thick conserves of tropical fruits such as mango or pineapple come as standard—as does good strong black coffee, taken with a generous dose of the local brown sugar. I remember, the first time I visited Guadeloupe, taking a photograph of a man cycling down the street, baguettes under one arm, fresh fish dangling on a line from the handlebars. Looking back upon the moment, I wonder why I thought it memorable. This is France, after all, and the correct standards must be observed, even under the tropical sun.

The harbour of Les Saintes, looking across towards Guadeloupe

gratin de coeurs de palmiers
gratin of palm hearts

Gratins are a peculiar feature of cooking in the French tropics, whether in the Caribbean or the Indian Ocean, perhaps reflecting the fact that many of the French colonists moved here from the north of the *métropole* or mainland. But unlike in northern France, gratins are usually served as a side dish to the main course rather than in their own right. In restaurants you will often be offered a piece of broiled meat or fish served *avec ses gratins*—with a selection of different gratinated vegetables.

From my experience in the Caribbean the favorite is a gratin of christophènes, a sort of summer squash known as chouchoux in La Réunion, but that island also has a penchant for gratinated palm hearts. The white sauce is a peculiarity, made with water rather than fresh milk, the latter being rarer on the island. However, the *chapelure* of grated Gruyere and bread crumbs from a baguette is a very French touch.

Serves 4 as a side dish

8 canned palm hearts
4 tablespoons butter
1 small white onion, peeled and finely chopped
1 garlic clove, peeled and finely chopped
½ cup all-purpose flour
1½ cups water
juice of 1 lemon
1 egg yolk
salt and freshly ground black pepper
a good pinch of mace or, failing that, nutmeg
⅔ cup shredded Gruyere
2 tablespoons breadcrumbs from a stale baguette

Drain the palm hearts and rinse very well under cold running water. Preheat the oven to 350°F. Melt the butter and add the chopped onion and garlic; sweat gently, stirring a couple of times, until just soft but not browned, 5 minutes. Slowly stir in the flour until you have a thick mixture. Add the water, very slowly at first, stirring continuously to avoid lumps. When you have added all the water, allow to bubble gently 5 minutes or so, then remove from the heat and add the lemon juice, egg yolk, seasoning and spice.

Stir all well together, then spoon some of the sauce onto the base of a gratin dish, which you have chosen so that the palm hearts will just fit into it. Lay the palm hearts in a line over the sauce base and pour over the remainder of the sauce—it should just cover the hearts. Sprinkle over the cheese and bread crumbs and place in the preheated oven until bubbling and nicely browned on top, 50 minutes or so. Serve straight away.

accras aux crevettes
shrimp accras

Typically made with salt-cod, these little deep-fried dumplings, are served piping hot as an appetizer with the lethal ti-punch of the islands—high-proof white rum mixed with sugar and lime juice. On Marie Galante, the very dignified lady who ran the beach shack kindly gave me her recipe for this different and deliciously spiced version.

Serves 8 as a starter

2½ cups all-purpose flour
a good pinch of salt
1 heaped teaspoon baking soda
2 large eggs
scant ½ cup whole milk
4 tablespoons water
salt and freshly ground black pepper
½ teaspoon cayenne pepper
½ teaspoon four-spice powder
2 fat garlic cloves, peeled and finely chopped
4 spring onions, white parts finely chopped
1 tablespoon finely chopped chives
1 tablespoon finely chopped parsley
½ pound cooked peeled shrimp (you could also use crayfish), roughly chopped
groundnut oil

Sift the flour with the salt and baking soda. Whisk the eggs, then beat in the milk and water. Slowly sift in the flour mix, whisking all the time, until you have a smooth batter. Add all the remaining ingredients except the oil. Pour oil into a pan to a depth of about 1 inch and heat gently. When the oil is hot (test with a cube of bread, which should brown straight away) add the batter 1 teaspoon at a time, never cooking more than 5 accra at once. When the accra puff up and brown (a matter of a few minutes), remove with a slotted spoon and pat dry on paper towels.

salade de canard au vanille et aux agrumes
salad of duck with vanilla and citrus fruits

Réunion, like nearby Madagascar, is especially famous for its vanilla, an orchid which was first imported to the island at the beginning of the nineteenth century. Although vanilla is traditionally added to sweet dishes and for scenting sugar, vanilla beans are also used locally in savory dishes, especially with duck and chicken. For many years I was put off the combination by an unfortunate dish I first ate in Paris, but my faith was restored by this simple salade tiède of strips of duck marinated in a vanilla-scented vinaigrette, quickly flash-fried and then served on a bed of citrus fruits. Duck à l'orange became a classic for a reason—the sharpness of the fruit cuts through the fattiness of the bird. On La Réunion the fruit known as tangor, a graft of mandarin onto orange trees, is usually cooked with duck, but a mix of citrus fruits also works well.

Serves 4 as a first course

2 duck breasts , skin removed, flesh cut into
  thin strips

For the marinade:
2 vanilla beans
juice of 1 orange
juice of 1 lemon
a pinch each of salt and sugar
a splash of dark rum (optional)
4 tablespoons groundnut oil

For the salad:
2 oranges, peeled, the flesh cut across into fine
  slices, then diced
1 pink grapefruit, peeled, the segments again cut
  across, then diced
2 pink shallots, peeled and finely diced
salt and freshly ground black pepper

Split the vanilla beans lengthwise and scrape out the seeds into a bowl, then add the beans. Whisk together all the remaining ingredients for the marinade and add to the vanilla, together with the strips of duck. Leave to marinate for a couple of hours.

When you are nearly ready to serve, arrange the diced fruit on a serving plate and season. Heat a ridged grill pan until very hot and fry the marinated duck for a couple of minutes on either side. Pick the vanilla beans out of the marinade, then pour the rest over the duck. As soon as it bubbles, scatter the duck over the fruit. Give the hot marinade a quick whisk, pour over the salad and serve.

tuna tartare
tartare of tuna

The tiny Ile Sainte off Guadeloupe is especially favored by the yachting community, who make for the almost circular bay in search of lunch just as often as safe harbor. One Sunday morning I watched the local fisherman chop up a big yellowfin tuna and then followed the hunks of fish to a seaside restaurant, where it was served as a tuna tartare with impeccable chips. It goes without saying that the fresher the tuna, the better, although the marinade in lime juice helps 'cook' the fish.

Serves 4

1 pound very fresh tuna steak, in one
  thick-cut piece
juice of 1½ limes
1 teaspoon sea salt
2 tablespoons water
a good pinch of cayenne pepper
freshly ground black pepper
1 garlic clove, peeled and very finely chopped
½ onion or 2 shallots, peeled and finely chopped
½ teaspoon thyme leaves
1 tablespoon chopped parsley

Cut the tuna across the grain into 8 thick slices. Mix together the lime juice, salt, water, cayenne pepper, black pepper, garlic, onion and thyme and pour over the fish. Leave to stand for 1 hour, turning once; the fish will turn from rose red to a paler, milky color. Sprinkle with the parsley and serve.

terrine chaude de crabe à la creole
hot terrine of crab creole style

Many French Creoles from Louisiana moved to the French Caribbean, bringing their recipes with them. This dish from Guadeloupe is typically eclectic and sophisticated, using as it does sherry and spices: 1970s in feel and taste, it is no less delicious for that. Ideally, make it with fresh rather than frozen crab. A mix of the brown and white meat is essential.

Serves 4

2 large dressed crabs
2 tablespoons dark sherry such as Amontillado
juice of 1 lime plus another lime
Tabasco
a pinch each of cayenne pepper, paprika, mace and cinnamon
salt and freshly ground black pepper
a pinch of dried thyme
2 tablespoons finely chopped parsley, stalks removed
4 tablespoons white bread crumbs, ideally from the outside of a stale white baguette
2 small green peppers
4 tablespoons unsalted butter
2 garlic cloves, peeled and finely chopped

Mix the crabmeat with the sherry, lime juice, a few shakes of Tabasco, the spices, plenty of seasoning, the thyme and parsley and three quarters of the bread crumbs and leave to stand. Remove the stalks of the peppers, cut in half and scrape out the seeds. Finely dice the flesh.

Preheat the oven to 400°F. Heat half the butter over a gentle heat and sweat the peppers and garlic together for 10 minutes, until softened but not browned. Add the contents of the pan to the crab mixture. Butter a terrine dish (you could also use the well-cleaned crab shells) and pack in the crab mixture, pressing it down with the back of a wooden spoon. Sprinkle the remaining bread crumbs over the top and dot with the remaining butter. Bake in the oven until nicely browned on top, 20 minutes, and serve straight away, with quarters of lime.

requin à la normande
shark in the norman style

We were in a beach shack on Guadeloupe on the north-eastern side of the island. We asked after the fish dish of the day and were surprised to be told in perfect French that it was shark cooked in the Norman style, with cream and green peppercorns. When questioned, it turned out that the proprietor of the restaurant had moved to the sunny isle some five years before from a Norman coastal village. He conceded that sharkfish was not a classic Norman dish, but the sauce certainly was. A thick slice of halibut is a good substitute.

Serves 2

2 steaks of white fish, such as shark, halibut or marlin
sea salt and freshly ground black pepper
1 tablespoon all-purpose flour
a good knob of unsalted butter
a splash of white wine
1 tablespoon green peppercorns, drained and rinsed
¾ cup crème fraîche or sour cream

Preheat the oven to 300°C and put a serving dish in to keep warm. Season the fish, dust with flour and heat a non-stick skillet or, better still, a ridged grill pan. Melt the butter and fry the fish for 5 minutes or so on either side, depending upon thickness. Transfer the fish to the warmed serving dish and deglaze the pan with wine, stirring well to scrape up any residue. Add the peppercorns and the crème fraîche or sour cream, bubble for 2 minutes, pour over the fish and serve straight away.

filet de porc à l'ananas
pork tenderloin with pineapple

I have always been rather horrified by the 1970s classic of gammon with pineapple rings, so I was delighted to find on Martinique that the pork and tropical fruit combination has it roots in a very delicious dish. The key, of course, lies in good-quality pork, fresh fruit and delicate spicing.

Serves 4

2 pork tenderloins, trimmed of any fat
1 small or ½ large fresh pineapple
2 tablespoons groundnut oil
sea salt and freshly ground black pepper
good pinch of cayenne pepper
pinch of ground nutmeg or mace
2 sprigs fresh thyme
juice of ½ lime

Slice the pork into medaillons, cutting across the tenderloins at 1 inch intervals. Peel the pineapple, making sure that you remove all the eyes. Chop the flesh into bite-sized pieces.

Heat the oil in a heavy pan or skillet. Season and spice the pork and pineapple. Add to the hot oil and fry until the pork is cooked and the pineapple lightly browned, 3–4 minutes on either side. Sprinkle over the thyme leaves, stripped from the stalks, add a squeeze of lime and serve with beans and rice.

blaff
marinated white fish stew

A favorite of Martinique, this method of poaching fish is similar to the French court-bouillon—except the flavorings used include lime and chilli. The word blaff is believed to come from the local patois for broth, and the liquor the fish is cooked in should be served with it. The fish is usually served with plain boiled white rice and a side dish of sliced boiled green plantains would be typical.

Serves 4

1 large white fish steak or 4 separate ones,
  weighing in total around 3 pounds and cut
  1 inch thick—marlin is the best choice, but
  you could also use swordfish
4 cups water
2 teaspoons salt
3 limes
1 white onion, peeled and finely chopped
2 garlic cloves, peeled and chopped
1 red chilli, ideally the very hot
  Scotch bonnet variety
1 small green chilli
a few sprigs of parsley
2 bay leaves
a good pinch of dried thyme
8 peppercorns
dark rum

Place the fish steak(s) in a non-reactive pan into which they will just fit. Dissolve the salt in half the water and add the juice of 2 of the limes. Pour over the fish, which should be covered by the liquid. Leave for around 1 hour.

Meanwhile, mix the onion and garlic together. Deseed both chillies and chop the flesh very finely. Tie together the parsley and bay leaves. Put all these in another non-reactive pan large enough to take the fish flat and add the thyme, peppercorns and a good splash of rum together with the rest of the water and the juice of the remaining lime. Bring to the boil and turn down to barely a simmer for 20 minutes.

Remove the fish from the marinade and slip into the simmering liquor. Cook 15–20 minutes, depending upon the thickness and variety of fish. It is ready when it starts to flake. Fish out the bundle of parsley and bay leaves and serve the fish steaks straight away on a bed of rice, spooning the broth over the fish.

the caribbean marketplace

Most French markets are special but those of the Caribbean are beyond that—they are different. They are quite simply an assault on the senses. First there are the vibrant colors, which come not just from the fruits, vegetables, herbs and spices (and often a backdrop of bright blue sea) but from the clothes of the traders. The ladies of Martinique and Guadeloupe have a particular penchant for red and yellow checked dresses and headscarves; the fishermen, who often set up their stalls beside the market proper at the water's edge for ease of cleaning the fish, tend to go for a line in garish football T-shirts.

Then there is the hubbub. Caribbean market traders are especially fine at backchat. Look for too long and indecisively at the bottles of home-made rum punch, flavored with local fruits such as guava, passion fruit and mango, and you are likely to be informed of just how long the bottles have sat under the sun (not to mention the work that went into making them). Consider a few spices and you will be given a recipe

for chicken Colombo. All this will be delivered as merely an interruption to the conversations going on in the local patois, probably over some taped music and sometimes even local song. And then there are the aromas, of ripe fruit, heady spices, just-caught fish being gutted and sliced.

Every Caribbean market is an experience, whether it be the large covered markets of the capital cities of Pointe-à-Pitre and Fort-de-France or the small local markets such as that of Grand Bourg (literally, big town—it is something of a misnomer) on Marie Galante. One of my favorites is that of Basse Terre on the southern tip of Guadeloupe. On the same site that has been used as a local market since the early nineteenth century (and before that as a prison and site of executions), open to the elements but with a modern over-arching structure to protect the traders from the sun and the rain, looking straight out to the Caribbean, it is a central part of everyday local life. Which is just what a market should be.

poulet sauce fruit de passion
chicken in passion fruit sauce

When I first ate this dish at a simple family hotel on Martinique, I wondered whether the warm winds that swept over the terrace as we sat staring out to sea at the islands bathed in the light of a full moon might have made it taste especially delicious. Trying it in rather less exotic surroundings in London I found it just as delectable. The passion fruit both tenderizes the chicken and gives it an unusual sharp sweetness.

Serves 4

4 chicken drumsticks
4 chicken thighs
juice and pulp of 4 passion fruit
juice of 1 lime
salt and freshly ground black pepper
a pinch of turmeric
1 tablespoon groundnut oil

Put the chicken in a heatproof serving dish. Mix together all the remaining ingredients and pour over the chicken. Turn the pieces in the marinade and leave to stand for at least 4 hours, turning once or twice during the process.

To cook, preheat the oven to 350°F. Bake the chicken pieces for about 1 hour in their marinade, turning once halfway through. Serve with white rice.

cari de crevettes
shrimp cari

The cooking of the Ile de la Réunion is brightly colored, with plenty of turmeric used to give a deep yellow hue. 'Cari', whether of chicken, pork, lobster or even eel is a favorite local dish. I find it especially suited to the big Indian Ocean shrimp that are now widely available. With it serve a *rougail*, or fresh mango chutney (see next recipe).

Serves 4

16 large uncooked shrimp, in their shells, heads removed
2 onions
2 tablespoons groundnut oil
3 garlic cloves, peeled and finely chopped
1 inch fresh ginger, peeled and finely chopped
½ teaspoon sea salt
freshly ground black pepper
½ teaspoon turmeric
½ teaspoon chilli powder
several sprigs of fresh thyme
4 tomatoes, diced

Rinse the shrimp well under cold running water. Peel the onions and chop finely. Cook the onions in a heavy pan with the oil over a medium heat, stirring occasionally, for around 30 minutes, until well browned. Now add the garlic and ginger and continue to cook for another 5 minutes, stirring regularly.

Add the salt and pepper, spices, thyme and tomato and cook for a further 5 minutes, then add the shrimp and turn to coat in the sauce. Pour in just sufficient water barely to cover the shrimp and simmer for about 10 minutes, turning the shrimp halfway through, until the shellfish is cooked and you have a thick sauce.

rougail de mangue
mango rougail

Serves 4

1 large slightly under-ripe mango
½ teaspoon sea salt
freshly ground black pepper
½ teaspoon cayenne pepper
½ teaspoon turmeric

Peel the mango, remove the flesh from the stone and dice the flesh finely. Sprinkle over the salt, add enough water just to cover and leave to stand for 20 minutes—it will be lightly pickled. Drain the mango and pat dry. Add the peppers and turmeric and mix thoroughly.

flan au coco
coconut flan

I owe this recipe to Madame Francine, a modest lady who produces simple, delicious home cooking on the island of Martinique. She giggled when I asked her for her recipe for this local version of crème caramel—but it's so simple, she said. 'Some people add their own touch, a little orange zest soaked in rum, or a touch of cinnamon. I just like a little lime zest to lift it.'

Serves 4

5 large eggs
1½ cups canned condensed milk
1½ cups canned coconut milk
½ teaspoon lime zest
½ teaspoon groundnut oil
scant ¾ cup brown sugar
4 tablespoons water

Preheat the oven to 350°F.

Beat the eggs well then mix in the condensed and coconut milks together with the lime zest.

Lightly oil a non-stick mold and pour in the egg and milk mixture. Place the mold in a pan of water (a bain-marie) and bake until set, 50–60 minutes. Leave to cool slightly then loosen the sides with a sharp knife and carefully turn the flan out onto a deep plate. Melt the sugar with the water and bubble for 2–3 minutes to form a sugar syrup (but be careful not to cook too fiercely or too long or you will end up with toffee). Leave the syrup to cool, then pour over the flan.

bananes flambées au rhum
bananas flambéed in rum

antillaise fruit salad

A visit to a rum distillery is an essential element of a trip to the French Caribbean. Many of the rummeries still retain the old colonial houses, which give a good impression of the gracious living of the sugar cane plantation owner. On Martinique, for example, the nineteenth-century Creole mansion at Habitation Clément near St François is sited on top of the hill above the distillery and is open to the air on all sides to catch the breezes. On the verandah there are plantation chairs in which to sit and sip your barrel-aged rum while you smoked your cigar, after a splendid dinner at the long mahogany dining table. Upstairs hardwood beds, four-poster in order to hang the mosquito nets, are there for the guests to sleep it off.

Nowadays, of course, this is a lifestyle long gone but there remain plenty of distilleries, mostly owned corporately. The white *rhum agricole*, or farmer's rum, of Marie Galante is especially fierce (typically 58 per cent alcohol), while the dark rums of Martinique are more subtle, especially those aged in oak barrels, sometimes for many years. Martinique also retains plenty of banana plantations, despite the economic problems of exporting the fruit, and even has varieties specific to the island. The mixture of bananas, cane sugar syrup (known locally as sirop de batterie) and rum is the most popular adult dessert throughout the islands, especially when served with home-made vanilla ice cream flecked with seeds from the fragrant local vanilla beans.

Serves 4

4 ripe bananas
4 tablespoons unsalted butter
2 tablespoons brown sugar syrup or 2 tablespoons brown sugar melted with 1 tablespoon water
2 tablespoons rum

Peel the bananas and split in half lengthways. Fry in the butter for a few minutes on either side, until golden brown. Add the sugar syrup and bubble for 1 minute. Heat the rum in a ladle, set light to it and pour over the bananas at the table. A few scoops of home-made or at least good quality vanilla ice cream is a splendid accompaniment.

Mangoes, bananas, passion fruit and starfruit, known locally as carambole, all find their way into local fruit salads in season, but I am a purist on this one and prefer a simple mix of pineapple and papaya, delicately spiced.

Serves 4

½ cup brown sugar
¾ cup water
juice and zest of 1 lime
2 tablespoons dark rum
2 cloves
1 cinnamon stick
a pinch of mace or nutmeg
1 papaya
1 pineapple

Whisk the sugar into the water and add the lime juice and zest, rum and spices. Bring to the boil and simmer for 10 minutes. Leave to stand until cool. Just before serving, chop the papaya and pineapple into chunks, pour over the lime syrup, and serve.

index

abricots de Rousillon au Muscat 165
accras aux crevettes 194
aillade 127
aligot 94
almonds
    macaroons 149
    pear and almond tart 60
Alps 114–117
Alsace-Lorraine 20–1
anchovies
    Collioure 158
    mimosa salad 158
    olive paste 171
    pissaladière 172
    red mullet in the style of Nice 175
    salade niçoise in a roll 171
Antillaise fruit salad 202
apples
    black pudding with apples 57
    green apple sorbet 58
    pheasant Norman style 56
    red cabbage with chestnuts and 31
    tarte tatin 85
    thin apple tart 59
apricots poached in Muscat wine 165
Aquitaine 1245
Armagnac
    frozen Armagnac and prune mousse
    134
Arras marketplace 42
artichokes
    artichoke stew 65
    roast veal with artichoke hearts 73
asperge blanc au jambon et trois sauces 22
Auvergne hotpot 94

bacon
    Auvergne hotpot 94
    dandelion salad 32
    fava beans with bacon 186
    stewed beef 180
    tartiflette 116
    trout with 146
    warm salad with eggs and bacon 16
baeckhöfe 31
baked eggs 65
bananas flambéed in rum 202
bananes flambées au rhum 202

Basque country 138–9
Bassin de Marennes Oléron 133
Bayonne ham 143
Bayonne ham with eggs and peppers
    143
beans
    cassoulet 162
    fava beans with bacon 186
    pistou soup 168
    salad from Périgueux 127
    vegetable and meat stew 146
Beaune cellars 104
beef
    casserole of pork, lamb, beef and
    potato 31
    in jelly 111
    raclette 119
    steak tartare 17
    steak with Roquefort butter 97
    stewed 180
    stewed in beer 46
beer
    beef stewed in 46
    soup 40
beetroot salad 14
beignets de fleurs de courgettes 173
beurre de Montpellier 160
biscottins au fleur d'oranger 181
black pudding with apples 57
blackcurrant sorbet 112
blaff 198
blanquette de veau 16
boeuf en daube 180
boudins noirs aux pommes 57
boeuf à la mode 111
bread
    cheese fondue 120
    fresh foie gras with spiced bread 26
    'lost' 47
    salade niçoise in a roll 171
Bresse, poulet de 109
Breton fisherman's stew 68
brill with hollandaise sauce 45
Brittany 623
Burgundy 100–1
butter
    Montpellier butter 160
    radishes with butter 13

river fish with white butter sauce 78
skate in black butter 70
steak with Roquefort butter 97

cabbage
    guinea hen with cabbage 46
    red cabbage with chestnuts and
    apples 31
    soup with foie gras 25
    vegetable and meat stew 146
cailles aux raisins 108
caneton aux coings et figues 54
carbonnade de boeuf 46
cari de crevettes 201
Caribbean marketplace 200
carottes rapées 14
carottes Vichy 91
carrots
    Crécy soup 13
    grated 14
    vegetable and meat stew 146
    Vichy style 91
    casserole of pork, lamb, beef and
    potato 31
cassis 112
cassola de langoustines 155
cassoulet 162
cassoulet de seiches 163
cassoulet of cuttlefish 163
cauliflower cream soup 40
céleri rémoulade 14
celeriac salad 14
Central France 889
cèpes à la bordelaise 128
ceps with garlic and parsley 128
Céret cherries 159
Champagne 36–7
champagne 45
    fruit salad with 47
    salmon fillets in champagne sauce 45
cheese
    Corsican cheesecake 191
    fondue 120
    fresh goat's cheese with raspberry
    coulis 82
    hot goat's cheese salad with honey
    and walnuts 154
    Maroilles cheese tart 43

omelet with soft cheese and mint 186
onion soup with cheese 103
oysters in cheese sauce 66
plateau de fromages 86
pears with Fourme d'Ambert 97
pistou soup 168
potato with cheese 94
raclette 119
sardines baked with brocciu and
    herbs 188
steak with Roquefort butter 97
tartiflette 116
cherries
    Céret 159
    cherry pudding 98
    duck breast with cherries 158
    sour cherries flamed in alcohol 123
chestnuts
    chestnut soup 185
    Corsican chestnut festival 185
    red cabbage with chestnuts and
    apples 31
chèvre frais au coulis de framboises 82
chicken
    cockerel in red wine 110
    cooked in cider 73
    cooked in Riesling 28
    in passion fruit sauce 200
    in the Basque style 145
    liver parfait 26
    with morels 120
chicory gratin 41
chilled leek and potato soup 91
chocolate
    Nancy chocolate cake 34
    St-Emilions 137
    truffles 149
chou rouge aux marrons et pommes 31
choucroute festival 27
Christmas desserts 181
cider
    artichoke stew 65
    chicken cooked in 73
    duck with quince and figs 54
    lobster with tarragon 69
    monkfish Armoricaine 72
    mussels Norman style 50
    pheasant Norman style 56

pork chops in 54
civet de lièvre 81
civet de sanglier 164
clafoutis aux cerises 98
cockerel in red wine 110
coconut flan 201
coq au vin 110
coquilles St-Jacques à la Provençale 178
coquilles St-Jacques au Muscadet 68
Corsica 1823
Corsican cheesecake 191
Corsican chestnut festival 185
côtes d'agneau grillés avec leur aïoli 160
côtes de porc au cidre 54
cotriade 68
courgettes farcies 174
crab
    hot terrine of crab Creole style 197
    in the Breton style 66
crabes Bretons 66
cream
    frozen Armagnac and prune mousse
        134
    gratin dauphinois 119
    medallions of venison with cream
        sauce 29
    peas with lettuce and cream 80
    raspberry gratin 35
Crécy soup 13
crevettes au pastis 177
crudités: carottes rapées 14
cuttlefish, cassoulet of 163

darnes de saumon au champagne 45
dandelion salad 32
douillons 60
duck
    breast with cherries 158
    cassoulet 162
    salad of duck with vanilla and citrus
        fruits 195
    vegetable and meat stew 146
    with quince and figs 54

eaux de vie 34
eggs
    baked 65
    Bayonne ham with eggs and peppers
        143
    Corsican cheesecake 191
    floating islands 19
    frozen Armagnac and prune mousse
        134
    mimosa salad 156
    omelet 50
    omelet with soft cheese and mint 186
    poached in red wine 104
    raspberry gratin 35
    salade niçoise in a roll 171

souffléed omelet 123
    Swiss chard omelet 177
    warm salad with eggs and bacon 16
escargots en chaussons 103
étouffée de cabri 188

faisan à la Normande 56
fava beans with bacon 186
fèves au lard 186
fiadone 191
figs
    duck with quince and figs 54
    pigeon salad with girolles, figs and
        walnuts 131
filet de porc à l'ananas 198
fish
    Breton fisherman's stew 68
    marinated white fish stew 198
    river fish with white butter sauce 78
    see also brill, mackerels, red mullet,
        salmon, salt cod, sardines, sea bass,
        shark, tuna
flambéed peaches 111
flamiche au Maroilles 43
flan au coco 201
floating islands 19
foie gras
    cabbage soup with 25
    fresh, with spiced bread 26
    marché au gras 128
    salad from Périgueux 127
foie gras frais avec son pain d'épices 26
fondue Savoyarde 120
Fourme d'Ambert 97
fraises des bois au vin rouge 86
French onion soup with cheese 103
French West Indies 1923
fresh goat's cheese with raspberry
    coulis 82
fricassée d'artichauts 65
fried frog's legs 106
fritelles d'herbes 186
frog's legs, fried 106
frozen Armagnac and prune mousse
    134
fruit salad
    Antillaise 202
    with champagne 47

galettes 73
game 81
garbure Béarnaise 146
garlic
    aillade 127
    ceps with garlic and parsley 128
    grilled lamb chops with garlic
        mayonnaise 160
    langoustines with red peppers and
        garlic 155

olive paste 171
ratatouille 174
soup 140
gâteau de chocolat de Nancy 34
gherkins
    sauce gribiche 15
grapes
    picking 134
    quails cooked with 108
grated carrots 14
gratin dauphinois 119
gratin de coeurs de palmiers 194
gratin de framboises 35
gratin d'endives 41
gratin of palm hearts 194
green apple sorbet 58
grilled lamb chops with garlic
    mayonnaise 160
griottes flambées 123
guinea hen
    sauté with wild mushrooms 78
    with cabbage 46

ham
    raclette 119
    vegetable and meat stew 146
    white asparagus with smoked ham
        and three sauces 22
    with eggs and peppers 143
hare, jugged 81
herbs
    herb fritters 186
    sardines baked with brocciu and
        herbs 188
herrings
    salad of wine-marinated herrings
        with potatoes in oil 39
hollandaise sauce 22
    brill with 45
homard à l'estragon 69
honey, hot goat's cheese salad with
    walnuts and 154
horseradish, knuckle of pork with 28
hot goat's cheese salad with honey and
    walnuts 154
hot terrine of crab Creole style 197
huîtres aux saucisses 132
huîtres gratinées 66

iced melon soup 127
Ile-de-France 10–11
Ile de la Réunion 19–23
îles flottantes 19

jambon de Bayonne 143
jambon de Bayonne avec sa pipérade 143
jarret de porc au raifort 28
jugged hare 81

kid stew 188
kidneys with mustard 15
knuckle of pork with horseradish 28

lamb
    casserole of pork, lamb, beef and
        potato 31
    grilled lamb chops with garlic
        mayonnaise 160
    spring lamb stew 78
langoustines with red peppers and
    garlic 155
Languedoc-Roussillon 150–1
lapin à la moutarde 106
lapin aux pruneaux 131
leeks
    chilled leek and potato soup 91
    in vinaigrette 15
    vegetable and meat stew 146
lemons
    lemon tart 18
    salad of duck with vanilla and citrus
        fruits 195
lentilles à l'Auvergnate 92
lentils in the Auvergne style 92
lettuce
    peas with lettuce and cream 80
    salade niçoise in a roll 171
    warm salad with eggs and bacon 16
lobster with tarragon 69
Loire 745
'lost' bread 47
lotte à la Basquaise 144
lotte à l'Armoricaine 72
loup de mer en papillote 178

macarons 149
macaroons 149
    chocolate St-Emilions 137
magret de canard aux cerises 158
mango rougail 201
maquereaux Dieppoise 53
marché au gras 128
marinated white fish stew 198
Maroilles cheese tart 43
médaillons de biche à la crème 29
medallions of venison with cream
    sauce 29
melon soup, iced 127
mineral water 92
mint, omelet with soft cheese and 186
mirabelles, tart with 82
monkfish
    Armoricaine 72
    in the Basque style 144
Montpellier butter 160
mouclade 132
moules à la Normande 50

moules marinières 43
mousseline sauce 22
Muscadet, scallops in 68
mushrooms
  ceps with garlic and parsley 128
  chicken with morels 120
  mushroom soup 116
  pigeon salad with girolles, figs and
walnuts 131
  sauté of guinea hen with wild
   mushrooms 78
  scallops in Muscadet 68
  white veal stew 16
mussels
  marinières 43
  mouclade 132
  Norman style 50
mustard
  rabbit in mustard sauce 106
  veal kidneys with 15

Nancy chocolate cake 34
navarin printanier 78
Nice market 172
Normandy 489
North of France 36–7
oeufs en cocotte 65
oeufs en meurette 104
oillade 140
olives
  olive paste 171
  pissaladière 172
  veal with green olives 190
omelet 50
  souffléd 123
  with soft cheese and mint 186
omelette au brocciu et menthe 186
omelette soufflée 123
onions
  Onion Johnnies 69
  onion soup with cheese 103
  onion tart 25
  pissaladière 172
  ratatouille 174
oranges
  orange-flower water cookies 181
  salad of duck with vanilla and citrus
   fruits 195
oysters
  Bassin de Marennes Oléron 133
  in cheese sauce 66
  with sausage 132

pain perdu 47
palm hearts, gratin of 194
pan bagnat 171
parfait d'Armagnac aux pruneaux 134
parfait de foies de volaille 26
Paris 10–11

Parisian brasserie waiters 12
partridges in the Auvergne style 93
passion fruit
  chicken in passion fruit sauce 200
peaches
  flambéed 111
  white peach and tomato salad 152
pears
  in red wine 137
  pear and almond tart 60
  pear turnovers 60
  with Fourme d'Ambert 97
peas with lettuce and cream 80
pêches flambées 111
peppers
  chicken in the Basque style 145
  ham with eggs and peppers 143
  langoustines with red peppers and
   garlic 155
  mimosa salad 156
  monkfish in the Basque style 144
  ratatouille 174
  salt cod salad with peppers 140
perdrix à l'Auvergnate 93
petits pois à la française 80
pheasant Norman style 56
pigeon salad with girolles, figs and
  walnuts 131
Pilgrim's way 95
pineapple
  pork fillet with 198
pintade aux choux 46
pissaladière 172
pistou soup 168
plateau de fromages 86
plum tart 32
poireaux vinaigrette 15
poires au Fourme d'Ambert 97
poires au vin rouge 137
poisson de rivière au beurre blanc 78
Poitou-Charentes 124–5
porc aux pruneaux de Tours 77
pork
  Auvergne hotpot 94
  casserole of pork, lamb, beef and
   potato 31
  cassoulet 162
  chops in cider 54
  fillet with pineapple 198
  knuckle with horseradish 28
  with prunes 77
pork fillet with pineapple 198
potage aux champignons 116
potage Crécy 13
potatoes
  Breton fisherman's stew 68
  cabbage soup with foie gras 25
  casserole of pork, lamb, beef and
   potato 31

chilled leek and potato soup 91
Crécy soup 13
gratin dauphinois 119
potato with cheese 94
raclette 119
salad of wine-marinated herrings
  with potatoes in oil 39
tartiflette 116
vegetable and meat stew 146
watercress soup 77
potée Auvergnate 94
poule au pot 145
poule au Riesling 28
poulet au cidre 73
poulet aux morilles 120
poulet Basquaise 145
poulet de Bresse 109
poulet sauce fruit de passion 200
Provence 166–7
prunes
  frozen Armagnac and prune mousse
   134
  pork with 77
  rabbit with 131
pumpkin pie 39

quails cooked with grapes 108
quince, duck with figs and 54

rabbit
  in mustard sauce 106
  with prunes 131
raclette 119
radis au beurre 13
radishes with butter 13
raie au beurre noir 70
raspberries
  fresh goat's cheese with raspberry
   coulis 82
  raspberry gratin 35
ratatouille 174
red cabbage with chestnuts and apples
  31
red mullet in the style of Nice 175
requin à la Normande 197
Rhône valley 100–1
rhubarb tart 35
Riesling, chicken cooked in 28
river fish with white butter sauce 78
roast veal with artichoke hearts 73
rognons de veau à la moutarde 15
rôti de veau aux fonds d'artichauts 73
rougail de mangue 201
rougets à la Niçoise 175
Roussillon apricots poached in Muscat
  wine 165

St-Emilions au chocolat 137
St Michel sheep 55

salad from Périgueux 127
salad of duck with vanilla and citrus
  fruits 195
salad of wine-marinated herrings with
  potatoes in oil 39
salade de betteraves 14
salade de canard au vanille et aux agrumes
  195
salade de chèvre chaud au miel et noix 154
salade de fruits au champagne 47
salade de morue au poivrons 140
salade de pêches blanches et tomates 152
salade de Périgueux 127
salade de pigeon au girolles, figues et noix
  131
salade de pissenlits 32
salade d'harengs marinés au vin blanc avec
  pommes de terre à l'huile 39
salade mimosa 156
salade niçoise in a roll 171
salade tiède aux oeufs et lardons 16
salmon fillets in champagne sauce 45
salt cod salad with peppers 140
sardinade 152
sardines au four avec brocciu et herbes 188
sardines baked with brocciu and herbs
  188
sauce gribiche 15
sauce hollandaise 22
sauce mousseline 22
sausage
  cassoulet 162
  oysters with 132
sauté de cuisses de grenouilles 106
sauté de pintade aux champignons
  sauvages 78
sauté of guinea hen with wild
  mushrooms 78
scallop shell 95
scallops
  in Muscadet 68
  in the Provençale style 178
sea bass in paper parcels 178
shark in the Norman style 197
sheep of St Michel 55
shrimp
  shrimp accras 194
  shrimp cari 201
  with pastis 177
skate in black butter 70
ski slopes, lunch on 119
snails in pockets 103
socca in Nice market 172
sole Norman style 53
sole normande 53
sorbet au pommes vertes 58
sorbet de cassis 112
soufflé glacé à la verveine 98
souffléed omelet 123

soupe à la bière 40
soupe à l'oignon gratinée 103
soupe au cresson 77
soupe au pistou 168
soupe aux choux avec foie gras 25
soupe de marrons 185
soupe glacée de melon 127
sour cherries flamed in alcohol 123
spiced bread, fresh foie gras with 26
spring lamb stew 78
steak au beurre de Roquefort 97
steak tartare 17
steak with Roquefort butter 97
stewed beef 180
strawberries, wild, in red wine 86
Sunday lunch 145
Swiss chard omelet 177

tapenade 171
tarragon, lobster with 69
tart with mirabelles 82
tarte à l'oignon 25
tarte au citron 18
tarte au rhubarbe 35
tarte aux mirabelles 82
tarte aux poires et amandes 60
tarte aux quetsches 32
tarte fine aux pommes 59
tarte tatin 85
tartiflette 116
Tatin sisters 85
terrine chaude de crabe à la creole 197

thin apple tart 59
thon rôti 188
tomatoes
    monkfish in the Basque style 144
    pistou soup 168
    ratatouille 174
    red mullet in the style of Nice 175
    white peach and tomato salad 152
tourte au potiron 39
trouchia 177
trout with bacon 146
truffes au chocolat 149
truites au lard 146
tuna
    roasted 188
    salade niçoise in a roll 171
    tartare of 195
tuna tartare 195
turbotin sauce hollandaise 45

vanilla
    floating islands 19
    salad of duck with vanilla and citrus
      fruits 195
veal
    kidneys with mustard 15
    roast with artichoke hearts 73
    white veal stew 16
    with green olives 190
veau aux olives 190
vegetable and meat stew 146
velouté de choufleur 40

vendange 134
venison medallions with cream sauce
    29
verveine-flavoured iced soufflé 98
vichyssoise 91
vinaigrette 22

waiters in Paris, 12
walnuts
    aillade 127
    hot goat's cheese salad with honey
      and walnuts 154
    pigeon salad with girolles, figs and
      walnuts 131
    salad from Périgueux 127
warm salad with eggs and bacon 16
water, mineral 92
watercress soup 77
white asparagus with smoked ham
    and three sauces 22
white peach and tomato salad 152
white veal stew 16
wild boar stew 164
wild strawberries in red wine 86
wine
    beef in jelly 111
    Breton fisherman's stew 68
    casserole of pork, lamb, beef and
      potato 31
    cheese fondue 120
    chicken cooked in Riesling 28
    chicken liver parfait 26

cockerel in red wine 110
crab in the Breton style 66
eggs poached in red wine 104
iced melon soup 127
jugged hare 81
mackerels in the style of Dieppe 53
mussels marinières 43
pork with prunes 77
rabbit with prunes 130
Roussillon apricots poached in
    Muscat wine 165
salad of wine-marinated herrings with
    potatoes in oil 39
scallops in Muscadet 68
sour cherries flamed in alcohol 123
stewed beef 180
wild boar stew 164
wild strawberries in red wine 86

zucchini
    zucchini flower fritters 173
    ratatouille 174
    stuffed 174

acknowledgements

With thanks to:

Everyone at Kyle Cathie for their work on the book, especially Caroline Taggart and Vicki Murrell; Richard Jung and Linda Tubby for making the food look so beautiful; my agent Anthony Topping and his colleagues at Greene and Heaton; Natalie Goulet and all her colleagues at Maison de la France for providing information and assisting on trips; Xavier Olivieri for hosting my visit to Corsica and Nicola Célie for doing the same in the Pas-de-Calais; Patricia Parnell for help on Hine and Krug; Naomi Dulfer at Air France for helping me to get to both Corsica and the French Caribbean; Jonathan Little for providing genial company even while taking photographs; our many neighbors in la Bastide, in particular Veronique Baux for helping on recipes and her husband Daniel for providing wild boar, Louis for his supply of fresh vegetables, Jennie and Brian for keeping the kitchen in order in our absence and Marie and Didier for some inspirational meals; Monsieur Mic and Chris for more memorable meals in Coustouge; Michael and Marcos back in London for enthusiastic recipe testing; my brother and sister-in-law Philip and Martine for patiently answering my endless questions and looking after me in Alsace; my parents for introducing me to French food, language and culture at an early age; and, as ever, Jonathan Gregson, who knows more about French history than I ever shall.

Photographic acknowledgements

All food photography by Richard Jung.

page 9 Greg Elms/Lonely Planet Images; 10 *A Bar at the Folies-Bergere*, 1881–82 (oil on canvas), Edouard Manet (1832–83)/© Samuel Courtauld Trust, Courtauld Institute of Art Gallery,/Bridgeman Art Library; 11 *Traffic Island on Boulevard Haussmann*, 1880 (oil on canvas), Gustave Caillebotte (1848–94)/Private Collection, Giraudon/Bridgeman Art Library; 12 Mark Cator/Impact Photos; 14 *Marché des Innocents*/Bridgeman Art Library; 20 Sarah Woodward; 21 Richard Turpin/Aspect Picture Library; 26 Jonathan Little; 27 Sarah Woodward; 34 Robert Harding Picture Library; 35 Robert Harding Picture Library; 36 *Maisons-Alfort*, 1898, Jean Baptiste Armand Guillaumin (1841–1927)/Galerie Daniel Malingue, Paris, France/Bridgeman Art Library; 37 Sarah Woodward; 42 *The Hotel de Ville, Arras*, 1856 (oil on card), Lewis John Wood (1813–1901)/Musée des Beaux-Arts, Arras, Giraudon/Bridgeman Art Library; 49 *Rouen Cathedral, Effects of Sunlight, Sunset*, 1892 (oil on canvas), Claude Monet (1840–1926), Musée Marmottan, Paris, Giraudon/ Bridgeman Art Library; 55 Bruno Morandi/ Robert Harding Picture Library; 59 Rob Moore/The Travel Library; 61 Diana Mayfield/Lonely Planet Images; 62 Stuart Black/The Travel Library; 63 Stuart Black/The Travel Library; 72 *Breton Peasants*, 1894 (oil on canvas),Paul Gauguin (1848–1903)/Musée d'Orsay, Paris, Lauros/Giraudon/Bridgeman Art Library; 74 Bruno Barbier/Robert Harding Picture Library; 75 Gavin Hellier/Robert Harding Picture Library; 81 *Le Château de Chambord*, 1722 (oil on canvas), Pierre-Denis Martin (1663–1742)/Château de Versailles, Lauros/Giraudon/ Bridgeman Art Library; 85 *Still Life of Apples and Biscuits*, 1880–82 (oil on canvas), Paul Cézanne (1839–1906)/Musée de l'Orangerie, Paris, Lauros/Giraudon/Bridgeman Art Library; 88 Sarah Woodward; 89 Sylvain Grandadam/Robert Harding; 92 Steve Day/The Travel Library; 95 *The Supper at Emmaus*, 1601 (oil and tempera on canvas), Michelangelo Merisi da Caravaggio (1571–1610)/National Gallery, London/ Bridgeman Art Library; 100 John Miller/Robert Harding Picture Library; 101 (left) Stuart Black/The Travel Library; (right) Jonathan Little; 104 Adam Woolfitt/Robert Harding Picture Library; 109 CIVB; 112 David Kitchen; 114 Jonathan Little; 115 Robert Harding Picture Library; 124 Hine, 16 Quai de l'Orangerie, Jarnac, France; 125 (left) Clare Roberts/The Travel Library; (right) Richard Turpin/Aspect Picture Library; 128 Sarah Woodward; 133 Richard Turpin/Aspect Picture Library; 134 David Gallant/Impact Photos; 139 Stuart Black/The Travel Library; 143 Sarah Woodward; 144 Stuart Black/The Travel Library; 145 *The Hunt Lunch*, detail of the diners, 1737 (oil on canvas), Jean François de Troy (1679–1752)/ Louvre, Paris, Giraudon/Bridgeman Art Library; 150 Jonathan Little; 151 © Succession H Matisse/DACS 2006. Kyle Cathie Limited has paid DACS' visual creators for the use of their artistic works ⬛ 152 Sarah Woodward; 156 Jonathan Little, 159 Jonathan Little; 162 Geoff Hayes; 166 *The Olive Pickers, Saint-Remy*, 1889 (oil on canvas), Vincent van Gogh (1853–90)/ Private Collection, Peter Willi/Bridgeman Art Library; 167 Richard Turpin/Aspect Picture Library; 168 Richard Jung; 171 Richard Jung; 172 Richard Jung; 175 Stuart Black/The Travel Library; 183 Jonathan Little; 185 Jonathan Little; 186 Sarah Woodward; 191 Jonathan Little; 193 Sarah Woodward; 194 Sarah Woodward; 200 Sarah Woodward